Ext JS 4 Web Application Development Cookbook

Over 110 easy-to-follow recipes backed up with real-life examples, walking you through basic Ext JS features to advanced application design using Sencha's Ext JS

Stuart Ashworth

Andrew Duncan

open source
community experience distilled

PACKT PUBLISHING

BIRMINGHAM - MUMBAI

Ext JS 4 Web Application Development Cookbook

First published: August 2012

Production Reference: 1170812

Published by Packt Publishing Ltd.
Livery Place
35 Livery Street
Birmingham B3 2PB, UK.

ISBN 978-1-84951-686-0

www.packtpub.com

Cover Image by Ed Maclean (edmaclean@gmail.com)

About the Authors

Stuart Ashworth is a professional web developer and an all-round web geek currently living in Glasgow, Scotland with his girlfriend Sophie and wee dog, Meg. After graduating with a first-class honors degree in Design Computing from the University of Strathclyde, he earned his stripes at a small software company in the city.

Stuart has worked with Sencha technologies for over three years, creating various large and small-scale web applications, mobile applications, and framework plugins along the way.

At the end of 2010, Stuart and Andrew formed SwarmOnline, later becoming an official Sencha partner. Since then they have worked on projects with a number of local, national, and international clients ranging from small businesses to large multinational corporations.

Stuart enjoys playing football, snowboarding, and visiting new cities. He blogs about Sencha technologies on the SwarmOnline website as much as possible and can be contacted through Twitter, e-mail, or the Sencha forums.

Andrew Duncan's passion for the Internet and web development began from a young age, where he spent much of his time creating websites and installing/managing a 2 km square wireless mesh network for his local, rural community.

After graduating in Business and Management from the University of Glasgow, Andrew was inspired to set up a business offering web development, training, and consultancy as SwarmOnline. During expansion, he partnered with Stuart at the end of 2010. His experience is now expansive, having worked with a large variety of small, medium, and multinational businesses for both the public and private-sector markets.

Sencha's technologies first became of interest to Andrew more than three years ago. His knowledge and enthusiasm was recognized in the Sencha Touch App contest where SwarmOnline secured a top 10 place. This talent did not go unrecognized as Sencha soon signed SwarmOnline as their first official partner outside the US.

When not immersed in technology, Andrew lives in Glasgow's West End with his girlfriend, Charlotte. He enjoys skiing, curling, and DIY projects. Andrew can be found on `swarmonline.com/blog`, by e-mail, and on Twitter.

Credits

Authors

Stuart Ashworth

Andrew Duncan

Reviewers

Aafrin Fareeth

Yiyu Jia

Peter Kellner

Joel Watson

Acquisition Editor

Usha Iyer

Lead Technical Editor

Dayan Hyames

Technical Editors

Apoorva Bolar

Madhuri Das

Project Coordinator

Michelle Quadros

Proofreader

Martin Diver

Indexer

Hemangini Bari

Graphics

Manu Joseph

Production Coordinators

Shantanu Zagade

Aparna Bhagat

Cover Work

Shantanu Zagade

Peter Kellner, a Microsoft ASP.NET MVP since 2007, is founder and president of ConnectionRoad, and a seasoned software professional specializing in high quality, scalable, and extensible web applications. His experience includes building and leading engineering teams both on and off shore. Peter is actively engaged in the software community being the primary leader of Silicon Valley Code Camp, which attracted over 2,000 people in 2011 with over 200 sessions. He also organizes the San Francisco Sencha Users Group. In his free time he and his wife Tammy can be found biking the Santa Cruz Mountains. In 2003 they rode across the United States in 27 days.

Joel Watson is a web enthusiast, working for the past eight years in website design and development. He loves exploring web technologies of all sorts, and particularly enjoys creating web experiences that leverage the newest features of HTML5 and its related technologies.

When he's not coding, Joel enjoys spending time with his wife and two daughters, playing guitar, and watching cheesy sci-fi and anime.

About the Reviewers

Aafrin Fareeth is a self-made programmer who fell in love with codes during his high school. Since then he has mastered several languages, such as C++, Java, PHP, ASP, VB, VB.NET, and is on a quest to master more languages. He specializes in web application development, security testing, and forensic analysis.

> I would like to thank my family and friends who have been very supportive, Nor Hamirah for her continuous encouragement and motivation, Jovita Pinto, and Reshma Sundaresan for this wonderful opportunity.

Yiyu Jia has been developing web applications since 1996. He worked as a technical leader and solutions architect on various projects with Java and PHP as the major backend languages. He also has professional experience in interactive TV middleware and home gateway projects. He is especially interested in designing multi-channel web applications.

Yiyu Jia is also the main founder of the novel data-mining research topic—Promotional Subspace Mining (PSM), which aims at finding out useful information from subspaces in very large data sets. He can be reached at the given e-mail address—yiyu.jia@gmail.com. His blog and website are http://yiyujia.blogspot.com and http://www.idatamining. org respectively.

www.PacktPub.com

Support files, eBooks, discount offers, and more

You might want to visit www.PacktPub.com for support files and downloads related to your book.

Did you know that Packt offers eBook versions of every book published, with PDF and ePub files available? You can upgrade to the eBook version at www.PacktPub.com, and as a print book customer, you are entitled to a discount on the eBook copy. Get in touch with us at service@packtpub.com for more details.

At www.PacktPub.com, you can also read a collection of free technical articles, sign up for a range of free newsletters and receive exclusive discounts and offers on Packt books and eBooks.

http://PacktLib.PacktPub.com

Do you need instant solutions to your IT questions? PacktLib is Packt's online digital book library. Here, you can access, read, and search across Packt's entire library of books.

Why Subscribe?

- ▶ Fully searchable across every book published by Packt
- ▶ Copy and paste, print, and bookmark content
- ▶ On demand and accessible via web browser

Free Access for Packt account holders

If you have an account with Packt at www.PacktPub.com, you can use this to access PacktLib today and view nine entirely free books. Simply use your login credentials for immediate access.

For Charlotte, Sophie, and our families.
Thank you for the support and encouragement you gave us while writing this book.

Table of Contents

Preface

Ext JS 4 is Sencha's latest JavaScript framework for developing cross-platform web applications. Built upon web standards, Ext JS provides a comprehensive library of user interface widgets and data manipulation classes to turbo-charge your application's development. Ext JS 4 builds on Ext JS 3, introducing a number of new widgets and features including the popular MVC architecture, easily customizable themes, and plugin-free charting.

This book works through the framework from the fundamentals to advanced features and application design. More than 110 detailed and practical recipes demonstrate all of the key widgets and features the framework has to offer. With this book, and the Ext JS framework, you will learn how to develop truly interactive and responsive web applications.

Starting with the framework fundamentals, you will work through all of the widgets and features the framework has to offer, finishing with extensive coverage of application design and code structure.

Over 110 practical and detailed recipes describe how to create and work with forms, grids, data views, and charts. You will also learn about the best practices for structuring and designing your application and how to deal with storing and manipulating data. The cookbook structure is such that you may read the recipes in any order.

The Ext JS 4 Web Application Development Cookbook will provide you with the knowledge to create interactive and responsive web applications, using real-life examples.

What this book covers

Chapter 1, Classes, Object-Oriented Principles, and Structuring your Application, covers how to harness the power of Ext JS 4's new class system, architect your application using the Model-View-Controller (MVC) pattern, and extend the framework's functionality.

Chapter 2, Manipulating the Dom, Handling Events, and Making AJAX Requests, covers topics such as working with the Document Object Model (DOM), selecting, creating, and manipulating elements. We'll look at how to add built-in animations to your elements and how to create custom animations.

We'll talk through creating your first AJAX request and encoding/decoding the data either in JSON or HTML format.

Other topics include handling events, working with dates, detecting browser features, and evaluating object types/values.

Chapter 3, Laying Out your Components, explores the layout system in Ext JS 4 and demonstrates how to use these layouts to place your user-interface components. The layouts we will work with are FitLayout, BorderLayout, HBoxLayout, VBoxLayout, ColumnLayout, TableLayout, AccoridionLayout, CardLayout, AnchorLayout, and AbsoluteLayout. The final recipe will combine a number of these layouts to create a framework for a rich desktop-style application.

Chapter 4, UI Building Blocks – Trees, Panels, and Data Views, looks at how creating and manipulating the basic components that Ext JS provides is fundamental to producing a rich application. In this chapter, we will cover three fundamental Ext JS UI components and explore how to configure and control them within your applications.

Chapter 5, Loading, Submitting, and Validating Forms, introduces forms in Ext JS 4. We begin by creating a support-ticket form in the first recipe.

Instead of focusing on how to configure specific fields, we demonstrate more generic tasks for working with forms. Specifically, these are populating forms, submitting forms, performing client-side validation, and handling callbacks/exceptions.

Chapter 6, Using and Configuring Form Fields, will focus on how we configure and use Ext JS 4's built-in form fields and features to hone our forms for a perfect user experience.

We will cover various form fields and move up from configuring the fields using their built-in features to customizing the layout and display of these fields to create a form that creates a smooth and seamless user experience.

Chapter 7, Working with the Ext JS Data Package, will cover the core topics of the Data Package. In particular, we will demonstrate Models, Stores, and Proxies, and explain how each is used for working with your applications' structured data.

Chapter 8, Displaying and Editing Tabular Data, will cover the basics of simple grids to advanced topics such as infinite scrolling and grouping. We will also demonstrate how to edit data easily, customize how we present data, and link your grids with other Ext JS components.

Chapter 9, Constructing Toolbars with Buttons and Menus, looks at toolbars, buttons, and menus as they are the foundation for giving users the means to interact with our applications. They are a navigation and action-launching paradigm that almost all computer users are familiar with, and so making use of them in your applications will give users a head start in finding their way around.

This chapter will explore these crucial components and demonstrate how to add them to your application to provide an interactive and dynamic user experience.

Chapter 10, Drawing and Charting, will demonstrate the new charting and drawing features introduced to Ext JS 4. In particular, you will discover how to chart data for presentation in numerous ways.

We will take you through the `Ext.draw` package which, as you will learn, is used as the basis of the charting package that we explore later. The first recipes introduce the tools available for drawing shapes and text before moving onto the fully featured `Ext.chart` classes that enable you to quickly create and integrate attractive, interactive charts into your apps.

Chapter 11, Theming your Application, describes the tasks involved in customizing the look and feel of your Ext JS application. You will learn the basics of SASS and Compass and move on to compiling the framework's SASS. We will then explore how to customize your theme with SASS options and custom mixins. Finally we will demonstrate how to take care of legacy browsers using the Sencha SDK Tools' slicer tool.

Chapter 12, Advanced Ext JS for the Perfect App, covers advanced topics in Ext JS that will help make your application stand out from the crowd. We will start by explaining how to extend and customize the framework through plugins where we will write a plugin to toggle textfields between an editable and display state. The next recipes will focus on the MVC pattern that has become the recommended way of structuring your applications. These recipes will start by explaining the file and class structure we need leading into how to connect your application's parts together. Finally we will take one of our earlier examples and demonstrate how to create it while following the MVC pattern. We will also focus on `Ext.Direct` and how it can be used to handle server communications in conjunction with forms and stores. Other advanced topics such as state, advanced exception handling, history management, and task management will also be described.

Appendix, Ext JS 4 Cookbook - Exploring Further, contains an additional 20 recipes with more useful hints and tips to help you to get the most out of Sencha's Ext JS 4 framework. Following the same format as the book, these extra recipes cover a wide variety of topics and we hope they further broaden your knowledge of the framework.

 This appendix is not present in the book but is available as a free download from `http://www.packtpub.com/sites/default/files/downloads/Appendix_Ext JS 4 Cookbook_Exploring Further.pdf`.

What you need for this book

Before getting started with this book make sure you have your favorite text editor ready and a browser with some developer tools and a JavaScript debugger. We recommend Google Chrome (with Developer Tools) or Firefox (with Firebug).

All the recipes require the Ext JS 4 SDK. This is available as a free download from Sencha's website http://www.sencha.com/products/extjs/. Additionally, some make use of the Sencha SDK Tools, which can be downloaded from http://www.sencha.com/products/sdk-tools/.

Although each recipe is a standalone example, we need to include the SDK and add the `Ext.onReady` method to our HTML file, which will execute the passed function when everything is fully loaded. Prepare an HTML file with the following, which can be used as the starting point for most of the recipes:

```html
<html>
<head>
<link rel="stylesheet" type="text/css" href="extjs/resources/css/ext-all.css">
    <script type="text/javascript" src="extjs/ext-all-debug.js">
    </script>
    <script type="text/javascript">

        Ext.onReady(function () {

            //Recipe source code goes here

        });
    </script>
</head>
<body>
</body>
</html>
```

The example source code supplied with this book can be executed as a standalone project or by importing each chapter's folder into the Ext JS SDK package's examples folder.

Who this book is for

The Ext JS 4 Web Application Development Cookbook is aimed at both newcomers and those experienced with Ext JS who want to expand their knowledge and learn how to create interactive web applications with Ext JS 4.

Conventions

In this book, you will find a number of styles of text that distinguish between different kinds of information. Here are some examples of these styles, and an explanation of their meaning.

Code words in text are shown as follows: "We can include other contexts through the use of the `include` directive."

A block of code is set as follows:

```
Ext.define('Cookbook.Smartphone', {

  mixins: {
    camera: 'HasCamera'
  }

});
```

When we wish to draw your attention to a particular part of a code block, the relevant lines or items are set in bold:

```
...
fields: [...
{
        name: 'PublishDate',
        type: 'date',
        dateFormat: 'd-m-Y'
}
...]
...
```

Any command-line input or output is written as follows:

Windows: gem install compass

Mac OS X: sudo gem install compass

New terms and **important words** are shown in bold. Words that you see on the screen, in menus or dialog boxes for example, appear in the text like this: "The repeated questions will be dynamically added to the form by pressing an **Add Another Guest** button."

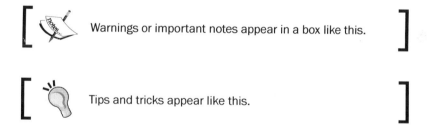

Warnings or important notes appear in a box like this.

Tips and tricks appear like this.

Reader feedback

Feedback from our readers is always welcome. Let us know what you think about this book—what you liked or may have disliked. Reader feedback is important for us to develop titles that you really get the most out of.

To send us general feedback, simply send an e-mail to `feedback@packtpub.com`, and mention the book title through the subject of your message.

If there is a topic that you have expertise in and you are interested in either writing or contributing to a book, see our author guide on `www.packtpub.com/authors`.

Customer support

Now that you are the proud owner of a Packt book, we have a number of things to help you to get the most from your purchase.

Downloading the example code

You can download the example code files for all Packt books you have purchased from your account at `http://www.packtpub.com`. If you purchased this book elsewhere, you can visit `http://www.packtpub.com/support` and register to have the files e-mailed directly to you.

Errata

Although we have taken every care to ensure the accuracy of our content, mistakes do happen. If you find a mistake in one of our books—maybe a mistake in the text or the code—we would be grateful if you would report this to us. By doing so, you can save other readers from frustration and help us improve subsequent versions of this book. If you find any errata, please report them by visiting `http://www.packtpub.com/support`, selecting your book, clicking on the **errata submission form** link, and entering the details of your errata. Once your errata are verified, your submission will be accepted and the errata will be uploaded to our website, or added to any list of existing errata, under the Errata section of that title.

Piracy

Piracy of copyright material on the Internet is an ongoing problem across all media. At Packt, we take the protection of our copyright and licenses very seriously. If you come across any illegal copies of our works, in any form, on the Internet, please provide us with the location address or website name immediately so that we can pursue a remedy.

Please contact us at `copyright@packtpub.com` with a link to the suspected pirated material.

We appreciate your help in protecting our authors, and our ability to bring you valuable content.

Questions

You can contact us at `questions@packtpub.com` if you are having a problem with any aspect of the book, and we will do our best to address it.

1
Classes, Object-Oriented Principles and Structuring your Application

In this chapter, we will cover:

- ▶ Creating custom classes using the new Ext JS class system
- ▶ Using inheritance in your classes
- ▶ Adding mixins to your classes
- ▶ Scoping your functions
- ▶ Dynamically loading Ext JS classes
- ▶ Aliasing your components
- ▶ Accessing components with component query
- ▶ Extending Ext JS components
- ▶ Overriding Ext JS functionality

Introduction

In this chapter, you will learn how to harness the power of Ext JS 4's new class system, and extend the framework's functionality.

Creating custom classes using the new Ext JS class system

Although JavaScript is not a class-based language, it is possible to simulate classes using its prototypal structure. Ext JS 4 introduces an entirely new way of defining classes, compared with Ext JS 3. Consequently, when developing with Ext JS 4 your JavaScript's structure will be more closely in line with that of other object oriented languages.

This recipe will explain how to define classes using the new system, and give some detail about the features it has to offer. We will do this by creating a custom class to model a vehicle, with a method that will alert some details about it.

How to do it...

The `Ext.define` method is used to define new classes. It uses a string-based definition, leaving the framework to take care of the namespacing and concrete defining of the class:

1. Call the `Ext.define` method with our class name and configuration object.

   ```
   // Define new class 'Vehicle' under the 'Cookbook' namespace
   Ext.define('Cookbook.Vehicle', {
       // class configuration goes here
   });
   ```

2. Add properties and methods to the configuration object:

   ```
   Ext.define('Cookbook.Vehicle', {
       Manufacturer: 'Aston Martin',
       Model: 'Vanquish',

       getDetails: function(){
           alert('I am an ' + this.Manufacturer + ' ' + this.Model);
       }
   });
   ```

Class Definition

> **Downloading the example code**
>
> You can download the example code files for all Packt books you have purchased from your account at http://www.packtpub.com. If you purchased this book elsewhere, you can visit http://www.packtpub.com/support and register to have the files e-mailed directly to you.

3. We now add the `Ext.define` method's optional third parameter, which is a function that is executed after the class has been defined, within the scope of the newly created class:

```
Ext.define('Cookbook.Vehicle', {
    Manufacturer: 'Aston Martin',
    Model: 'Vanquish',

    getDetails: function(){
        alert('I am an ' + this.Manufacturer + ' ' + this.Model);
    }
}, function(){
    Console.log('Cookbook.Vehicle class defined!');
});
```

Call back function loaded after class is fully defined. (handwritten annotation)

4. Finally, we create an instance of the new class and call its `getDetails` method:

```
var myVehicle = Ext.create('Cookbook.Vehicle');

alert(myVehicle.Manufacturer); // alerts 'Aston Martin'

myVehicle.getDetails(); // alerts 'I am an Aston Martin Vanquish'
```

Creating an object using class (handwritten annotation)

How it works...

1. The `Ext.define` method handles the creation and construction of your class, including resolving the namespaces within your class name.

   Namespaces allow us to organize classes into logical packages to keep code organized and prevents the global scope from becoming polluted. In our example, Ext JS will create a package (essentially just an object) called `Cookbook`, which contains our `Vehicle` class as a property. Your namespaces can be infinitely deep (that is, as many dots as you wish) and are automatically created by the framework.

2. The first parameter of this method identifies the class name as a string. Class names are always given as strings (when defined and when instantiated) so they can be dynamically loaded when needed, meaning you can start to instantiate a class before it has been loaded.

3. The second parameter of this method accepts a standard JavaScript object that defines all of the properties and methods of your class. These can be accessed, as you would expect, from an instance of the class.

4. The third parameter of `Ext.define`'s is an optional callback function that gets executed once the class has been fully defined and is ready to be instantiated.

5. Internally every class that is defined is turned into an instance of the `Ext.Class` class by the `Ext.ClassManager`. During this process, the manager runs through a series of pre and post processing steps. These processors each take care of initializing one part of the class and are called in the following order:

Preprocessors

- □ **Loader:** Loads any other required classes if they don't already exist, recursing through this process for each class loaded
- □ **Extend:** Now that all the required classes have been loaded, we can extend from them as required by our `extend` config option
- □ **Mixins:** Any Mixins that have been defined are now handled and merged into our class
- □ **Config:** Any properties in the `config` configuration option are processed and their get/set/apply/reset methods are created
- □ **Statics:** If the class has any static properties or methods these are handled at this stage

6. Once all of these pre-processors have completed their work our new class is ready to be instantiated. However, it will continue to work through its post-processors that perform the following actions:

Post Processors

- □ **Aliases**: It creates the necessary structure to allow the class to be created through an `xtype`
- □ **Singleton**: If the class has been defined as a singleton its single instance is created here
- □ **Legacy**: To help with backward compatibility a class can have alternate names that are mapped to the class

At this point our class is fully created, and all that is left to do is to execute the callback function (defined as the third parameter to `Ext.define`) to signal the class definition being complete. The full process can be seen in the following diagram:

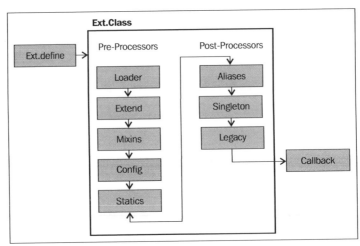

This model is extremely flexible and allows you to include your own pre or post processor at any stage in the sequence by using the `registerPreProcessor` and `registerPostProcessor` methods.

All Ext JS 4 classes inherit from a common base class, named `Ext.Base`. This class contains several methods that provide basic functionality to all created subclasses, for example `override` and `callParent`. When we define a new class using the `Ext.define` method, and don't specify an explicit base class, then the framework will automatically use `Ext.Base` as its base inside the Extend preprocessor. If we do specify a base class then that class will, at the root of its inheritance tree, extend `Ext.Base`. The following diagram shows how our custom class fits into this structure:

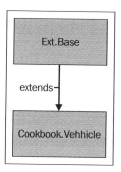

There's more...

The new Ext JS class system also takes care of a lot of the heavy lifting for you when it comes to defining your properties, configuration options, and their associated getter and setter methods.

If you define these configuration options within a `config` object, the class system (inside its Config pre-processor) will automatically generate `get`, `set`, `reset`, and `apply` methods. This reduces the amount of code that needs to be maintained and downloaded.

The following code sample utilizes this `config` option and takes advantage of the free code that the framework will create. This code is initialized by calling the `initConfig` method within the constructor, which is executed when your class is instantiated.

Constructors are special methods that are executed when a class is instantiated (either using the `Ext.create(..)` or `new` syntax) and are used to prepare the object in any way needed. For example, it could be used to set up default property values.

config pre-processor

Utilizes config option... this creates the getters & setters

```
Ext.define('Cookbook.Vehicle', {
    config: {
        Manufacturer: 'Aston Martin',
        Model: 'Vanquish'
    },

    constructor: function(config){
        // initialise our config object
        this.initConfig(config);
    },

    getDetails: function(){
        alert('I am an ' + this.Manufacturer + ' ' + this.Model);
    }
});

// create a new instance of Vehicle class
var vehicle = Ext.create('Cookbook.Vehicle');

// display its details
vehicle.getDetails();

// update Vehicle details
vehicle.setManufacturer('Volkswagen');
vehicle.setModel('Golf');

// display its new details
vehicle.getDetails();
```

Can use get & set methods now w/oot explicitly defining them.

By using this approach it is the equivalent of defining your class with the explicit methods shown as follows:

```
Ext.define('Cookbook.Vehicle', {
    Manufacturer: 'Aston Martin',
    Model: 'Vanquish',

    getManufacturer: function(){
        return this.Manufacturer;
    },
    setManufacturer: function(value){
        this.Manufacturer = value;
    },
```

```
    resetManufacturer: function(){
        this.setManufacturer('Aston Martin');
    },
    applyManufacturer: function(manufacturer){
        // perform some action to apply the value (e.g. update a DOM
element)
        return manufacturer;
    },

    getModel: function(){
        return this.Model;
    },
    setModel: function(value){
        this.Model = value;
    },
    resetModel: function(){
        this.setModel('Vanquish');
    },
    applyModel: function(model){
        // perform some action to apply the value (e.g. update a DOM
element)
        return model;
    },

    getDetails: function(){
        alert('I am an ' + this.Manufacturer + ' ' + this.Model);
    }
});
```

> Notice that we return the property's value within our
> `apply` methods. This is important as this method is
> called by the property's `set` method, so the new value is
> applied appropriately, and its return value is stored as the
> property's value.

Sometimes we will want to perform some extra actions when calling these generated
methods. We can do this by explicitly defining our own version of the method that will
override the generated one. In our example, when calling the `apply` method, we want to
update a DOM element that contains the `Vehicle`'s name, so the change is reflected on
the screen. First we add some markup to hold our `Vehicle`'s data:

```
<span id="manufacturer"></span>
<span id="model"></span>
```

Now we override the `applyManufacturer` and `applyModel` methods to perform an update of each DOM element when the properties are changed:

```
Ext.define('Cookbook.Vehicle', {
    config: {
        Manufacturer: 'Aston Martin',
        Model: 'Vanquish'
    },

    constructor: function(config){
        // initialise our config object
        this.initConfig(config);
    },

    getDetails: function(){
        alert('I am an ' + this.getManufacturer() + ' ' + this.getModel());
    },

    applyManufacturer: function(manufacturer){
        Ext.get('manufacturer').update(manufacturer);
        return manufacturer;
    },

    applyModel: function(model){
        Ext.get('model').update(model);
        return model;
    }
});
// create a Vehicle and set its Manufacturer and Model
var vehicle = Ext.create('Cookbook.Vehicle');
vehicle.setManufacturer('Volkswagen');
vehicle.setModel('Golf');
```

(handwritten note: gets 'manufacturer' element from the DOM & updates it)

See also

▶ The next recipe explaining how to include inheritance in your classes.

▶ The *Adding mixins to your class* recipe, which describes what Mixins are and how they can be added to your classes.

▶ Dynamically Loading ExtJS Classes which explains how to use the dynamic dependency loading system that the framework provides.

Using inheritance in your classes

More often than not when defining a new class, we want to extend an existing Ext JS class or component so that we inherit its current behavior and add our own new functionality.

This recipe explains, how to extend an existing class and add new functionality through new methods and by overriding existing ones.

We will define a very simple class that models a `Vehicle`, capturing its `Manufacturer`, `Model`, and `Top Speed`. It has one method called `travel`, which accepts a single parameter that represents the distance to be travelled. When called, it will show an alert with details of the vehicle, how far it travelled, and at what speed.

How to do it...

1. Define our base `Vehicle` class, which provides us with our basic functionality and from which we will extend our second class:

```
Ext.define('Cookbook.Vehicle', {
    config: {
        manufacturer: 'Unknown Manufacturer',
        model: 'Unknown Model',
        topSpeed: 0
    },

    constructor: function(manufacturer, model, topSpeed){
        // initialise our config object
        this.initConfig();

        if(manufacturer){
            this.setManufacturer(manufacturer);
        }
        if(model){
            this.setModel(model);
        }
        if(topSpeed){
            this.setTopSpeed(topSpeed);
        }
    },

    travel: function(distance){
        alert('The ' + this.getManufacturer() + ' ' + this.
getModel() + ' travelled ' + distance + ' miles at ' + this.
getTopSpeed() + 'mph');
    }
```

Handwritten annotations:
- `} Config parameters` (next to config block)
- `— Initializes config object` (next to `this.initConfig();`)
- `— changes the manufacturer` (next to `this.setManufacturer(manufacturer);`)
- `" " model` (next to `this.setModel(model);`)
- `" " speed.` (next to `this.setTopSpeed(topSpeed);`)

executes after an object is created.

```
}, function(){
    console.log('Vehicle Class defined!');
});
var vehicle = Ext.create('Cookbook.Vehicle', 'Aston Martin',
'Vanquish', 60);
vehicle.travel(100);  // alerts 'The Aston Martin Vanquish
travelled 100 miles at 60mph
```

2. Define a sub-class `Cookbook.Plane` that extends our base `Vehicle` class and accepts a fourth parameter of `maxAltitude`:

```
Ext.define('Cookbook.Plane', {
    extend: 'Cookbook.Vehicle',

    config: {
        maxAltitude: 0
    },

    constructor: function(manufacturer, model, topSpeed,
maxAltitude){
        // initialise our config object
        this.initConfig();

        if(maxAltitude){
            this.setMaxAltitude(maxAltitude);
        }

        // call the parent class' constructor
        this.callParent([manufacturer, model, topSpeed]);
    }
}, function(){
    console.log('Plane Class Defined!');
});
```

extends the Vehicle class

only needs to configure new variable... others will be configured in parent class

calls parent class

3. Create an instance of our `Cookbook.Plane` sub-class and demonstrate that it has the properties and methods defined in both the `Vehicle` and `Plane` classes:

```
var plane = Ext.create('Cookbook.Plane', 'Boeing', '747', 500,
30000);

plane.travel(800);
```

Alerts The Boeing 747 travelled 800 miles at 500mph (inherited from the Vehicle class)

```
alert('Max Altitude: ' + plane.getMaxAltitude() + ' feet');
```

Alerts 'MaxAltitude: 30000 feet' (defined in the `Plane` class)

How it works...

The `extend` configuration option, used when defining your new subclass, tells the `Ext.Class'` Extend preprocessor (which we talked about in the previous recipe) what class your new one should be inherited from. The preprocessor then merges all of the parent class' members into the new class' definition, giving us our extended class.

By extending the `Vehicle` class in this way our class diagram will look like the one shown as follows. Notice that the `Plane` class still inherits from the `Ext.Base` class through the Vehicle class' extension of it:

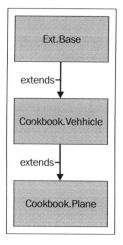

The `callParent` method is a very quick way of executing the parent class' version of the method. This is important to ensure that the parent class is constructed correctly and will still function as we expect. In previous versions of Ext JS, this was achieved by using the following syntax:

```
Plane.superclass.constructor.apply(this, arguments);
```

The new `callParent` method effectively still does this but it is hidden from the developer, making it much easier and quicker to call.

There's more...

We can expand on this idea by adding new functionality to the `Plane` class and override the base class' `travel` method to incorporate this new functionality.

A plane's `travel` method is a little more complicated than a generic vehicle's so we're going to add `takeOff` and `land` methods to the class:

```
Ext.define('Cookbook.Plane', {
    ...

    takeOff: function(){
        alert('The ' + this.getManufacturer() + ' ' + this.getModel()
    + ' is taking off.');
    },

    land: function(){
        alert('The ' + this.getManufacturer() + ' ' + this.getModel()
    + ' is landing.');
    }

    ...
});
```

We can then override the `travel` method of the Vehicle class to add in the `takeOff` and `land` methods into the Plane's `travel` procedure:

```
Ext.define('Cookbook.Plane', {
    ...

    travel: function(distance){
        this.takeOff();

        // execute the base class' generic travel method
        this.callParent(arguments);
```

(handwritten annotation): calls base classes version of this method.

```
        alert('The ' + this.getManufacturer() + ' ' + this.getModel()
  + ' flew at an altitude of ' + this.getMaxAltitude() + 'feet');

        this.land();
    }

    ...

});
```

This method extends the `travel` functionality given to us by the `Vehicle` class by alerting us to the fact that the plane is taking off, flying at a specific altitude, and then landing again.

The important part of this method is the call to the `callParent` method. This executes the base class' `travel` method, which runs the `Vehicle`'s implementation of the `travel` method. Notice that it passes in the `arguments` variable as a parameter. This variable is available in all JavaScript functions and contains an array of all the parameters that were passed into it.

We can see this in action by creating a new `Plane` object and calling the `travel` method:

```
var plane = Ext.create('Cookbook.Plane', 'Boeing', '747', 500, 30000);

plane.travel(800); // alerts 'The Boeing 747 is taking off'
              // 'The Boeing 747 travelled 800 miles at 500mph'
              // 'The Boeing 747 flew at an altitude of 30000 feet'
              // 'The Boeing 747 is landing.'
```

See also

▶ The very first recipe in this chapter that covers how classes work.

▶ The recipe describing *Dynamically loading Ext JS classes*, which teaches you about how these classes can be loaded on the fly.

▶ The *Extending Ext JS components* recipe, which explains how to use inheritance to extend the functionality of the framework.

Adding mixins to your class

Mixins are classes that can be included in another class, merging its members (methods and properties) into it. This technique provides us with a form of multiple inheritance where the `mixin` class' methods and properties can be accessed as if they were part of the parent class.

Form of multiple inheritence

By making use of mixins we can package small and reusable bits of functionality into an encapsulated class, and merge it into classes which require that functionality. This reduces repetition and removes the need for the class to be extended directly. One example of a `Mixin` used within the framework is the `Ext.form.Labelable` class, which gives the component it is mixed into the ability to have a label attached to it.

How to do it...

1. Define our simple `mixin` class called `HasCamera` with a single method called `takePhoto`:

```
Ext.define('HasCamera', {
    takePhoto: function(){
        alert('Say Cheese! .... Click!');
    }
});
```

2. Define a `skeleton` class and use the `mixins` configuration option to apply our `HasCamera` mixin to our `Cookbook.Smartphone` class.

skeleton class

```
Ext.define('Cookbook.Smartphone', {
    mixins: {
        camera: 'HasCamera',
    }
});
```
Short name we gave our mixin.   *Class Name that is being mixed in*

3. We can now call our mixin's `takePhoto` method as part of the `Smartphone`'s class within a `useCamera` method:

```
Ext.define('Cookbook.Smartphone', {
    mixins: {
        camera: 'HasCamera'
    },

    useCamera: function(){
        this.takePhoto();  — calls method defined in
    }                          mixins class
});
```

4. Instantiate the `Smartphone` class and call the `useCamera` method:

```
var smartphone = Ext.create('Cookbook.Smartphone');
smartphone.useCamera(); // alerts 'Say Cheese! .... Click!'
```

How it works...

By using the `mixins` configuration option we tell the class defining process to use the mixins preprocessor to merge all of the `mixin` class' members into the main class. This now means that all of the methods and properties defined as part of the `HasCamera` class can be accessed directly from the parent class' instance.

The name we give to our mixin in this configuration object allows us to reference it within our class' code. We will explore this later in the recipe.

Step 4, shows how we can access the `HasCamera` class' methods from the parent class by simply calling them as if they are part of the `Smartphone` class itself.

There's more...

We might be required to override the functionality provided by our `mixins` class as we often would when using traditional inheritance.

In our example, we might want to introduce a `focus` routine into the `takePhoto` process to ensure that our subject is in focus before taking a photo. As we have done in previous recipes, we declare a method called `takePhoto` that will override the one added by the `HasCamera` Mixin, and another method to perform our `focus` operation:

```
Ext.define('Cookbook.Smartphone', {
    mixins: {
        camera: 'HasCamera'
    },

    useCamera: function(){
        this.takePhoto();
    },

    takePhoto: function(){
        this.focus();

        this.takePhoto();
    },

    focus: function(){
        alert('Focusing Subject...');
    }
});
```

[handwritten annotations]
— *Overrides mixin method*
— *should calls the mixin version of the method... however it calls itself → will be fixed later*

At this point we are in trouble because our new `takePhoto` method needs to reference the original `takePhoto` method defined in the `HasCamera` class. However, at the moment it is pointing back to itself and will cause an infinite loop.

We get around this by calling the `mixins` method directly from its prototype, which can be accessed using the name we assigned it in Step 3. Our `takePhoto` method now becomes:

```
takePhoto: function(){
    this.focus();

    this.mixins.camera.takePhoto.call(this);
}
```

[handwritten: Proper way to call mixin methods]

[handwritten: name we defined for mixin]

See also

▶ The first recipe, *Creating custom classes using the new Ext JS class system*, for a recap about defining classes.

▶ Overriding Ext JS' functionality describes how to customize the framework's default behaviour by defining new versions of key methods.

▶ See the *Adding functionality with plugins* recipe, in *Chapter 12, Advanced Ext JS for the Perfect App* to help understand how plugins can be used and how they differ from mixins.

Scoping your functions

Making sure that you execute your functions in the correct scope is one of the harder tasks faced by new (and experienced!) JavaScript developers.

We would recommend studying the scoping rules of JavaScript to get a full understanding of how it works, but we will start this recipe with an explanation of exactly what scope is, how it changes, and how it affects our code.

What is Scope?

Scope refers to the context that a piece of code is executing in and decides what variables are available to it. JavaScript has two types of scope: global scope and local scope. Variables and functions declared in the global scope are available to code everywhere. Common examples are the `document` and `window` variables. Local Scope refers to variables and functions that have been declared within a function, and so are contained by that function. Therefore, they can't be accessed from code above it in the scope chain.

The **scope chain** is the way that JavaScript resolves variables. If you are trying to access a variable within a function, which has not been declared as a local variable within it, the JavaScript engine will traverse back up the chain of functions, (that is, scopes) looking for a variable matching its name. If it finds one then it will be used, otherwise an error will be thrown. This also means that local variables will take precedence over global variables with the same name.

We will explore a couple of examples to demonstrate how this works.

1. The first example shows a simple variable being declared in the global scope and it being alerted—no surprises there!

```
var myVar = 'Hello from Global Scope!';
alert(myVar); //alerts 'Hello from Global Scope!'
```

2. If you run the next example, you will now see two alerts; the first will say `Hello from Global Scope!` and the second `Hello from MyFunction!`. Our `myFunction` function is able to access the `myVar` variable because it was declared in the global scope and so can be found on the function's scope chain:

```
var myVar = 'Hello from Global Scope!';

function myFunction(){
   myVar = 'Hello from MyFunction!';
}

alert(myVar); //alerts 'Hello from Global Scope!'

myFunction();

alert(myVar); //alerts 'Hello from MyFunction!'
```

3. We now add an alert to the `myFunction` function and add the `var` keyword in front of the `myVar` assignment within it. This keyword creates a local variable as part of the `myFunction`'s scope with the same name as the one created in the global scope. The alert inside the `myFunction` function will now alert `Hello from MyFunction!` But the two alerts outside the function will alert the original global `myVar`'s value. This is because the `myVar` variable that was modified in the `myFunction` function is a new local variable, and so doesn't affect the global version:

```
var myVar = 'Hello Global Scope!';

function myFunction(){
   var myVar = 'Hello from MyFunction!';
   alert(myVar);
```

```
}

alert(myVar); //alerts 'Hello from Global Scope!'

myFunction(); //alerts 'Hello from MyFunction!'

alert(myVar); //alerts 'Hello from Global Scope!'
```

4. Finally, we will demonstrate the use of the `this keyword.` This keyword exists everywhere and provides us with a reference to the context (or scope) that the current piece of code is executing in. Consider the following example where a new object is created using the `MyObject`'s constructor function. If we then `console.log` the contents of the `this` keyword, we see that it refers to the new object that we have created. This means that we can define properties on this object and have them contained within this object, and so, inaccessible from any other scope:

```
function MyClass(){
    console.log(this);
}

var myClass = new MyClass();
```

5. If we add a property to the `this` object in our constructor, we can alert it once a new instance has been created. Notice that if we try to alert `this.myProperty` outside the scope of the `MyClass` object, it doesn't exist because `this` now refers to the browser window:

```
function MyClass(){
    console.log(this);
    this.myProperty = 'Hello';
}

var myClass = new MyClass();

alert(myClass.myProperty); // alerts 'Hello'

alert(this.myProperty); // alerts 'undefined'
```

Scope and Ext JS

When dealing with scope in Ext JS we are generally concerned with making sure our functions are executing in the scope of the correct class (whether it is a component, store, or controller). For example, by default an `Ext.button.Button`'s click event will execute its handler function in the scope of itself (that is, `this` refers to the `Ext.button.Button` instance). It's likely that we want the button's handler to execute in the scope of the parent class (for example, a grid panel) and so we must force a different scope upon it.

We will now explore ways in which we can change the scope a function executes in using Ext JS' in-built functionality. By following these steps we will see how Ext JS makes it easy to ensure `this` refers to what you want it to!

How to do it...

Ext JS provides us with a method that allows us to force a function to execute in the scope we specify, meaning we can specify what the `this` keyword refers to within the function.

1. Define two objects, each with a property and a function:

```
var cat = {
    sound: 'miaow',
    speak: function(){
        alert(this.sound);
    }
};
var dog = {
    sound: 'woof',
    speak: function(){
        alert(this.sound);
    }
};

cat.speak(); // alerts 'miaow'
dog.speak(); // alerts 'woof'
```

2. Use the `Ext.bind` method to force the `dog` object's `speak` method to execute in the scope of the `cat` object by passing it as its second parameter:

```
Ext.bind(dog.speak, cat)(); // alerts 'miaow'
```

How it works...

The `Ext.bind` method creates a wrapper function for the `speak` method that will force it to have its scope set to the object that is passed in, overriding the default scope value. This new function can be executed immediately (as our example did) or stored in a variable to be executed at a later point.

By using it we redefine the `this` keyword used within the function to refer to what was passed in as the second parameter. This is the reason that in Step 2 the alert displayed the value stored in the cat's `sound` property rather than the dog's.

There's more...

Getting the scope of a function correct is especially important within event handlers. Ext JS provides a scope config option that can be used to explicitly set the scope an event handler is executed in.

Consider the following example where we define a button and attach a handler to its click event, which will show an alert of the current scope's `text` property:

```
var button = Ext.create('Ext.button.Button', {
    text: 'My Test Button',
    listeners: {
        click: function(button, e, options){
            alert(this.text);
        }
    },
    renderTo: Ext.getBody()
});

button.show();
```

By default, `this` refers to the button itself and displays `My Test Button`. But what if we want to execute the function in the scope of another object, like this one?

```
var exampleObject = {
    text: 'My Test Object'
};
```

Our initial reaction would be to use the `Ext.bind` method, which we looked at earlier in the recipe, and would look something like this:

```
listeners: {
    click: Ext.bind(function(button, e, options){
        alert(this.text);
    }, exampleObject)
}
```

This technique works well and functions correctly. However, there is a more succinct method in the form of the scope config option, which can be added as shown in the following code:

```
listeners: {
    click: function(button, e, options){
        alert(this.text);
    },
    scope: exampleObject
}
```

Added to Listeners

The scope object is effectively a short hand way of using `Ext.bind` and gives us the same outcome with less code.

If you were to include multiple event handlers within the `listeners` property the `scope` value would be applied to them all. If you want to specify a different scope value for each event, you can use the following syntax:

```
listeners: {
    click: {
        fn: function(button, e, options){
            alert(this.text);
        },
        scope: this
    },
    afterrender: {
        fn: function(button, options){
            // do something...
        },
        scope: otherObject
    }
}
```

See also

▶   The recipe *Handling event on elements and components* in *Chapter 2, Manipulating the Dom, Handling Events, and Making AJAX Requests* for further examples.

Dynamically loading Ext JS classes

Ext JS 4 gives us the ability to only load the parts of the framework we need, as and when we need them. In this recipe, we will explore how to use the framework to automatically load all our class dependencies on the fly.

How to do it...

We are going to use the `Vehicle` and `Plane` classes that we created in the Using inheritance recipe earlier to demonstrate dynamic loading.

1.   Configure the `Ext.Loader` class to enable it and map our namespaces to a physical path. This should be added before your `Ext.onReady` call:

```
Ext.Loader.setConfig({
    enabled: true,
    paths: {
        'Cookbook': 'src/Cookbook'
    }
});
```

2. Create individual files in the `src/Cookbook` folder for the `Vehicle` and `Plane` classes, naming each the same as the class name (excluding the namespace).

3. Call the `Ext.require` method, inside our `Ext.onReady` function, passing in the class we need, and a callback function, which is executed after the class and all its dependencies have loaded, containing our code:

```
Ext.require('Cookbook.Vehicle', function(){
    var van = Ext.create('Cookbook.Vehicle', 'Ford', 'Transit',
60);
    van.travel(200);
});
```

4. Execute the code and monitor your **Developer Tools** console and HTML tabs and you will see the `Ext.define`'s callback being displayed and the new script tag being injected into the HTML:

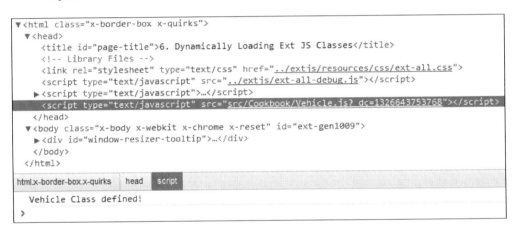

```
▼<html class="x-border-box x-quirks">
  ▼<head>
      <title id="page-title">6. Dynamically Loading Ext JS Classes</title>
      <!-- Library Files -->
      <link rel="stylesheet" type="text/css" href="../extjs/resources/css/ext-all.css">
      <script type="text/javascript" src="../extjs/ext-all-debug.js"></script>
     ►<script type="text/javascript">…</script>
      <script type="text/javascript" src="src/Cookbook/Vehicle.js? dc=1326643753768"></script>
    </head>
  ▼<body class="x-body x-webkit x-chrome x-reset" id="ext-gen1009">
     ►<div id="window-resizer-tooltip">…</div>
    </body>
  </html>
```

| html.x-border-box.x-quirks | head | script |

```
  Vehicle Class defined!
>
```

How it works...

The initial configuration of the `Ext.Loader` class is vital for our classes to be loaded correctly, as it defines how class names are mapped to file locations so the `Loader` class knows where to find each class it is required to load. It also highlights the need for strict naming conventions when it comes to creating your files.

In our example, the paths configuration tells the Loader that any required classes within the `Cookbook` namespace should be loaded from the `src/Cookbook` directory.

We then call the `Ext.require` method, (an alias of the `Ext.Loader.require` method) which takes the class name specified and resolves its URL based on the paths configuration, and if it hasn't already been loaded previously, injects a script tag into the HTML page to load it. Once this load has happened the specified callback function is executed where you can create instances of the class with the knowledge that it has been fully loaded.

The `Ext.require` method accepts either a single or array of string values that will all be loaded prior to the callback being executed.

There's more...

One of the great things about the `Ext.Loader` class is that it is recursive and won't stop until all the files needed by the original required classes are loaded. This means that it will load all classes referenced in the extend, mixins, and requires configuration objects.

We will demonstrate this by creating an instance of `Cookbook.Plane`, which extends the `Cookbook.Vehicle` class. If we execute the following code, and monitor your developer tool as we did before, we will see both classes being loaded and created:

```
Ext.require('Cookbook.Plane', function(){
    var plane = new Ext.create('Cookbook.Plane', 'Boeing', '747', 500,
35000);
    plane.travel(200);
});
```

See also

▶   See the very first recipe covering the details of how to define and work with classes.

▶   A fixed folder structure is required for dynamic loading. See the recipe *Creating your application's folder structure* in *Appendix, Ext JS 4 Cookbook-Exploring Further* for a detailed explanation.

Aliasing your components

Aliasing allows you to define a shorthand name for a component class. This is particularly useful as it means you don't always have to reference the full class name, which, if you are following Sencha's naming convention, can become fairly long. Additionally, aliasing allows you to define an `xtype` for your component.

This `xtype` is not only a shortcut to the full component name but brings advantages such as improved performance.

Instead of explicitly creating components during initialization a component with an `xtype` can be created implicitly as an object config. If you don't instantiate everything as an object, you can defer creation and rendering of the component to save resources until they are actually required.

We will demonstrate aliasing by creating a panel inside a viewport.

How to do it...

1. We start by defining our class and specifying an `alias` config option with a "widget" prefix:

```
Ext.define('Customer.support.SupportMessage', {
    extend: 'Ext.panel.Panel',
    alias: 'widget.supportMessage',
    title: 'Customer Support',
    html: 'Customer support is online'
});
```

2. The panel `Customer.support.SupportMessage` can be instantiated lazily by using its `xtype`:

```
Ext.application({
    name: 'Customer',
    launch: function(){
        Ext.create('Ext.container.Viewport', {
            layout: 'fit',
            items: [{
                xtype: 'supportMessage'
            }]
        });
    }
});
```

How it works...

`Ext.reg()` doesn't exist in Ext JS 4, instead we register aliases with the `alias` config option.

When the application is first loaded, the class definitions are parsed and a dictionary of class `aliases` is created. This is contained within the framework's component manager (`Ext.ComponentManager`).

We're required to name our aliases with a prefix, "widget." However, when using the alias the prefix is not required.

The aliases are, as you would expect, simply a reference to the class. As we haven't instantiated the class (yet) we're able to save memory and resources. This is particularly helpful when our widgets are nested deeply as resources are not wasted on components that are not required or even rendered.

As we destroy our components, the framework releases the resources, but keeps the alias reference in the component manager, so that we can re-create the same component time and time again.

Calling the alias is done using the `xtype` config option, which is where you provide the alias name.

There's more...

There are other ways to define aliases for your components.

- ▶ `Ext.ClassManager.setAlias(string class, string alias)`: This registers the alias for a class
- ▶ `Ext.Base.createAlias(string/object alias, string/object origin)`: This will create an alias for existing prototype methods.

See also

- ▶ Aliasing is used throughout this book in a variety of topics and recipes, however, the recipe *Constructing a complex form layout*, in *Chapter 5, Loading, Submitting, and Validating Forms* is a good example of using xtypes.

Accessing components with component query

Ext JS 4 introduces a new helper class called `Ext.ComponentQuery`, which allows us to get references to Ext JS Components using CSS/XPath style selector syntax. This new class is very powerful and, as you will find out, is leveraged as an integral part of the MVC architecture system.

In this recipe we will demonstrate how to use the `Ext.ComponentQuery` class to get references to specific components within a simple application. We will also move onto exploring how this query engine is integrated into the `Ext.Container` class to make finding relative references very easy.

Finally we will look at adding our own custom selector logic to give us fine-grain control over the components that are retrieved.

Getting ready

We will start by creating a simple application, which consists of a simple `Ext.panel.Panel` with a toolbar, buttons, a form, and a grid. This will form the basis of our examples as it has a number of components that we can query for.

```
var panel = Ext.create('Ext.panel.Panel', {

    height: 500,
    width: 500,
    renderTo: Ext.getBody(),
```

```
layout: {
    type: 'vbox',
    align: 'stretch'
},
items: [{
    xtype: 'tabpanel',
    itemId: 'mainTabPanel',
    flex: 1,
    items: [{
        xtype: 'panel',
        title: 'Users',
        id: 'usersPanel',
        layout: {
            type: 'vbox',
            align: 'stretch'
        },
        tbar: [{
            xtype: 'button',
            text: 'Edit',
            itemId: 'editButton'
        }],
        items: [{
            xtype: 'form',
            border: 0,
            items: [{
                xtype: 'textfield',
                fieldLabel: 'Name',
                allowBlank: false
            }, {
                xtype: 'textfield',
                fieldLabel: 'Email',
                allowBlank: false
            }],
            buttons: [{
                xtype: 'button',
                text: 'Save',
                action: 'saveUser'
            }]
        }, {
            xtype: 'grid',
            flex: 1,
            border: 0,
            columns: [{
                header: 'Name',
                dataIndex: 'Name',
                flex: 1
            }, {
                header: 'Email',
                dataIndex: 'Email'
            }],
```

```
            store: Ext.create('Ext.data.Store', {
                fields: ['Name', 'Email'],
                data: [{
                    Name: 'Joe Bloggs',
                    Email: 'joe@example.com'
                }, {
                    Name: 'Jane Doe',
                    Email: 'jane@example.com'
                }]
            })
        }]
    }]
}, {
    xtype: 'component',
    itemId: 'footerComponent',
    html: 'Footer Information',
    extraOptions: {
        option1: 'test',
        option2: 'test'
    },
    height: 40
}]
});
```

How to do it...

The main method of the `Ext.ComponentQuery` class is the `query` method. As we have mentioned, it accepts a CSS/XPath style selector string and returns an array of `Ext.Component` (or subclasses of the `Ext.Component` class) instances that match the specified selector.

1. **Finding components based on xtype**: We generally use a component's xtype as the basis for a selector and can retrieve references to every existing component of a xtype by passing it in to the query method. The following snippet will retrieve all `Ext.Panel` instances:

    ```
    var panels = Ext.ComponentQuery.query('panel');
    ```

2. Just like in CSS we can include the concept of nesting by adding a second xtype separated by a space. In the following example, we retrieve all the `Ext.Button` instances that are descendants of an `Ext.Panel` instance:

    ```
    var buttons = Ext.ComponentQuery.query('panel button');
    ```

     If you have custom classes whose xtypes include characters other than alphanumeric (for example, a dot or hypen) you cannot retrieve them in this way. You must instead query the `xtype` property of the components using the following syntax:

    ```
    var customXtypeComponents = Ext.
    ComponentQuery.query('[xtype="My.Custom.
    Xtype"'];
    ```

3. **Retrieving components based on attribute values**: Along with retrieving references based on xtype, we can query the properties a component possesses to be more explicit about which components we want. In our sample application we have given the **Save** button an `action` property to distinguish it from other buttons. We can select this button by using the following syntax:

    ```
    var saveButton = Ext.ComponentQuery.query('button[action="saveUs
    er"]');
    ```

    This will return all `Ext.Button` instances that have an `action` property with a value of `saveUser`.

4. **Combining selectors**: It is possible to combine multiple selectors into one query in order to collect references to components that satisfy two different conditions. We do this by simply comma separating the selectors. The following code will select all `Ext.Button` and `Ext.form.field.Text` component instances:

    ```
    var buttonsAndTextfields = Ext.ComponentQuery.query('button,
    textfield');
    ```

5. **Finding components based on ID**: A component's `id` and `itemId` can be included in a selector by prefixing it with the # symbol. This syntax can be combined with all the others we have seen so far but IDs should be unique and so should not be necessary. The following code snippet will select a component with an ID of `usersPanel`:

```
var usersPanel = Ext.ComponentQuery.query('#usersPanel');
```

6. **Retrieving components based on attribute presence**: One useful feature of the component query engine is that we can select components based on an attribute simply being present, regardless of its value. This can be used when we want to find components that have been configured with specific properties but don't know the values they might have. We can demonstrate this with the following code that will select all `Ext.Component` that have the property `extraOptions`.

```
var extraOptionsComponents = Ext.ComponentQuery.query('component[e
xtraOptions]');
```

7. **Using Components' Member Functions**: It's also possible to execute a component's member function as a part of the selection criteria. If the function returns a truthy result then that component will be included (assuming the other criteria is met) in the result set. The following code shows this in action and will select all text fields who are direct children of a form and whose `isValid` method evaluates to true:

```
var validField = Ext.ComponentQuery.query('form >
textfield{isValid()}');
```

How it works...

The `Ext.ComponentQuery` is a singleton class that encapsulates the query logic used in our examples. We have used the `query` method, which works by parsing each part of the selector and using it in conjunction with the `Ext.ComponentManager` class. This class is responsible for keeping track of all the existing `Ext.Component` instances, and is used to find any matching components.

There's more...

There is one other method of the `Ext.ComponentQuery` class to introduce and a further four methods that are part of the `Ext.container.AbstractContainer` class.

Evaluating a component instance's type

The component query class allows us to evaluate a component reference we already have to find out if it matches a certain criteria. To do this we use the `is` method, which accepts a selector identical to the ones that the `query` method accepts and will return true if it does match. The following code determines if our main `Ext.Panel` (referenced in the `panel` variable) has an xtype of panel.

```
var isPanel = Ext.ComponentQuery.is(panel, 'panel');
```

Ext.container.AbstractContainer ComponentQuery methods

There are four methods available in the `Ext.container.AbstractContainer` class (which all container classes extend from; for example panels), which utilizes the component query engine and allow us to query using that component as the root. These methods are `query`, `child`, `up` and `down`. The `query` method is identical to the query method available in the `Ext.ComponentQuery` class but uses the container instance as the root of the query and so will only look for components under it in the hierarchy.

The `up` and `down` methods retrieve the first component, at any level, either above or below the current component in the component hierarchy that matches the selector passed in.

Finally, the `child` method retrieves the first direct child of the current instance that matches the selector.

Using and creating the pseudo-selectors

Pseudo-selectors allow us to filter the retrieved result array based on some criteria that may be too complex to represent in a plain selector. There are two built-in pseudo-selectors: `not` and `last`. These can be added to a selector using a colon. The following example shows a selector that will retrieve the last text field.

```
var lastTextfield = Ext.ComponentQuery.query('textfield:last');
```

It is very simple for us to create our own custom pseudo-selectors; we will demonstrate how to add a pseudo-selector to retrieve components that are visible.

We start by creating a new function on the `Ext.ComponentQuery.pseudos` object called `visible`, which accepts one parameter that will contain the array of matches found so far. We will then add code to loop through each item, checking if it's visible and, if it is, adding it to a new filtered array. We then return this new filtered array.

```
Ext.ComponentQuery.pseudos.visible = function(items) {
    var result = [];

    for (var i = 0; i < items.length; i++) {

        if (items[i].isVisible()) {
            result.push(items[i]);
        }
    }

    return result;
};
```

We can now use this in a selector in the same way as we did before. The following query will retrieve all visible components:

```
var visibleComponents = Ext.ComponentQuery.query('component:visible');
```

> ▸ The recipes about MVC in Chapter 12, *Advanced Ext JS for the Perfect App* make use of component queries extensively.

Extending Ext JS components

It is regarded as best practice to create each of your components as extensions of Ext JS' own components and store them in separate files. This approach aids code reuse, helps organize your code and makes maintenance a much easier task. In this recipe, we will discuss how to go about extending an Ext JS component to create a pre-configured class and then configuring it to make our own custom component.

How to do it...

We will define an extension of the `Ext.panel.Panel` class to create a simple display panel.

1. Define a new class under the `Cookbook` namespace, which extends the `Ext.panel.Panel` class:

```
Ext.define('Cookbook.DisplayPanel', {
    extend: 'Ext.panel.Panel'
});
```

2. Override the `Ext.panel.Panel`'s `initComponent` method and call the parent class' `initComponent` method:

```
Ext.define('Cookbook.DisplayPanel', {
    extend: 'Ext.panel.Panel',

    initComponent: function(){
        // call the extended class' initComponent method
        this.callParent(arguments);
    }
});
```

3. Add our own component configuration to the `initComponent` method by applying it to the class itself:

```
initComponent: function(){
    // apply our configuration to the class
    Ext.apply(this, {
        title: 'Display Panel',
        html: 'Display some information here!',
        width: 200,
        height: 200,
```

```
        renderTo: Ext.getBody()
    });

    // call the extended class' initComponent method
    this.callParent(arguments);
}
```

4. Create an instance of our preconfigured class and show it:

```
var displayPanel = Ext.create('Cookbook.DisplayPanel');
displayPanel.show();
```

How it works...

Our first step creates our new class definition and tells the framework to give our new class all the functionality that the `Ext.panel.Panel` has, through the use of the `extend` config option.

We then introduce an override for the `initComponent` method, which is used by each component to add its own configuration and perform any actions that are needed to set the component up. In order to ensure that this component behaves as it should, we call the parent class' `initComponent` method (in this case, `Ext.panel.Panel`) using the `callParent` method.

Next, we give our new class the configuration we want. We do this by using the `Ext.apply` method, which merges our configuration object into the class itself.

We are now able to instantiate our new class using its defined name and it will automatically be configured with all the properties we applied in the `initComponent` method. This means we can create a `DisplayPanel` anywhere in our code and only have to define it once.

There's more...

We can take this idea further by integrating our own functionality into an extended component by overriding its functions. We are going to create a custom `TextField` that includes some information text below the field to help the user complete the form field correctly:

1. First we create our basic structure for extending the `Ext.form.field.Text` component:

```
Ext.define('Cookbook.InfoTextField', {

    extend: 'Ext.form.field.Text'

});
```

2. Next, we override the `onRender` function, which is used to render the component to the page. In our override, we immediately call the parent's `onRender` method, so the field is fully rendered before our code is executed. We then use the `Ext.core.DomHelper` class to insert a new `div` element, after the textfield, containing the value from the component's `infoText` property:

```
Ext.define('Cookbook.InfoTextField', {
    extend: 'Ext.form.field.Text',
    onRender: function(){
        this.callParent(arguments);

        // insert our Info Text element
        Ext.core.DomHelper.append(this.getEl(), '<div>' + this.
infoText + '</div>');
    }
}, function(){
    console.log('Cookbook.InfoTextField defined!');
});
```

3. We can now create our new `InfoTextField` class wherever we like and display any value that we would like using the `infoText` config option, like this:

```
var infoTextField = Ext.create('Cookbook.InfoTextField', {
    renderTo: Ext.getBody(),
    fieldLabel: 'Username',
    infoText: 'Your Username must be at least 6 characters long.'
});

infoTextField.show();
```

See also

▶ *Creating custom classes with the new Ext JS class system* for an explanation on creating classes and their structure.

▶ We extend classes throughout this book, however, if you would like to see it in action we suggest you take a look at *Modeling a data object*, in *Chapter 7*, *Working with the Ext JS Data Package*.

▶ The next recipe covers overriding in more detail.

Overriding Ext JS' functionality

To save the hassle of editing the framework directly (not recommended) when you are looking to alter its behaviour Ext JS provides a very useful override feature. By keeping framework behaviour changes separate you can remove them easily if necessary and keep track of your updates when upgrading to a newer version of the framework.

Altering framework code is strongly discouraged as other developers may not realize your changes and be unpleasantly surprised by the non-standard behavior!

Overriding allows you to take an existing class and either modify the behavior of existing functions or add completely new ones. This greatly increases the flexibility of the framework as it provides a very straightforward way to completely alter the out-the-box behaviour.

Achieving this in Ext JS 4 is done with the `Ext.override` method, which is an alias of `Ext.Base.override`.

`Ext.override(Object originalCls, Object overrides)` takes the original class and merges the new (or updated) functions you wish to create for the class.

It's perhaps worth pointing out that `Ext.override` will overwrite any members with the same name, so if you wish to simply extend their functionality you may be required to include the code from the original function.

To demonstrate overriding we will add new functions to an existing class.

How to do it...

1. Let's start by defining a class and giving it a `welcome` method:

    ```
    Ext.define('Simple.Class', {
        welcome: function() {
            alert('Welcome to the app');
        }
    });
    ```

2. We provide `Ext.override` with the original class and add new functions:

    ```
    Ext.override(Simple.Class, {
        goodBye: function() {
            alert('Goodbye');
        },

        runAll: function() {
            this.welcome();
            this.goodBye();
        }
    });
    ```

3. Next, instantiate our class and call the new `runAll()` method:

```
var app = new Simple.Class();
app.runAll();   // Welcome to the app
                // Goodbye
```

4. The override can also be written like this:

```
Simple.Class.override({
  //New members...
});
```

How it works...

The override method of `Ext.Base` takes the original class and loops around the new functions that you've created by adding them to the prototype of the existing class and replacing any existing ones with the new definitions.

There's more...

There are a number of other features in the framework that help you override and perform similar tasks.

Ext.Base.callParent

If you are looking to extend the behavior of an existing function, you can now easily call the original function passing any required arguments using the `callParent` method.

Let's take the example from the recipe *Extending Ext JS Components*. The recipe shows how to add information text under a specified text field.

We can amend that example and force our information text to appear on all text fields throughout the application with a very simple override.

```
Ext.define('Cookbook.overrides.TextField', {
    override: 'Ext.form.field.Text',

    onRender: function(){
        this.callParent(arguments);

        Ext.core.DomHelper.append(this.el, '<div>' + this.infoText +
'</div>');
    }
});
```

We use the usual Ext.define function and give our override a name; this can be any name we want. Instead of including an extend configuration like we normally would, we add the override option, which is a string representation of the class we want to apply the override to.

Just like the *Extending Ext JS Components* recipe we override the text field's onRender function and want to call the parent's onRender method so the field is fully rendered before our code is executed. We do this by including this.callParent(arguments), which will execute the Ext.form.field.Text class' onRender function.

If we wanted to skip the Ext.form.field.Text class' onRender function and execute its parent class' (that is, Ext.form.field.Base) onRender function, (if we were, for example, providing a complete customization of the text Field's rendering process) we do this by calling Ext.form.field.Text.superclass.onRender.apply(this, arguments).

Now we define infoText in our text field's config options and it will display the field;

```
Ext.application({
    launch: function(){
        Ext.create('Ext.container.Viewport', {
            layout: 'fit',
            items: [{
                xtype: 'form',
                defaultType: 'textfield',
                items: [{
                    fieldLabel: 'Security Question',
                    name: 'securityQuestion',
                    allowBlank: false,
                    infoText: 'You are required to write a security
question for your account.'
                }, {
                    fieldLabel: 'Security Answer',
                    name: 'securityAnswer',
                    allowBlank: false,
                    infoText: 'Please provide the answer to your
security
                }]
            }]
        });
    }
});
```

Ext.Base.borrow

With `Ext.Base.borrow` you can borrow another class' members and add them directly to the prototype of your class.

Ext.Base.implement

`Ext.Base.implement` is similar to override, but will always replace members with the same name and not give you the ability to call the original method. Just like `Ext.Base.override`, it's intended for adding methods or properties to the prototype of a class.

See also

- ▸ *Creating custom classes using the new Ext JS class system*, explains how the class system works and its structure.
- ▸ The recipe *Handling session timeouts with TaskManager* in *Appendix, Ext JS 4 Cookbook-Exploring Further*, is a further demonstration on overriding classes.

2
Manipulating the Dom, Handling Events, and Making AJAX Requests

In this chapter, we will cover:

- ▸ Selecting DOM elements
- ▸ Traversing the DOM
- ▸ Manipulating DOM elements
- ▸ Creating new DOM elements
- ▸ Handling events on elements and components
- ▸ Delegating event handling of child elements
- ▸ Simple animation of elements
- ▸ Custom animations
- ▸ Parsing, formatting, and manipulating dates
- ▸ Loading data through AJAX
- ▸ Encoding and decoding JSON date

Introduction

This chapter will cover topics about working with the **Document Object Model** (**DOM**), selecting, creating, and manipulating elements. We'll look at how to add built-in animations to your elements and how to create custom animations.

We'll walk through creating your first AJAX request and encoding/decoding the data either in JSON or HTML format.

Other topics include, handling events, working with dates, detecting browser features, and evaluating object types/values.

Selecting DOM elements

When creating interactive and responsive web applications it's vital to be able to access DOM elements for manipulation and processing. Ext JS provides multiple methods of retrieving references to those DOM elements, which we will explore in this recipe.

Ext JS wraps basic DOM elements up in a class called `Ext.Element`, which is what we generally deal with when retrieving DOM elements and manipulating them. It provides a large number of helpful methods to make life easy for us.

How to do it...

Imagine an HTML page, with the Ext JS 4 library loaded into it, containing the following HTML fragment:

```
<h1 id="book-title">Ext JS 4 Cookbook</h1>
<h2>Authors</h2>
<ul id="authors">
    <li>Stuart Ashworth</li>
    <li>Andrew Duncan</li>
</ul>

<h2>What's new in Ext JS 4?</h2>
<ul id="whats-new">
    <li>Charting</li>
    <li>Drawing</li>
    <li>Data Package</li>
    <li>Enhanced Grid</li>
    <li>Powerful Theming</li>
</ul>
```

We will now use the `Ext.get()` method to retrieve a reference to the div containing the book's title and alert it to the user:

```
var bookTitleEl = Ext.get('book-title');
alert('Book Title ID: ' + bookTitleEl.id);
```

How it works...

The `Ext.get()` method accepts a single parameter that can be either a DOM element's ID, a DOM node, or an existing `Ext.Element` instance. The method returns an instance of `Ext.Element`, which wraps the underlying DOM node, giving it additional functionality for further manipulation.

 The `Ext.Element`'s underlying DOM node can be accessed through the `dom` property of an `Ext.Element` instance. For example, `varbookTitleDomNode = Ext.get('book-title').dom`.

When an ID is passed into this method, the framework uses the browser's `document.getElementById` method, and after retrieving the DOM node, it creates a wrapping `Ext.Element` instance and then caches it to make future retrievals faster.

If a DOM node is given to the method, then the framework skips the initial step outlined above and simply wraps the DOM node in an `Ext.Element` instance and caches it.

Finally, when an `Ext.Element` instance is passed to the method, it refreshes the element's `dom` property with the latest contents using the `document.getElementById` method.

The `Ext.get` method only returns a single element, so when you want to deal with multiple matches consider using either the `Ext.select` or `Ext.query` methods, which we will describe further.

There's more...

There are two other noteworthy methods provided by the framework that makes much more advanced DOM node retrieval possible.

Ext.select

The `Ext.select` method allows us to retrieve a collection of DOM nodes based on CSS selectors. The returned object from this method is an instance of either the `Ext.CompositeElement` or `Ext.CompositeElementLite` class.

These two classes contain a collection of DOM elements (all wrapped in `Ext.Element` instances) that were matched and allows us to perform any method available on all of the elements in the collection. Both classes support all the methods of the `Ext.Element` and `Ext.fx.Anim` classes.

If, for example, we wanted to hide all the author `<li>` tags in our previous HTML snippet, we can do so by calling the `Ext.select` method passing in a CSS selector. We are then able to call the `hide` method, which is added to the `Ext.CompositeElement` class from the `Ext.Element` class.

```
var authorsListItemEls = Ext.select('ul#authors li');
authorsListItemEls.hide();
```

The `Ext.select` method accepts two further parameters:The second parameter is a Boolean value that determines if each node is given its own unique `Ext.Element` instance. When `true`, an `Ext.CompositeElement` instance is returned, giving each selected element its own wrapping `Ext.Element` instance. When `false`, an `Ext.CompositeElementLite` instance is returned, which uses the shared flyweight object to wrap each node.

The last parameter allows you to specify the root that the select will start from. This accepts either an ID or an `Ext.Element` object.

It is also useful to note that an `Ext.Element` instance has its own `select` method which forces itself to be the root of the select and so will only look at elements below it in the DOM's hierarchy.

Ext.query

`Ext.query`, an alias for `Ext.DomQuery.select`, selects an array of raw DOM nodes based on the specified CSS/XPath selector. This method is ideal when you require fast performance and only need to deal with DOM nodes directly without the framework's wrapping class and functionality.

The previous example can be rewritten using `Ext.query` and the console output seen in the following screenshot, showing an array of DOM node references:

```
console.log(Ext.query('ul#authors li'));
```

```
>>> Ext.query('ul#authors li')
[ li#ext-gen1010, li#ext-gen1011 ]
```

Similarly to the `select` method an `Ext.Element` instance has its own `query` method, which forces the query's root to be that element.

The Ext JS 4 documentation has numerous examples of selector syntax that this method can accept.

See also

▸ The next three recipes, which explain how to traverse, manipulate, and create DOM elements.

Traversing the DOM

It is important to be able to move around the DOM based on the current context and retrieve references to surrounding elements. In this recipe, we will discover how to use Ext JS to traverse the DOM and access elements based on the context of the current element we are working with.

Getting ready

We will use the HTML snippet from the previous recipe, *Selecting DOM elements,* to demonstrate how to traverse the DOM, so make sure it is handy!

How to do it...

We will first discuss how to access a DOM element's siblings.

1. First we retrieve the `Ext.Element` instance that will be the root of our traversal. In this case we will use the Data Package item in the *"What's new in Ext JS 4"* list, simply because it is in the middle of the list. We do this using the `item` method which returns the item at the specified position in our returned collection:

```
var dataPackageEl = Ext.select('ul#whats-new li').item(2);
```

2. Get the previous list item ('Drawing') using the `prev` method:

```
var drawingEl = dataPackageEl.prev();
alert(drawingEl.dom.innerHTML); // alerts 'Drawing'
```

3. Get the next list item ('Enhanced Grid') using the `next` method:

```
var enhancedGridEl = dataPackageEl.next();
alert(enhancedGridEl.dom.innerHTML); // alerts 'Enhanced Grid'
```

4. It is also possible to get the first and last child of an `Ext.Element` using the `first` and `last` methods respectively:

```
var whatsNewEl = Ext.get('whats-new');
var chartingEl = whatsNewEl.first();
alert(chartingEl.dom.innerHTML); // alerts 'Charting'

var owerfulThemingEl = whatsNewEl.last();
alert(powerfulThemingEl.dom.innerHTML); // alerts 'Powerful
Theming'
```

Each of the methods described can be passed a selector string in order to be more specific about the element returned. For example, using `el.next('.my-class')` will return the next element with the `my-class` CSS class.

How it works...

Each of the methods described use the `Ext.Element`'s `matchNode` method to navigate the DOM until it finds the relevant element that is being asked for.

Both the `next` and `prev` methods described only retrieve elements that are siblings of the root element, that is moving sideways in the DOM hierarchy rather than up or down). The `first` and `last` methods deal with the first level of children contained in the root element.

There's more...

In addition to traversing siblings (that is, accessing elements on the same level within the DOM hierarchy) Ext JS offers ways of moving up and down the tree gaining access to parents and children of an element.

Direct parents and children

We can demonstrate this by retrieving the parent `<ul>` element of one list element using the `parent` method of the `Ext.Element` class:

```
var dataPackageEl = Ext.select('ul#whats-new li').item(2);
alert(dataPackageEl.parent().id); // alerts 'whats-new'
```

We are also able to move back down the tree by using the `child()` method, which returns the first element that matches the specified selector, as follows:

```
var whatsNewEl = Ext.get('whats-new');

// get the first child LI element
var firstListItemChildEl = whatsNewEl.child('li');

alert(firstListItemChildEl.dom.innerHTML); // alerts 'Charting'
```

The `child` method only returns direct children of the root element and so won't go deeper than one level.

Multiple level traversal

It is often necessary to traverse the DOM without restricting the number of levels we pass through in order to find a match. Fortunately, Ext JS provides us with the `up` and `down` methods, which don't impose such restrictions

The `up` method moves up the tree from the current `Ext.Element` until it finds an element matching the specified selector, which it then returns. If it fails to find a match it will return null. We can also specify the maximum depth the traversal will go to, as the method's second parameter, in terms of a number or as a specific Element that we don't want to go past.

The `down` method works in a very similar way but moves down the hierarchy to any depth until it finds a matching element without the option to restrict it.

See also

▶ The previous recipe which discusses how to retrieve references to specific DOM elements.

▶ To find out about manipulating DOM elements see the next recipe which explains this in detail.

▶ To learn about creating your own DOM elements on the fly, go to the *Creating new DOM elements* recipe later in this chapter.

Manipulating DOM elements

So far we have discussed selecting elements and traversing through them. We will now explore how to manipulate those elements once we have got our hands on them.

We will start by changing the style of an element by updating its inline styles and then by adding CSS classes. Following this we will explore how to show and hide elements.

Getting ready

Once again we will use the HTML snippet defined in the *Selecting DOM elements* recipe.

How to do it...

1. Firstly, we will make the book's title bigger, color it red, and give it a bottom border by updating those specific styles using the `setStyle` method.

2. Retrieve a reference to the element, in this case the book's title heading:

    ```
    var bookTitleEl = Ext.get('book-title');
    ```

3. Update the element's font-size style by itself.

    ```
    bookTitleEl.setStyle('font-size', '1.5em');
    ```

4. Make the heading red and give it a bottom border at the same time:

    ```
    bookTitleEl.setStyle({
        color: 'red',
        borderBottom: '3px solid red'
    });
    ```

5. Finally, we will change the styling of the heading by adding a new CSS class to its element that will center the book's title. Define our new CSS class in the head of our HTML document:

    ```
    <style type="text/css">
        .book-title
        {
            text-align: center;
        }
    </style>
    ```

6. Add the class to our book title element using the `addCls` method:

    ```
    bookTitleEl.addClass('book-title');
    ```

 You can remove the class again by using the `removeCls` method, passing it the name of the CSS class that you would like to remove.

How it works...

The `setStyle` method can either accept two parameters, acting as a name/value pair, or a single parameter with multiple styles in a configuration object format.

In step 2, we make the change by specifying the CSS style we want to update and the new value we want to give it.

Step 3 makes use of the alternative syntax where a configuration object containing multiple name/value pairs is passed to the method, which loops through them, updating them each in turn.

 Notice that we specified the border-bottom CSS style as a camel-cased property name (borderBottom). This is because JavaScript doesn't allow hyphens in property names and so Ext JS converts this for us using the normalize method of Ext.Element.

Under the surface, the framework is simply accessing the DOM's style collection and updating the individual styles. The following code snippet is taken directly from the framework and shows the styles being updated:

```
me.dom.style[ELEMENT.normalize(style)] = value;
```

Finally, the addCls method updates the DOM node's className property with the specified class name. Alternatively, the method accepts an array of class names and will apply all of these to the element.

After executing the code in this recipe, you can inspect the HTML from FireBug (or Developer Tools) and you will see that the styles and classes have been applied. The following screenshot shows the HTML after this code has been executed:

```
<html class="x-border-box x-quirks">
    <head>
    <body id="ext-gen1009" class="x-body x-gecko x-reset">
        <h1 id="book-title" class="book-title" style="font-size: 2em; color: red;
        border-bottom: 3px solid red;">Ext JS 4 Cookbook</h1>
        <h2>Authors</h2>
        <ul id="authors">
        <h2>What's new in Ext JS 4?</h2>
        <ul id="whats-new">
    </body>
</html>
```

There's more...

There are a huge number of further possibilities for manipulating DOM elements, unfortunately, too many to discuss in this recipe. However, we will go over a few of the most popular methods and how to use them.

Showing and hiding an element

The following code snippet will hide the book's title and then, after three seconds, show it again with a simple animation:

```
bookTitleEl.hide();

setTimeout(function(){
    bookTitleEl.show(true)
}, 3000); // execute after 3000 ms
```

We pass `true` to the `show` method to indicate that we want it to animate the transition. This could also be a proper animation config object, allowing you to customize the transition.

The visibility mode of an `Ext.Element` instance becomes important when hiding it. This setting determines whether the CSS style properties—visibility or display are used or if an offset value is used to hide it. By passing `Ext.Element.VISIBILTY` to the `setVisibilityMode` method of an `Ext.Element` instance, the element is hidden but retains its space in the document. Using `Ext.Element.DISPLAY` will mean that the element does not retain any space and the document's elements will rearrange to suit. Finally, the `Ext.Element.OFFSETS` will move the element off-screen so it isn't visible.

Updating the contents of an element

The `Ext.Element` class provides us with a handy `update` method, which updates the element's `innerHTML` property with the new HTML we pass it:

```
bookTitleEl.update('How to Make AWESOME Web Apps');
```

See also

▶ The previous two recipes discussing selecting DOM elements and traversing them.

▶ The *Chapter 3, Laying Out Your Components*, which discusses how to create your own DOM elements.

▶ To read more about the animation options that could have been used with the `hide` method discussed in the *There's More...* section, see the two animation recipes, later in this chapter.

Creating new DOM elements

After working through examples for selecting, traversing, and manipulating DOM elements, we will now move onto creating new ones and injecting them into our pages.

Initially, we will demonstrate how to create a simple list item element with some basic configuration. We will then move onto exploring how to control the position of our new element.

Getting ready

As with the previous DOM recipes, we will use the same HTML snippet defined in the first recipe of this chapter.

How to do it...

In this recipe, we are going to add a new item to the What's new in Ext JS 4? list:

1. First, we define the configuration of our new element using a simple JavaScript object:

```
var newClassSystemConfig = {
    tag: 'li',
    html: 'New Class System'
};
```

2. Next, we get a reference to the element we want to insert our new element into. In this case our What's New list:

```
var whatsNewListEl = Ext.get('whats-new');
```

3. Finally, we use the Ext.core.DomHelper class to create a new element, based on our configuration (in the newClassSystemConfig variable), and append it to the list:

```
var newClassSystemEl = Ext.core.DomHelper.append(whatsNewListEl,
newClassSystemConfig);
```

4. By inspecting the HTML with our browser's developer tools, we can see the newly inserted HTML (highlighted in the following screenshot):

```
▼<html class="x-border-box x-quirks">
  ▶<head>…</head>
  ▼<body class="x-body x-webkit x-chrome x-reset" id="ext-gen1021">
      <h1 id="book-title">Ext JS 4 Cookbook</h1>
      <h2>Authors</h2>
    ▶<ul id="authors">…</ul>
      <h2>What's new in Ext JS 4?</h2>
    ▼<ul id="whats-new">
        <li>Infinite Scrolling</li>
        <li id="ext-gen1022">Charting</li>
        <li>Drawing</li>
        <li>Data Package</li>
        <li>Enhanced Grid</li>
        <li>Powerful Theming</li>
        <li>New Class System</li>
        <li id="ext-gen1023">New Class System</li>
        <li>Component Query</li>
        <li>Row Editor</li>
      </ul>
    </body>
  </html>
```

How it works...

The `Ext.core.DomHelper` class provides us with various methods to make creating and inserting new elements very quick and easy. Inside the framework, the `append` method calls the class' `createDom` method, which parses our configuration object and builds a DOM node to match the specification. It is then inserted into the page as the last child of the element passed. In this case our `What's New` list element.

The `createDom` method parses all the properties of the configuration object as attributes of the newly created DOM element except for four reserved properties, which are:

- ▶ `tag`: this is used to define the element's tag (for example, `div`)
- ▶ `children` (or `cn`): this is used to define an array of sub elements defined in the same way
- ▶ `cls`: this will be mapped to the element's class attribute
- ▶ `html`: the content to be assigned to the inner HTML of the element

The `append` method can also accept a plain HTML string, instead of a configuration object, which will be inserted into the document in exactly the same way. For example:

```
var newClassSystemEl = Ext.core.DomHelper.append(whatsNewListEl,
'<li>New Class System</li>');
```

There's more...

The framework gives us full control over where new elements are inserted. By utilizing other methods of the `Ext.core.DomHelper` class, we can create new elements anywhere on our page.

It also provides a way for leveraging the power of the `Ext.Template` class by compiling element configurations into reusable templates.

Inserting a new element before or after an existing element

The `insertBefore` method of `Ext.core.DomHelper` allows us to insert a new element before an existing element, as a sibling to it. For example, we can insert a new `What's New` list item at the top of the list (that is, before the first item):

```
var whatsNewListEl = Ext.get('whats-new');

Ext.core.DomHelper.insertBefore(whatsNewListEl.first(), {
    tag: 'li',
    html: 'Infinite Scrolling'
});
```

The `insertAfter` method can be used in exactly the same way to insert the new element after the one passed in as the first parameter.

Using templates to insert elements

Templates allow us to create HTML strings that contain data placeholders. These templates can be merged with a data object giving us an HTML string with its placeholders replaced with the values from the data object.

The `Ext.Template` class can be used to append (or insertBefore/insertAfter) the output of this merge process to an existing element. We can use `Ext.core.DomHelper`'s `createTemplate` method to initially generate this template.

We start by creating a template using the same configuration object syntax that we used earlier. Our template has one placeholder, named `newFeature`:

```
var itemTpl = Ext.core.DomHelper.createTemplate({
    tag: 'li',
    html: '{newfeature}'
});
```

We then use the `Ext.Template`'s `append()` method to insert the new element. The method accepts an ID or element as its first parameter to indicate which element the output should be appended to. The second parameter provides the data object to be applied to the template:

```
itemTpl.append('whats-new', {newFeature: 'Row Editor'});
```

See also

► The previous three recipes, which go into further details about selecting, traversing, and manipulating DOM elements.

► The recipes in *Chapter 4, UI Building Blocks—Trees, Panels, and Data Views,* explaining templates in more detail.

Handling events on elements and components

Ext JS is an event driven framework and so it is important to be able to listen for raised events and react to them to control the flow of your application. These events could be raised through user interaction, for example, a button being clicked or keyboard keys being pressed, or internally within the framework, for example a store being loaded with data or a component being hidden.

In this recipe, we will explain how to listen for components' events and execute code when they are raised.

We will start off by listening for a simple click event on an element to explain the syntax and composition of an event handler. We will then move on to alternative ways of defining listeners.

Getting ready

We will set up a simple HTML page, which references the library and contains a single element within the `<body>` tag as shown as follows:

```
<div id="my-div">Ext JS 4 Cookbook</div>
```

How to do it...

1. Firstly, inside the `Ext.onReady` function, we retrieve a reference to the element (in the form of an `Ext.Element` instance). See the *Selecting DOM Elements* recipe, for more details:

```
var el = Ext.get('my-div');
```

2. We then attach an event handler function to the click event of the element using the `on` method. In our example, the function will show an alert when the event is raised:

```
el.on('click', function(e, target, options){
    alert('The Element was clicked!');
    alert(this.id);
}, this);
```

Notice the output of the `alert(this.id);` line. The scope, defined by `this` being passed in as the third parameter, is the browser's window. Try changing this parameter to `el` and see what the alert displays.

How it works...

The `Ext.Element`'s on method is an alias of the `addListener` method, and comes from the mixed in `Ext.util.Observable` class. This method tells the element that whenever the element's click event (defined by the first parameter) is raised, execute the function that is supplied as the second parameter. This can be either an anonymous function or a reference to a previously defined function.

The third parameter indicates what scope the handling function will execute in (that is, what the `this` keyword will refer to). See the *Scoping your functions* recipe, in *Chapter 1*.

There's more...

It is possible to attach handlers to multiple events at once and to also define these handlers when configuring components at the start of their lifecycle. We will now demonstrate how to achieve this with two short examples.

Defining multiple event handlers at once

The on method also accepts an alternative parameter set that allows multiple event handlers to be assigned at once. By specifying a JavaScript object as the first parameter, with name/value pairs specifying the event name and its handling function, they will all be assigned at once. By defining a `scope` property within this object the handler functions will all be executed within this scope.

```
el.on({
    click: function(e, target, options){
        alert('The Element was clicked!');
        alert(this.id);
    },
    contextmenu: function(e, target, options){
        alert('The Element was right-clicked!');
        alert(this.id);
    },
    scope: this
});
```

Defining event handlers in config objects

Ext JS components (for example, grids, panels, stores, and so on) all allow event handlers to be defined when they are configured using the `listeners` config option. Event handlers are defined in this config option in an identical fashion to the method described earlier.

In the following short example, we create a simple `Ext.panel.Panel` and bind an event listener to its `afterrender` event, showing an alert:

```
Ext.create('Ext.panel.Panel', {
    title: 'Ext JS 4 Cookbook',
    html: 'An Example Panel!',
    renderTo: Ext.getBody(),
    width: 500,
    listeners: {
        afterrender: function(){
            alert('The Panel is rendered!');
        },
        scope: this
    }
});
```

See also

▶ The first recipe of this chapter explaining how to select DOM elements.

▶ The *Scoping your functions* recipe in *Chapter 1, Classes, Object-Oriented Principles and Structuring your Application*.

Delegating event handling of child elements

Event handlers are a common cause of memory leaks and can cause performance degradation when not managed carefully. The more event handlers we create the more likely we are to introduce such problems, so we should try to avoid creating huge numbers of handlers when we don't have to.

Event delegation is a technique where a single event handler is created on a parent element, which leverages the fact that the browser will bubble any events raised on one of its children to this parent element. If the target of the original event matches the delegate's selector then it will execute the event handler, otherwise nothing will happen.

This means that instead of attaching an event handler to each individual child element, we only have to create a single handler on the parent element and then, within the handler, query which child element was actually clicked, and react appropriately.

In this recipe, we will discover how to make use of event delegation when attaching event handlers to the items within a list. We will listen for click events on each of the list items and alert their `innerHTML` contents when they are clicked.

Getting ready

Once again we will make use of the HTML snippet from the first recipe of this chapter.

How to do it...

1. Retrieve a reference to the `What's New` list element:

```
var whatsNewEl = Ext.get('whats-new');
```

2. Attach an event handler to the list's click event and specify we want to delegate this event to the list items (that is LI tags), by passing a configuration object to the `on` method's fourth argument, containing the `delegate` property:

```
whatsNewEl.on('click', function(e, target, options){
    alert(target.innerHTML);
}, this, {
    delegate: 'li'
});
```

When you run this code and click each of the list items you will see an alert with each of the items' contents.

How it works...

When attaching event handlers the framework builds up a dynamic function based on the configuration options passed in.

In our example, only the delegate option has been used, but you can also specify additional options such as:

- ▸ - `stopEvent`
- ▸ - `preventDefault`
- ▸ - `stopPropagation`
- ▸ - `delay`
- ▸ - `buffer`

When a delegate is specified, the dynamic function contains a simple call to the `Ext.EventObject`'s `getTarget` method passing in the contents of the `delegate` property. If this call returns a value then we know that the event has occurred on a valid element and so it is fired, passing in this target element into the handler as the second argument.

In our example, the dynamically generated function contains the following code:

```
// output of the Ext.EventManager.createListenerWrap() method
if (!Ext) {
    return;
}

e = Ext.EventObject.setEvent(e);

var t = e.getTarget("li", this);
if (!t) {
    return;
}
fn.call(scope || dom, e, t, options);
```

As you can see, the highlighted line shows the delegate being used and the function only actually calling the event's handler function (fn) if a match was made.

We could achieve identical functionality if we omitted the delegate option and included the getTarget call in our own handler function. An equivalent event handler is shown in the following code block:

```
whatsNewEl.on('click', function(e, target, options){
    var t = e.getTarget("li", this);

    if (!t) {
        return;
    }

    alert(target.innerHTML);
}, this);
```

There are couple of obvious advantages of using this technique over attaching an event handler to each element:

- ▶ We create fewer event handlers which means less memory is used and fewer opportunities exist for memory to leak
- ▶ If you were to add new child elements, the event handler is already set up to react to events on this new element

There's more...

When using event delegation we often need to perform different actions depending on which of the child elements the event is raised upon. For example, if we had the following toolbar, we would want to execute a different function when each of the links were clicked:

```
<div id="toolbar">
  <a href="javascript:void(0);">Add</a> |
  <a href="javascript:void(0);">Edit</a> |
  <a href="javascript:void(0);"Delete</a>
</div>
```

Firstly, we decorate each of the links with a class to distinguish it from the others. This will be used when deciding which of the links was actually clicked:

```
<div id="toolbar">
  <a href="javascript:void(0);" class="add">Add</a> |
  <a href="javascript:void(0);" class="edit">Edit</a> |
  <a href="javascript:void(0);" class="delete">Delete</a>
</div>
```

We then add our click event handler to the toolbar `div` and delegate it with an `a` tag selector:

```
toolbarEl.on('click', function(e, target, options){

}, this, {
    delegate: 'a'
});
```

We use the `getTarget` method of the `Ext.EventObject` parameter to decide which of the child elements the event originated from. We do this by passing a selector to it which will return a matching element if it was found in the chain of elements involved in the event. When the `getTarget` call returns an element (which evaluates to true in an IF statement) we can then call the correct method for that link.

```
toolbarEl.on('click', function(e, target, options){
    if(e.getTarget('a.add')){
        addItem();
    } else if(e.getTarget('a.edit')){
        editItem();
    } else if(e.getTarget('a.delete')){
        deleteItem();
    }
}, this, {
    delegate: 'a'
});
```

See also

▶ The previous recipe titled, *Handling events on elements and components*.

▶ The recipe in *Chapter 1*, called *Scoping your functions*.

Simple animation of elements

Animating elements can be achieved easily with Ext JS. This recipe will demonstrate adding simple animations and transitions to an element or Ext JS component.

How to do it...

1. Start by adding an element to the body of your HTML:

   ```
   <div id="animate"></div>
   ```

2. Now style the DIV to help us see the animations working:

   ```
   <style type="text/css">
      #animate {
         margin: 50px auto;
         width: 200px;
         background-color: #444;
         height: 200px;
      }
   </style>
   ```

3. Inside your `Ext.onReady` function get the element:

   ```
   var el = Ext.get('animate');
   ```

4. The first animation to try is `puff`. This effect expands the element in all directions while fading it out. Call the `puff` method passing in some `FX` options:

   ```
   el.puff({
      easing: 'easeOut',
      duration: 1000,
      useDisplay: false
   });
   ```

5. Having seen the box 'puff' we can substitute the method for one of the many other pre-defined animations. Remove or comment-out `el.puff()`:

   ```
   /*
   el.puff({
      easing: 'easeOut',
      duration: 1000,
      useDisplay: false
   });
   */
   ```

6. Add the following to make your element switch off. This will collapse your element into itself, in the same way a TV might:

```
el.switchOff({
    easing: 'easeIn',
    duration: 2000,
    remove: false,
    useDisplay: false
});
```

7. Having tried both `puff` and `switchOff` now try any of the following (remembering to comment out the animations you are not trying to use):

```
// slides the element into view from the direction specified
// t = top, b = bottom, l = left, r = right
el.slideIn('t', {
    easing: 'easeOut',
    duration: 500
});

// slides the element out of view in the direction specified
el.slideOut('t', {
    easing: 'easeOut',
    duration: 500,
    remove: false,
    useDisplay: false
});

// pulses a gray border (first parameter) 10 times (second
parameter)
el.frame("#444", 10, {
    duration: 1000
});

// fades the element out
el.fadeOut({
    opacity: 0,
    easing: 'easeOut',
    duration: 2000,
    remove: false,
    useDisplay: false
});
```

8. To see animations working on Ext JS components add an animation to an alert:

```
var messageBox = Ext.Msg.alert('Alert', 'This Message Box has an
animation');

messageBox.getEl().frame("red", 3, {
    duration: 500
});
```

How it works...

`Ext.fx.Anim` is the class that manages the animation of the element. It's made available to us through the use of `Ext.Element`.

`Ext.Element` has a number of methods that can be used for animating the element as we've seen in the examples. Depending on the method you are calling you can either animate it by passing `true` to the animate parameter or by passing it an object literal with animation options.

When the animation is called on the element, Ext JS, in essence, goes through a process of updating aspects of the element (for example, it's CSS) which alters its appearance on the browser. Each step of the process changes the element slightly to give the user the impression of a smooth transition.

There are a number of animation options that can be set to alter the behavior of your animation. The common `config` options we set were:

- `useDisplay: Boolean`: when this is set to false the element will be hidden using the `hide` method after the animation is complete, otherwise it will be hidden using `setDisplayed(false)`, which uses the CSS `display` property. By setting this to true the element will not take up any space in the document after it is hidden.

- `duration: Number`: this is the time (in milliseconds) that the animation will last.

- `easing: String`: the easing of the animation is a description of how the animation should calculate the intermediate values for the process. This gives you the ability to alter how the animation changes speed during the animation. We can set this with values such as, `backIn`, `easeIn`, `easeOut`, `bounceOut`, or `elasticeIn`.

See also

- The four recipes at the beginning of this chapter explaining DOM retrieval and manipulating.

- The next recipe, which goes into more detail about creating custom animations.

Custom animations

Ext JS 4 introduces a brand new animation builder which allows us to build keyframe animations in a similar style to those available with CSS3.

In this recipe, we will create a simple keyframe animation using the `Ext.fx.Animator` class. We will then move on to discuss how to have your application react to these custom animations by harnessing the built-in events and callbacks.

Keyframe animation is when the animator defines the characteristics (position, size, color, and so on) of the elements involved in the animation at specific points in time. The software (in this case the Ext JS framework) then uses these key points to calculate the characteristics of elements in the frames between the two keyframes. This creates a smooth transition between the two (or more) key frames and gives us a nice animation.

The example we will create in this recipe is that of a simple bouncing ball, which will change color after each bounce.

How to do it...

1. We start by creating an element to represent our ball and giving it some basic styles:

```css
<style type="text/css">
    #ball
    {
        border-radius: 50px;
        width: 100px;
        height: 100px;
        background-color: red;
        position: absolute;
        y: 50px;
        x: 100px;
    }
</style>

<div id="ball"></div>
```

2. We next create a new instance of `Ext.fx.Animator` and target the new ball DIV as the element we want to animate:

```javascript
Ext.create('Ext.fx.Animator', {
    target: 'ball'
});
```

3. We can now start defining our animation's duration and first and last keyframes. These two keyframes will define the start and end point of the animation:

```
Ext.create('Ext.fx.Animator', {
     target: 'ball',
     duration: 5000,
     keyframes: {
          0: {
               y: 50
          },
          100: {
               y: 300
          }
     }
});
```

4. Finally, we add the intermediate keyframes to produce the bouncing effect and color changes:

```
Ext.create('Ext.fx.Animator', {
     target: 'ball',
     duration: 5000, // 5 seconds
     keyframes: {
          0: {
               y: 50
          },
          20: {
               y: 300
          },
          40: {
               y: 175,
               backgroundColor: '#0000FF'
          },
          60: {
               y: 300
          },
          80: {
               y: 275,
               backgroundColor: '#00FF00'
          },
          100: {
               y: 300
          }
     }
});
```

How it works...

We initially tell our `Ext.fx.Animator` instance that the element we want to animate is the element with an ID of ball using the `target` config option. We also define the `duration`, in milliseconds, that our animation will run for.

Our `keyframes` configuration takes a JavaScript object defining properties based on the percentage of time elapsed and a configuration object defining the element's characteristics at that point.

For example, our 0 property tells the animator that after 0 percent of the 5 second duration (that is, at the very beginning) the element should have a y value of 50. The `100` property tells it that after 100 percent of our 5 second animation (that is, at the end) it should have a y value of `300`.

 It is mandatory to define a 0 and `100` keyframe, so the animation has an explicit start and end point.

Each of the intermediate keyframes tell the animator what the element should look like after that amount of time (for example, 20 => 20% of 5 second animation = 1 second). If a characteristic has a different value from the previous keyframes, then the animator will animate the transition between the two, be it moving it from position x to position y or changing color from red to blue.

Internally, the framework builds up a collection of `Ext.fx.Anim` instances based on these keyframe definitions and the animation's other properties (duration, easing, and so on) and executes them one after another creating this smooth animation.

There's more...

There are several other options and events available to customize our animations even further, and integrate them into our application's process. We will explore a few of these options further.

easing

The animation's `easing` config option allows us to define how the animator calculates the frames between the defined keyframes. This gives us control over the speed in which the transition occurs, for example, whether it speeds up in the middle or if it bounces back once reaching its desired position.

iterations

This config option allows you to have the animation repeat itself this number of times.

beforeanimate and afteranimate events

These two events allow you to execute some code before the animation starts and after it has completed. This allows us to perform application logic once an animation has taken place, for example, after animating the removal of an `Ext.view.View` item, we could make an AJAX call to the server removing the item from our database using this event.

keyframe event

The `keyframe` event fires before performing the animation between two keyframes. It passes in a reference to the `Ext.fx.Animator` itself and the current keyframe's index as its first and second parameters respectively.

See also

▶ The previous recipe, which covered simple animations on HTML elements.

▶ To read about how to listen for the `beforeanimate` and `afteranimate` events see the recipe called *Handling events on elements and components*.

Parsing, formatting, and manipulating dates

Dates crop up in every application in some form or another. Ext JS 4 provides a useful `Ext.Date` class that enhances the JavaScript `Date` object's functionality with a series of useful methods to help when working with dates.

 If you already have experience with PHP, you will be pleased to know that the formatting syntax for `Ext.Date` is a (comprehensive) subset of those available in PHP's `date` function.

How to do it...

1. Start by instantiating the `Date` object, passing in numbers to represent the year, month, day, hour, and minute:

```
var date = new Date(2011, 6, 6, 22, 30);
```

2. Add the following date/time patterns for formatting dates:

```
Ext.Date.patterns = {
    ISO8601Long: "Y-m-d H:i:sP",
```

```
    ISO8601Short: "Y-m-d",
    ShortDate: "n/j/y",
    FullDateTime: "l, F d, Y g:i:s A",
    LongTime: "g:i:s A",
    SortableDateTime: "Y-m-d\\TH:i:s",
    UniversalSortableDateTime: "Y-m-d H:i:sO"
};
```

3. With our defined patterns we can format the date and view our browser's console output:

```
// 2011-07-06 22:30:00+01:00
console.log(Ext.Date.format(date, Ext.Date.patterns.ISO8601Long));

//2011-07-06
console.log(Ext.Date.format(date, Ext.Date.patterns.
ISO8601Short));

//7/6/11
console.log(Ext.Date.format(date, Ext.Date.patterns.ShortDate));

//Wednesday, July 06, 2011 10:30:00 PM
console.log(Ext.Date.format(date, Ext.Date.patterns.
FullDateTime));

//10:30:00 PM
console.log(Ext.Date.format(date, Ext.Date.patterns.LongTime));

//2011-07-06T22:30:00
console.log(Ext.Date.format(date, Ext.Date.patterns.
SortableDateTime));

//2011-07-06 22:30:00+0100
console.log(Ext.Date.format(date, Ext.Date.patterns.
UniversalSortableDateTime));

//Wednesday, the 6th of July 2011 10:30:00 PM
console.log(Ext.Date.format(date, 'l, \\t\\he jS \\of F Y h:i:s
A'));
```

4. Parse the following strings as dates with the `Ext.Date.parse()` method:

```
//Mon Mar 07 2011 00:00:00 GMT+0000 (GMT Standard Time)
console.log(Ext.Date.parse("3", 'n'));

//Mon May 17 2010 00:00:00 GMT+0100 (GMT Daylight Time)
console.log(Ext.Date.parse("2010-05-17", "Y-m-d"));

//output: null as the date is invalid
console.log(Ext.Date.parse("2011-11-31", "Y-m-d", true));
```

5. Ext JS adds further functionality for working with dates:

```
//true
console.log(Ext.Date.between(new Date('07/01/2011'), new
Date('05/01/2011'), new Date('09/01/2011')));

//Thu Sep 30 2010 00:00:00 GMT+0100 (GMT Daylight Time)
console.log(Ext.Date.add(new Date('09/30/2011'), Ext.Date.YEAR,
-1));

//Sun Jul 31 2011 00:00:00 GMT+0100 (GMT Daylight Time)
console.log(Ext.Date.getLastDateOfMonth(new Date('07/01/2011')));

// true
console.log(Ext.Date.isDST(new Date('07/01/2011')));

//false
console.log(Ext.Date.isValid(2011, 29, 2));
```

How it works...

The `Ext.Date.patterns` object we defined in step 2 is our working set of recognized formats for our application. These aren't provided in the framework, however, they can be found on the `Ext.Date` documentation page for copying and editing. `Ext.Date` in Ext JS 4 is a series of static methods that are written specifically to manipulate and work with a JavaScript `Date` instance. `Ext.Date.parse` takes three arguments:

- ▶ `input`: string
- ▶ `format`: string
- ▶ `strict`: boolean (optional)

The purpose of `Ext.Date.parse` is to take a string input and return it as a `Date` object. We need to specify a format to allow the parser to ensure the date it returns is what we expect. Ext JS follows the same formatting syntax as PHP. So, if the input is 3 and the format is n (numeric representation of a month, without leading zeros), then the parser will interpret this as March. If the input were 3 and the format m (numeric representation of a month, with leading zeros) and strict were `true`, then parsing would fail as our input string would require the leading zero to be valid.

The complete list of formats can be found in the `Ext.Date` documentation.

There's more...

A useful property in `Ext.Date` is `defaultFormat`. When used with `Ext.util.Format.dateRenderer` and `Ext.util.Format.date`, dates will appear in a format you specify.

Setting a default format helps by ensuring your application displays dates in a format suited to the locale, for example, `Ext.Date.defaultFormat = 'd/m/Y';`.

`Ext.Date` has many other features that haven't been looked at in our examples, such as:

- `getDayOfYear(Date date)` is used for getting the numeric day of the year.
- `getDaysInMonth(Date date)` is used for getting the number of days in a given month.
- `getElapsed(Date dateA, [Date dateB])` is used for finding out the number of milliseconds between two dates. If you don't include the `dateB` parameter, it will default to the current date.
- `getGMTOffset(Date date, [Boolean colon])` is used for getting the GMT offset of a given date (for example, `+02:00`). If you exclude the colon parameter the output would be `+0200`.
- `getTimezone(Date date)` will return the abbreviated timezone name.

See also

- The recipe *Loading and Parsing Dates into a Date field* in *Chapter 6, Using and Configuring Form Fields*.

Loading data with AJAX

In this recipe, we will discover how to load data asynchronously using the `Ext.Ajax` class. We will demonstrate how to use the `Ext.Ajax.request` method for loading data and how to process the `XMLHttpRequest` response that's returned. Additionally, we will learn how to handle errors.

Getting ready

Make sure you have a web server installed and running on your development computer.

For the purposes of this demonstration your web server will need to serve JSON files. If you run into problems you may need to add a MIME type for JSON (application/json).

How to do it...

1. Create a file called `ajaxRequest.json` and add some JSON:

```
{
    "id": 1,
    "firstname": "John",
    "lastname": "Smith"
}
```

2. Create an Ajax request with Ext JS by adding the following inside the
   `Ext.onReady` function:

```
Ext.Ajax.request({
    url: 'ajaxRequest.json',
    success: function(response, options){
        console.log('The Success function was called.');
        console.log(response.responseText);
    },
    failure: function(response, options){
        console.log('The Failure function was called.');

        var statusCode = response.status;
        var statusText = response.statusText;
        console.log(statusCode + ' (' + statusText + ')');
    },
    callback: function(options, success, response){
        console.log('The Callback function was called.');
        console.log('Successful Request? ' + success);
    },
    timeout: 60000 //60 seconds (default is 30)
});
```

How it works...

`Ext.Ajax` is a singleton and a subclass of `Ext.data.Connection` that creates, opens, and sends the request using the `XMLHttpRequest` object in JavaScript. As a result, the request is made asynchronously.

Processing the response is done using the `callback` property and the `success/failure` properties.

In each of these the response parameter is the `XMLHttpRequest` objects response data. The data returned by the server is available in the `responseText` property.

There's more...

When making AJAX requests there are a number of other features in Ext JS for posting JSON or XML, caching, and cross-domain requests.

POST JSON or XML data

Defining the `params` config of an `Ext.Ajax.request` allows you to add parameters to a request. However, if you wish to POST JSON or XML, simply define either `xmlData` (object) or `jsonData` (object/string) properties in your `Ext.Ajax.request`.

If you define `xmlData` or `jsonData` and `params` at the same time all `params` will be appended to the URL.

Disabling client-side caching of Ajax requests

Adding `disableCaching: true` to an `Ext.Ajax.request` will add a unique parameter to the URL for GET requests. This can be of particular use for ensuring the client is always receiving up-to-date data.

Use Ext.data.JsonP for cross-domain

If you are looking to make cross-domain requests, you'll need to use `JSONP`. `Ext JS` provides an `Ext.data.JsonP` class for this purpose with similar configuration to `Ext.Ajax`. Here's a quick example:

```
Ext.data.JsonP.request({
    url: 'http://www.example.com/api/example',
    params: {
        apiKey: '1234'
    },
    callbackKey: 'myCallbackFn',
    success: function(){
        //task on successful request
    },
    failure: function(){
        //task on failed request
    },
    scope: this
});
```

See also

▶ The next recipe, for learning how to encode and decode JSON data.

▶ *Chapter 7, Working with the Ext JS Data Package*, explores the Ext JS 4 data package in further depth and demonstrates Models, Proxies, and Stores.

Encoding and decoding JSON data

JavaScript Object Notation (or JSON) is a lightweight data interchange format that's human readable and very useful for representing simple data structures and data objects.

As JSON is language independent, it's ideal for use with frameworks such as Ext JS.

Ext JS has an excellent range of functions that work with JSON. However, let's start at the beginning with encoding and decoding data in JSON format.

A useful tool when working with JSON is the online JSON validator JSON Lint, which validates and formats JSON. This is available at www.jsonlint.com.

How to do it...

1. Start by creating a JavaScript object. We're going to encode this object as JSON:

```
var objToEncode = {
    foo: "bar",
    id: 1,
    today: new Date(),
    isJson: true,
    size: ["Small", "Medium", "Large"],"
    obj: {
        item: "My Item"
    }
};
```

2. Encode the object as JSON using Ext.encode:

```
console.log(encodedJson);

/*
{
    "foo": "bar",
    "id": 1,
    "today": "2011-07-09T15:01:21",
    "isJson": true,
    "size": [
        "Small",
        "Medium",
        "Large"
    ],
    "obj": {
        "item": "My Item"
    }
}
*/
```

3. Decode the JSON back to an object using `Ext.decode()`:

```
var decodedJson = Ext.decode(encodedJson);

console.log(decodedJson.foo); //bar
console.log(decodedJson.id); //1
console.log(decodedJson.size[0]); //Small
console.log(decodedJson.obj.item); //My Item
```

How it works...

To demonstrate encoding and decoding JSON data we started by creating an object with a variety of data types.

The encoding and decoding is done by the `Ext.JSON` class. However, we've used the shorthand methods `Ext.encode` and `Ext.decode`. Encoding is done by the `doEncode` method, which determines what it's to be encoded to (for example, string, array, and so on) and returns the item as a string in JSON format.

Decoding is done by the `doDecode` method, which evaluates the JSON using the `eval` method:

```
doDecode = function(json) {
    return eval("(" + json + ')');
},
```

There's more...

The `Ext.JSON` class provides another useful method for encoding dates—`encodeDate`. This method returns a date as a JSON string in the following format: yyyy-mm-ddThh:mm:ss. It's easy to override the default date by setting your own, for example:

```
Ext.JSON.encodeDate = function(d) {
    return d.format('"d/m/Y"');
};
```

See also

▸ The next recipe as it demonstrates encoding/decoding HTML.

3
Laying Out Your Components

In this chapter, we will cover:

- ▶ Using a `FitLayout` to expand components to fill their parent
- ▶ Creating flexible vertical layouts with `VBoxes`
- ▶ Creating flexible horizontal layouts with `HBoxes`
- ▶ Displaying content in columns
- ▶ Collapsible layouts with accordions
- ▶ Displaying stacked components with the `CardLayout`
- ▶ Anchor components to their parent's dimensions
- ▶ Creating fullscreen applications with the `BorderLayout`
- ▶ Combining multiple layouts

Introduction

This chapter explores the layout system in Ext JS 4 and demonstrates how to use these layouts to place your user interface components. The layouts that we will be working with are `FitLayout`, `BorderLayout`, `HBox` layout, `VBox` layout, `ColumnLayout`, `TableLayout`, `AccoridionLayout`, `CardLayout`, `AnchorLayout`, and `AbsoluteLayout`. The final recipe will combine a number of these layouts to create a framework for a rich desktop-style application.

Using a FitLayout to expand components to fill their parent

The `FitLayout` makes it possible for you to expand a component to fill its parent container. The `FitLayout` is easy to use and requires no configuration. The screenshot shows how a `FitLayout` can be used to automatically expand a panel to take up its parent's entire area:

Fit Layout
Inner Panel
Panel content

How to do it...

1. Start by creating a simple `Ext.panel.Panel` and render it to the document's body. This panel will be the parent item that contains our inner, expanded-to-fit component:

```
Ext.create('Ext.panel.Panel', {
    title: 'Fit Layout',
    width: 500,
    height: 200,
    renderTo: Ext.getBody()
});
```

2. Now, add the inner panel by adding it to the parent's items collection:

```
Ext.create('Ext.panel.Panel', {
    title: 'Fit Layout',
    width: 500,
    height: 200,
    items: {
        title: 'Inner Panel',
        html: 'Panel content',
        bodyPadding: 10,
        border: true
    },
    renderTo: Ext.getBody()
});
```

3. Finally, apply the fit layout to the parent panel to have the inner panel expand:

```
Ext.create('Ext.panel.Panel', {
    title: 'Fit Layout',
    width: 500,
    height: 200,
    layout: 'fit',
    items: {
        title: 'Inner Panel',
        html: 'Panel content',
        bodyPadding: 10,
        border: true
    },
    renderTo: Ext.getBody()
});
```

The difference between step two and three can be seen by observing the border.

How it works...

The FitLayout works by defining the layout config option as fit in the parent container. This tells Ext JS that the child item should expand to fill the entire space available from its parent.

In the example, the parent panel has a fixed height and width. When layout: 'fit' is set, the child panel automatically expands to fill the space within the parent component.

There's more...

It's worth noting that the FitLayout will only work for the first child item of the parent container. If you have multiple items defined, the first will be displayed (as it will expand into the remaining space of its parent) and the others will not be visible.

See also

▶ The recipe demonstrating the CardLayout shows how the FitLayout can be extended.

▶ *Displaying a simple form in a window* recipe in *Chapter 4, UI Building Blocks—Trees, Panels, and Data Views*, is another example of the FitLayout in action.

Creating flexible vertical layouts with VBoxes

The VBoxLayout allows you to align components vertically down a container. The following screenshot shows three panels vertically aligned, dividing the available space between them:

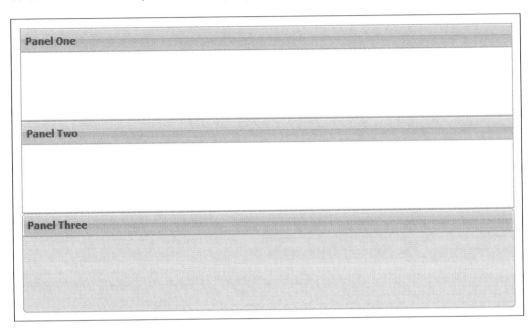

How to do it...

1. Start by creating a Viewport:

```
Ext.create('Ext.container.Viewport', {});
```

2. Define a layout for the Viewport with the following configuration:

```
Ext.create('Ext.container.Viewport', {
    layout: {
        type: 'vbox',
        align: 'stretch',
        padding: 10
    }
});
```

3. Finally add panels to the `items` collection and give them a `height` or `flex` configuration:

```
Ext.create('Ext.container.Viewport', {
    layout: {
        type: 'vbox',
        align: 'stretch',
        animate: true, //{ duration: 2000, easing: 'easeIn' },
        padding: 10
    },
    items: [{
        xtype: 'panel',
        title: 'Panel One',
        height: 100
    }, {
        xtype: 'panel',
        title: 'Panel Two',
        flex: 1
    }, {
        xtype: 'panel',
        title: 'Panel Three',
        frame: true,
        flex: 3
    }]
});
```

How it works...

The `Viewport` automatically consumes all available space in the browser. We've added a `layout` object to the `Viewport` with the type defined as a `vbox`. The `Vbox` layout automatically arranges child items vertically within their parent.

The `align` config option in this case is set to `stretch`. This means that all child items will be stretched horizontally to fill the width of the parent container (in this case the full width of the browser window).

The `padding` config option adds padding to all child items in the example. A value of `10` adds padding of 10px to the parent container giving a small space between the parent and its children.

Finally, and most importantly, the `height` or `flex` is set for each child. In this example, panel one has a fixed height of 100px. No matter how the height is defined for the other children, panel one will always be 100px high.

Panel two and panel three have a `flex` value defined. The `flex` config option relatively flexes the items vertically in the container. Panel two has `flex: 1` and Panel three has `flex: 3`, therefore, 25 percent of the remaining parent space (remember we've already used 100px with panel one) is given to panel two and 75 percent of the space is given to panel three.

Flex values are calculated by `((Container Height - Fixed Height of Child Components) / Sum of Flexes) * Flex Value` (assume parent is 1000px high). For example, `((1000 - 100) / (1 + 3)) * 1` (or 3).

There's more...

The `VBox` layout has some useful configuration options that are described as follows:

align: String

The `align` config option controls how child items are horizontally aligned in a `VBox` layout. Valid values are:

- ▶ `left`: This is the default value. All items in the `VBox` layout will be horizontally aligned to the left of the container and will use their `width` config to define how wide they are.
- ▶ `center`: All items will be horizontally aligned to the middle (or center) of the container.
- ▶ `stretch`: Each item will be horizontally stretched to fit the width of the container.
- ▶ `stretchmax`: This horizontally stretches all items to the width of the largest item creating a uniform look without having to individually define a width for each item.

pack: String

The `pack` config option controls how the child items are packed together. If the items do not stretch to the full height of the parent container (that is, have no flex values), it's possible to align them to the top, middle, or bottom using this option. Valid values are:

- ▶ `start`: This is the default value. It will align all items to the top of the parent container
- ▶ `center`: Center aligns all items to the middle (or center) of the container
- ▶ `end`: Aligns all items to the bottom of the container

▸ The next recipe demonstrating the `HBoxLayout`.

Creating flexible horizontal layouts with HBoxes

The `HBox` layout allows you to align components horizontally across a container. The screenshot shows three panels horizontally aligned, dividing the available space between them:

Panel One	Panel Two	Panel Three

How to do it...

1. Start by creating a `Viewport`:

   ```
   Ext.create('Ext.container.Viewport', {});
   ```

2. Define an `HBox` layout in the `Viewport` with the following configuration:

   ```
   Ext.create('Ext.container.Viewport', {
       layout: {
           type: 'hbox',
           align: 'stretchmax',
           pack: 'center'
       }
   });
   ```

3. Add three panels to the `items` collection, the first and third with fixed widths, and the second with a `flex` of 1 to take up the remaining browser space:

```
Ext.create('Ext.container.Viewport', {
    layout: {
        type: 'hbox',
        align: 'stretchmax',
        padding: 10
    },
    items: [{
        xtype: 'panel',
        title: 'Panel One',
        height: 200,
        width: 100
    }, {
        xtype: 'panel',
        title: 'Panel Two',
        flex: 1
    }, {
        xtype: 'panel',
        title: 'Panel Three',
        width: 100
    }]
});
```

How it works...

The `Viewport` automatically consumes the space available in the browser window. Defining an `HBox` layout ensures that Ext JS horizontally positions each child item giving the feeling of columns in this example.

The `align` configuration is `stretchmax` meaning that all child items will automatically be stretched to the height of the tallest child. Panel one's height is defined as `200`. With `align: 'stretchmax'`, panel two and three will also be stretched to 200px high.

Panel one and panel three both have their width defined as `100`. These panels now have a set width of 100px even when the user resizes their browser. They are not fluid.

Panel two, on the other hand, is set to flex with `flex: 1`. The HBox layout will calculate a width for panel two and will update this value when the user resizes the browser. Full details on how flex widths are calculated is provided in the recipe demonstrating the VBox layout.

There's more...

The HBox layout has some useful configuration options that are described as follows. These options are the same as the Vbox layout. However, they work on a horizontal layout.

align: String

The `align` config option controls how child items are vertically aligned in an HBox Layout. Valid values are shown as follows:

- ▶ `top`: This is the default value. All items in the HBox layout will be vertically aligned to the top of the container.
- ▶ `middle`: All items will be vertically aligned to the middle (or center) of the container.
- ▶ `stretch`: Each item will be vertically stretched to fit the height of the container.
- ▶ `stretchmax`: This vertically stretches all items to the height of the largest item creating a uniform look without having to individually define a height for each item.

pack: String

The `pack` config option controls how the child items are packed together. If the items do not stretch to the full width of the parent container, it's possible to align them to the left, middle, or right using this option. Valid values are as follows:

- ▶ `start`: This is the default value. It will align all items to the left of the parent container.
- ▶ `center`: This aligns all items to the middle of the container.
- ▶ `end`: It aligns all items to the right of the container.

See also

- ▶ The previous recipe on `VBoxLayout`. This recipe also explains in further detail how flex works.

Displaying content in columns

The `ColumnLayout` is used for creating multi-column layouts. The width of each column can be specified as fixed (in pixels), as a percentage, or a mixture of both.

This recipe will demonstrate creating a three column layout with one fixed width column and two columns with widths specified as percentages:

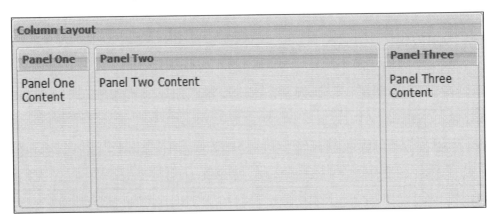

How to do it...

1. Start by creating a panel rendered to the document's body:

```
Ext.create('Ext.Panel', {
    title: 'Column Layout',
    width: 500,
    height: 200,
    renderTo: Ext.getBody()
});
```

2. Add three child panels to the parent's `items` collection:

```
Ext.create('Ext.Panel', {
    title: 'Column Layout',
    width: 500,
    height: 200,
    items: [{
        title: 'Panel One',
        html: 'Panel One Content'
    }, {
```

```
        title: 'Panel Two',
        html: 'Panel Two Content'
    }, {
        title: 'Panel Three',
        html: 'Panel Three Content'
    }],
    renderTo: Ext.getBody()
});
```

3. Give the parent a `ColumnLayout` configuration and define column widths for each child:

```
Ext.create('Ext.Panel', {
    title: 'Column Layout',
    width: 500,
    height: 200,
    layout: 'column',
    items: [{
        title: 'Panel One',
        columnWidth: .2,
        html: 'Panel One Content'
    }, {
        title: 'Panel Two',
        columnWidth: .8,
        html: 'Panel Two Content'
    }, {
        title: 'Panel Three',
        width: 100,
        html: 'Panel Three Content'
    }],
    renderTo: Ext.getBody()
});
```

4. The layout can be enhanced by giving each panel a frame and defining a fixed height for the child items:

```
Ext.create('Ext.Panel', {
    title: 'Column Layout',
    width: 500,
    height: 200,
    layout: 'column',
    frame: true,
    defaults: {
        height: 165,
        frame: true
    },
```

```
        items: [{
            title: 'Panel One',
            columnWidth: .2,
            html: 'Panel One Content'
        }, {
            title: 'Panel Two',
            columnWidth: .8,
            margin: '0 5 0 5',
            html: 'Panel Two Content'
        }, {
            title: 'Panel Three',
            width: 100,
            html: 'Panel Three Content'
        }],
        renderTo: Ext.getBody()
    });
```

How it works...

Steps 3 and 4 are where the magic happens. The parent panel's `layout` config is set to `column`. Ext JS now looks for either the `width` or `columnWidth` config option for child panels.

A fixed width is set on column three (`width: 100`). The framework now calculates the space remaining and assigns it to the first and second columns. The `columnWidth` property is a percentage (although represented as a decimal) and must total 1 (100 percent) across the items.

Panel one is 20 percent (defined as .2) and Panel two is 80 percent (defined as .8). Ext JS can now calculate the pixel widths for panel one and two and assign them accordingly.

In step 4, we further enhance the layout by adding `frame: true` (adds a frame to the panel) to the parent and `defaults` config object.

The default option is an object of config options that will be applied to the child items (not the parent panel). This is where the fixed height for each column is set and a frame added to the child panels.

Finally, the `margin` config option in panel two adds a 5px margin to the left and right of the component. The margin could have been defined as a number; however, this numeric value would apply the same margin to all four sides of the component.

See also

▶ The `HBox` layout is an alternative method of creating columns. See the previous recipe for more information.

Collapsible layouts with accordions

Accordion layouts allow us to present multiple containers in a fashion where only one of the containers is expanded and visible at any one time. The other containers are collapsed, leaving only their headers visible, each of which can be clicked on to expand that content area and collapse the others.

This layout style is useful when only one area of content is required to be displayed at once. This might be because there isn't enough space to display everything at once or only one area is relevant at a time.

In this recipe, we will describe how to create an accordion layout to display some simple information about Sencha products. A screenshot of our final goal can be seen as follows:

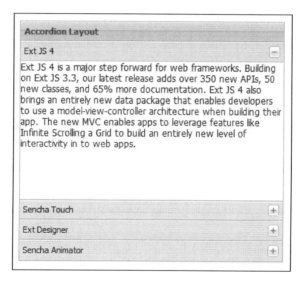

How to do it...

1. Once again we start by creating a simple `Ext.panel.Panel` and render it to the document's body. This panel will be the parent `item` that contains each of our accordion items:

```
Ext.create('Ext.panel.Panel', {
    title: 'Accordion Layout',
    width: 350,
    height: 400,
    renderTo: Ext.getBody()
});
```

2. Next, we create the four panels that will make up the accordion structure and add them to the parent panel's `items` collection:

```
Ext.create('Ext.panel.Panel', {
    title: 'Accordion Layout',
    width: 350,
    height: 400,
    renderTo: Ext.getBody(),
    items: [{
        title: 'Ext JS 4',
        html: 'Ext JS 4 ...' // full content omitted
    }, {
        title: 'Sencha Touch',
        html: 'Sencha Touch ...'
    }, {
        title: 'Ext Designer',
        html: 'Ext Designer ...'
    }, {
        title: 'Sencha Animator',
        html: 'With Sencha Animator...'
    }]
});
```

3. Note that we use the `title` option to give our accordion items a header bar that provides a clickable area to expand and collapse the content pane.

4. After creating this structure, our panel looks like the following screenshot. By default, it has adopted an Auto layout and the panels flow one after the other.

5. Finally, we apply the accordion layout to the parent panel and the framework takes care of the rest! It is simply a case of setting the `layout` configuration option to `'accordion'`:

```
Ext.create('Ext.panel.Panel', {
    title: 'Accordion Layout',
    width: 350,
    height: 450,
    layout: 'accordion',
    renderTo: Ext.getBody(),
    items: [{
        title: 'Ext JS 4',
        html: 'Ext JS 4 ...'
    }, {
        title: 'Sencha Touch',
        html: 'Sencha Touch ...'
    }, {
        title: 'Ext Designer',
        html: 'Ext Designer ...'
    }, {
        title: 'Sencha Animator',
        html: 'With Sencha Animator ...'
    }]
});
```

How it works...

By setting an `Ext.panel.Panel`'s layout to `accordion`, the framework automatically adds a **+/-** button to each child item's header and makes it clickable allowing the item to be expanded and collapsed. It also ensures that only one panel's content is visible at a time by collapsing the open panel when another is clicked.

We can also set the layout's `titleCollapse` configuration option to true, to make a click anywhere on the entire title bar collapse or expand, that accordion item.

See also

▸ The recipe covering the VBox layout, which the accordion layout extends from.

Displaying stacked components with CardLayouts

Ext JS gives us the ability to stack components on top of one another allowing us to only show a single item at once and have the option to switch between them as we wish. There are several possible use cases for this type of layout, for example, a wizard style form, a content carousel, or a tabbed layout.

The `Ext.tab.TabPanel` component is in fact based on the card layout and uses it to manage the tabs' layout.

In this recipe, we will demonstrate how to use the `Ext.layout.container.Card` layout manager to create a simple account creation wizard as shown in the following screenshot:

How to do it...

1. We start by creating our wrapping `Ext.panel.Panel` which will contain each of our cards:

```
var panel = Ext.create('Ext.panel.Panel', {
    title: 'Account Creation Wizard - Card Layout',
    width: 350,
    height: 300,
    renderTo: Ext.getBody()
});
```

2. We now create our three cards that will form each screen of our wizard. The first contains three form fields to gather the user's first and last names and an e-mail address:

```
var card1 = new Ext.panel.Panel({
    bodyStyle: 'padding: 20px',
    title: 'Personal Info',
    items: [{
        xtype: 'textfield',
        fieldLabel: 'First Name'
    }, {
        xtype: 'textfield',
        fieldLabel: 'Last Name'
    }, {
        xtype: 'textfield',
        fieldLabel: 'Email Address',
        vtype: 'email'
    }]
});
```

3. The second card contains two fields for the user's username and password:

```
var card2 = new Ext.panel.Panel({
    bodyStyle: 'padding: 20px',
    title: 'Account Info',
    items: [{
        xtype: 'textfield',
        fieldLabel: 'Username'
    }, {
        xtype: 'textfield',
        fieldLabel: 'Password',
        inputType: 'password'
    }]
});
```

4. Finally, we create a third card with a simple success message:

```
var card3 = new Ext.panel.Panel({
    bodyStyle: 'padding: 20px',
    title: 'Account Creation Successful!',
    html: 'Success!'
});
```

5. Now that we have our three cards defined we can add them to the wrapper panel we created earlier within its `items` array:

```
var panel = Ext.create('Ext.panel.Panel', {
    title: 'Account Creation Wizard - Card Layout',
    width: 350,
    height: 300,
    renderTo: Ext.getBody(),
    items: [card1, card2, card3]
});
```

6. If we looked at our progress so far in the browser, we will see the panels flow one after the other in the same way as the accordion example. To turn this into a `CardLayout`, we simply add the `layout` config option and assign it a value of `'card'` and it will transform the child panels, making them fill the parent and hide all except the first one:

```
var panel = Ext.create('Ext.panel.Panel', {
    title: 'Account Creation Wizard - Card Layout',
    width: 350,
    height: 300,
    layout: 'card',
    renderTo: Ext.getBody(),
    items: [card1, card2, card3]
});
```

7. After applying the `Ext.layout.container.Card` class to the parent panel we can see that the child panels are stacked on top of each other. We will now add some navigation buttons so that the user can move between the three cards as you would in a wizard. We do this by creating a toolbar and two buttons which, when pressed, tell the layout to move to the next or previous card, if one exists:

```
var panel = Ext.create('Ext.panel.Panel', {
    title: 'Account Creation Wizard - Card Layout',
    width: 350,
    height: 300,
    layout: 'card',
    renderTo: Ext.getBody(),
    items: [card1, card2, card3],
    bbar: ['->', {
        xtype: 'button',
        text: 'Previous',
        handler: function(btn) {
            var layout = panel.getLayout();

            if (layout.getPrev()) {
                layout.prev();
            }
        }
    }, {
        xtype: 'button',
```

```
            text: 'Next',
            handler: function(btn){
                var layout = panel.getLayout();

                if (layout.getNext()) {
                    layout.next();
                }
            }
        }]
    });
```

How it works...

The `Ext.layout.container.Card` layout extends the `Ext.layout.container.Fit` layout and so forces each of the parent panel's children to fill its available space. The layout then hides all but one of these children, giving the effect of a stack.

If you inspect our small example with your developer tools, you will see that each of the three cards have exactly the same dimensions but the second and third are set to `"display: none"`:

```
▼<div class="x-panel-body  x-panel-body-default x-panel-body-default x-layout-
  fit" id="ext-gen1020" style="width: 350px; height: 248px; left: 0px; top: 25px;
  ">
  ▶<div id="panel-1014" class="x-panel x-fit-item x-panel-default" role=
    "presentation" aria-labelledby="component-1031" style="width: 348px; height:
    246px; ">…</div>
  ▶<div id="panel-1018" class="x-panel x-fit-item x-panel-default" role=
    "presentation" aria-labelledby="component-1033" style="display: none;
    ">…</div>
  ▶<div id="panel-1021" class="x-panel x-fit-item x-panel-default" role=
    "presentation" aria-labelledby="component-1035" style="display: none;
    ">…</div>
  </div>
```

By calling the `next`, `prev`, or `setActiveItem` methods, the layout switches which of the cards is visible and hides the rest.

There's more...

The Card layout gives us the option to defer the rendering of its cards until they are activated. This is extremely useful when the cards have large amounts of content or lots of components within them as it means the browser isn't required to deal with laying out and rendering markup that is not immediately visible. This will give us a performance boost when dealing with such content-heavy card layouts.

To use this feature we simply set the `deferredRender` option to `true` within the `layoutConfig` configuration object. This config option is only applicable to card layouts and the components that use them (for example, tab panels).

See also

▶ The first recipe in this chapter that explores the `FitLayout`, which this layout extends from.

▶ The *Creating a tabbed layout* recipe in the next chapter which uses the `Ext.tab.Panel` component that is built upon the card layout.

Anchor components to their parent's dimensions

We can use the `Ext.layout.container.Anchor` class to size a child component relative to the dimensions of its parent. This class inherits from the `Ext.layout.container.Container` layout which means that by default a component that has the Anchor layout will have its children flow vertically within it one after another.

The Anchor layout gives us four options for defining the size of a child component. The first, and most popular, is a simple percentage value which is used to calculate the child's width and height based on the parent's dimensions (or the defined `anchorSize` property, see *There's more...* for further details).

The second option is a basic offset value that will size the child to the parent's full width (or height) minus the offset value, with the component anchored to the parent's left edge.

The third variation allows the child to be sized based on its static width and height and its parent's width and height by providing a value of `bottom` or `right`. Alternatively, a shorthand value of `b` or `r` can be used. This alternative can only be used when the child component has a fixed size or the parent component has an `anchorSize` defined.

Finally, we are able to specify a combination of percentages and offsets to give us maximum control over the layout.

During this recipe, we are going to walk through creating an anchor layout that makes use of these variations and demonstrates how to create a simple fluid layout.

How to do it...

We will create each of our example panels within an `Ext.window.Window` component, which is a subclass of the `Ext.panel.Panel` class that we have used in the previous recipe. By doing this, we can easily resize them to see the effect of our anchor configuration in real time.

1. We first create a panel anchored using percentages to its parent (an instance of Ext.window.Window). We apply the Anchor layout using the layout config option and configure the panel with the anchor property, passing it a string containing two percentages, in this case 100% and 35%, representing the width and height. Note that the width value comes first and the height second:

```
var win = Ext.create('Ext.window.Window', {
    x: 0,
    y: 0,
    width: 400,
    height: 400,
    title: 'Anchor Layout Panel - Percentages',
    layout: 'anchor',
    items: [{
        xtype: 'panel',
        title: 'Percentages',
        html: 'Panel Content',
        anchor: '100% 35%'
    }]
});

win.show();
```

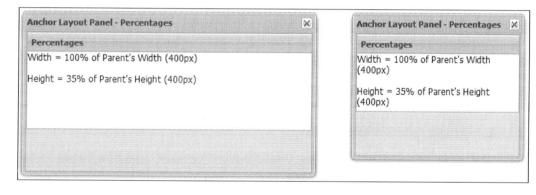

2. Next, we create a panel anchored using offsets. This time we give the anchor configuration option a string value containing two numbers, -150 and -100:

```
var win = Ext.create('Ext.window.Window', {
    x: 500,
    y: 0,
    width: 400,
    height: 400,
    title: 'Anchor Layout Panel - Offsets',
    layout: 'anchor',
    items: [{
        xtype: 'panel',
        title: 'Offsets',
```

```
            html: 'Panel Content',
            anchor: '-150 -100'
      }]
});

win.show();
```

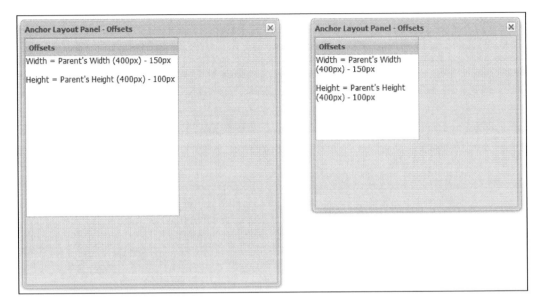

3. The use of the Sides variation can be demonstrated using the following code, where the child Panel is given a fixed height and width and the `anchor` option defined as `r b`:

```
var win = Ext.create('Ext.window.Window', {
    x: 0,
    y: 500,
    width: 400,
    height: 400,
    title: 'Anchor Layout Panel - Sides',
    layout: 'anchor',
    items: [{
        xtype: 'panel',
        title: 'Sides',
        height: 200,
        width: 200,
        html: 'Panel Content',
```

```
            anchor: 'r b'
       }]
   });

   win.show();
```

4. Finally, we can anchor a panel using a combination of offsets and percentages. We do this in exactly the same manner as the previous examples, separating the width and height of anchor values with a space:

```
var win = Ext.create('Ext.window.Window', {
    x: 500,
    y: 500,
    width: 400,
    height: 400,
    title: 'Anchor Layout Panel - Combination',
    layout: 'anchor',
    items: [{
        xtype: 'panel',
        title: 'Combination',
        html: 'Panel Content',
        anchor: '75% -150'
    }]
});

win.show();
```

How it works...

This layout works by parsing the defined anchor values and using them to calculate the child's dimensions based on the parent container's sizes. The first anchor value specifies the component's width and the second its height. These calculated dimensions are then applied to the component.

In Step 1, we use percentage values. These are used to calculate the final dimensions in the following way:

```
Width = 100% of Parent's Width (400px) = 400px
Height = 35% of Parent's Height (400px) = 140px
```

Step 2 shows our example use of offsets to calculate its dimensions, as follows:

```
Width = Parent's Width (400px) - 150px = 250px
Height = Parent's Height (400px) - 100px = 300px
```

In Step 3, the `anchor` config is given a value of `r b`. This is used in conjunction with the child components fixed dimensions and sizes them based on the difference between the parent and child's starting width subtracted from the parent container's actual width. This is shown in the following formula:

```
Width = Parent's actual width - (Parent's defined width - Child's
defined width)
Height = Parent's actual height - (Parent's defined height - Child's
defined height)
```

There's more...

Rather than having the parent's actual dimensions determining the children components size we can give the parent an additional configuration option called `anchorSize`. At present, this property will take the place of the parent's actual width and height when the layout calculates the relative sizes of its children.

The `anchorSize` configuration can be specified in two ways:

  ▸ The first way is:

```
anchorSize: 200 // if a single number is specified it defaults to
the component's width
```

  ▸ And the second way is:

```
anchorSize: {
   width: 200,
   height: 200
} // width and height explicitly set
```

See also

  ▸ See the next recipe that outlines how to use the `Absolute` layout to position components precisely within their container.

  ▸ The first recipe, in *Chapter 5, Loading, Submitting and Validating Forms* discusses constructing forms, which use the `Anchor` layout as their default.

Creating fullscreen applications with the BorderLayout

If you are looking to create a desktop style experience with your user interface then the `BorderLayout` is for you.

The `BorderLayout` is very much an application-oriented layout, supporting multiple nested panels, the ability to collapse regions by clicking on the regions' header or collapse icon, and the resizing of regions by clicking-and-dragging the splitter bar between them.

This recipe will demonstrate a simple `BorderLayout` using the maximum number of regions configurable (north, south, east, west, and center). The west and east regions will be collapsible, with the east region loading pre-collapsed. Resizing will be demonstrated on the south and west regions. These four borders will surround the center region, which regardless of your configuration is required for a `BorderLayout` to work:

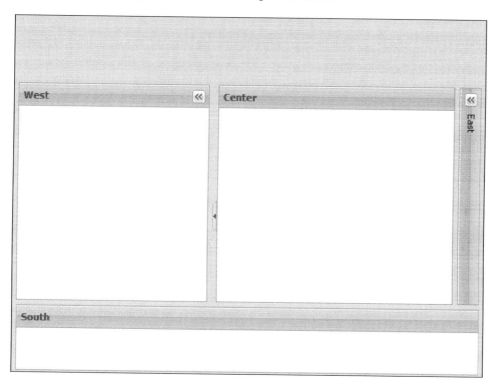

How to do it...

1. Start by creating a Viewport:

    ```
    Ext.create('Ext.container.Viewport', {});
    ```

2. Set the layout to border and add a center region to the `items` collection:

    ```
    Ext.create('Ext.container.Viewport', {
        layout: 'border',
        items: [{
            title: 'Center',
            region: 'center'
        }]
    });
    ```

A requirement of the `BorderLayout` is that it has a child item with a `center` region .

3. Next, add four further regions (north, south, east, and west) to the items collection. Specify a `height`, `width`, or `flex` for these regions:

    ```
    Ext.create('Ext.container.Viewport', {
        layout: 'border',
        items: [{
            region: 'north',
            height: 100,
            xtype: 'container'
        }, {
            title: 'West',
            region: 'west',
            flex: .3
        }, {
            title: 'Center',
            region: 'center'
        }, {
            title: 'East',
            region: 'east',
            width: 200
        }, {
            title: 'South',
            region: 'south',
            flex: .3
        }]
    });
    ```

4. The north and south regions can have a `height` or `flex` value to calculate height whereas west and east regions can have a `width` or `flex` value to calculate width.

5. Spread the regions apart with a 5px margin.

```
Ext.create('Ext.container.Viewport', {
    layout: 'border',
    items: [{
        region: 'north',
        margins: 5,
        height: 100,
        xtype: 'container'
    }, {
        title: 'West',
        region: 'west',
        margins: '0 5 0 5',
        flex: .3
    }, {
        title: 'Center',
        region: 'center'
    }, {
        title: 'East',
        region: 'east',
        margins: '0 5 0 5',
        width: 200
    }, {
        title: 'South',
        region: 'south',
        margins: '0 5 5 5',
        flex: .3
    }]
});
```

6. Additional functionality, such as resizing and collapsing regions, can be added in the following way:

```
Ext.create('Ext.container.Viewport', {
    layout: 'border',
    items: [{
        region: 'north',
        margins: 5,
        height: 100,
    }, {
        title: 'West',
        region: 'west',
        margins: '0 5 0 5',
```

```
            flex: .3,
            collapsible: true,
            split: true,
            titleCollapse: true
        }, {
            title: 'Center',
            region: 'center'
        }, {
            title: 'East',
            region: 'east',
            margins: '0 5 0 5',
            width: 200,
            collapsible: true,
            collapsed: true
        }, {
            title: 'South',
            region: 'south',
             margins: '0 5 5 5',
            flex: .3,
            split: true
        }]
    });
```

How it works...

The `BorderLayout`, as the name suggests, creates a layout of components that borders a center component. Therefore, a requirement of the `BorderLayout` is that one item must be specified as the center.

A Viewport renders itself to the document's body and automatically consumes the viewable area.

The center region, which you must include for a `BorderLayout` to work, automatically expands to consume the empty space left over from the other regions in your layout. It does this by having a pre-defined `flex` value of `1` for both height and width.

The north and south regions take a `height` or `flex` configuration. In this example, north has a fixed height of 100px and south a flex of `3`. The south and center's heights are calculated based on the height remaining in the browser window. In this example, the height of south is just under a third of the height of the center. The west and east regions, instead, take a width or flex configuration.

We add further functionality with `collapsed: true`, `collapsible: true`, `split: true`, and `titleCollapse: true` specified in the desired regions' configuration. They do the following:

▶ `collapsed: true` means the region will start collapsed (the regions need to be `Ext.panel.Panel` to be collapsible)

▶ `collapsible: true` allows the user to expand/collapse the panel by clicking on the toggle tool that's added to the header

▶ `titleCollapse: true` makes the panel collapse no matter where the user clicks on the panel's header

▶ `split: true` makes the region resizable by allowing the users to click-and-drag the dividing bar between regions

See also

▶ The next recipe, which expands on what we have covered here.

Combining multiple layouts

This chapter has demonstrated how to use individual layouts with Ext JS, however, it's time to bring everything together, combining some of the layouts to create the beginning of a desktop style Ext JS application.

This recipe will start with an `Ext.Viewport` to form the basis of a single page web application because it is a component that always expands to fill the browser window. We will then look at using a `BorderLayout` and combining it with:

▶ An `AccordionLayout` in the west region as a main menu

▶ A `CardLayout` in the center region

▶ A combination layout with the `HBoxLayout` and `VBoxLayout`, also in the center panel

▶ An `Ext.tab.Panel` to navigate between screens:

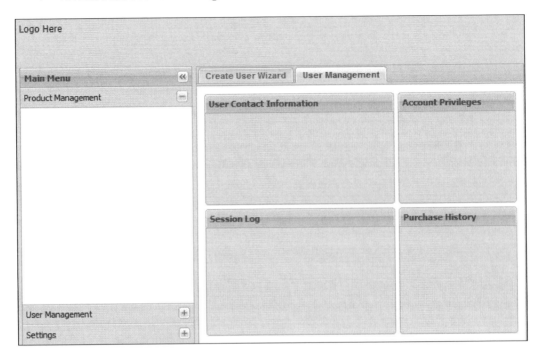

How to do it...

1. Start by specifying the panel for the west region. In this case, the west region will be a main menu:

```
var mainMenu = Ext.create('Ext.panel.Panel', {
    title: 'Main Menu',
    region: 'west',
    margins: '0 5 5 5',
    flex: .3,
    collapsible: true,
    titleCollapse: true,
    layout: 'accordion',
    layoutConfig: {
        animate: false,
        multi: true
    },
    items: [{
        title: 'Product Management'
    }, {
```

```
          title: 'User Management'
      }, {
          title: 'Settings'
      }]
  });
```

2. Next, add the panels that will make up the `CreateUserWizard` wizard. This `CardLayout` will eventually sit in the center region:

```
var card1 = new Ext.panel.Panel({
    bodyStyle: 'padding: 20px',
    title: 'Personal Info',
    border: false,
    items: [{
        xtype: 'textfield',
        fieldLabel: 'First Name'
    }, {
        xtype: 'textfield',
        fieldLabel: 'Last Name'
    }, {
        xtype: 'textfield',
        fieldLabel: 'Email Address',
        vtype: 'email'
    }]
});
var card2 = new Ext.panel.Panel({
    bodyStyle: 'padding: 20px',
    title: 'Account Info',
    border: false,
    items: [{
        xtype: 'textfield',
        fieldLabel: 'Username'
    }, {
        xtype: 'textfield',
        fieldLabel: 'Password',
        inputType: 'password'
    }]
});

var card3 = new Ext.panel.Panel({
    bodyStyle: 'padding: 20px',
    title: 'Account Creation Successful!',
    border: false,
    html: 'Success!'
});
```

```
var createUserWizard = Ext.create('Ext.panel.Panel', {
    title: 'Create User Wizard',
    layout: 'card',
    deferredRender: true,
    items: [card1, card2, card3],
    bbar: ['->', {
        xtype: 'button',
        text: 'Previous',
        handler: function(btn){
            var layout = cardPanel.getLayout();

            if (layout.getPrev()) {
                layout.prev();
            }
        }
    }, {
        xtype: 'button',
        text: 'Next',
        handler: function(btn){
            var layout = cardPanel.getLayout();

            if (layout.getNext()) {
                layout.next();
            }
        }
    }]
});
```

3. This step defines the **User Management** screen, which also sits in the center region:

```
var userManagementPanel = Ext.create('Ext.panel.Panel', {
    title: 'User Management',
    layout: {
        type: 'hbox',
        align: 'stretch',
        padding: 10
    },
    defaults: {
        flex: 1
    },
    items: [{
        xtype: 'container',
        margins: '0 5 0 0',
        layout: {
```

```
            type: 'vbox',
            align: 'stretch',
            animate: true
        },
        defaults: {
            flex: 1,
            frame: true
        },
        items: [{
            title: 'User Contact Information',
            margins: '0 0 5 0'
        }, {
            title: 'Session Log'
        }]
    }, {
        xtype: 'container',
        layout: {
            type: 'vbox',
            align: 'stretch',
            animate: true
        },
        defaults: {
            flex: 1,
            frame: true
        },
        items: [{
            title: 'Account Privileges',
            margins: '0 0 5 0'
        }, {
            title: 'Purchase History',
        }]
    }]
});
```

4. Now, add the center region. We'll make the center region a basic `Ext.tab.Panel` with the `CreateUserWizard` and `UserManagementPanel` as separate tabs:

```
var contentPanel = Ext.create('Ext.tab.Panel', {
    region: 'center',
    margins: '0 5 5 0',
    items: [createUserWizard, userManagementPanel]
});
```

5. Finally, bring everything together by creating an `Ext.container.Viewport` and specifying a `BorderLayout` for the viewport:

```
Ext.create('Ext.container.Viewport', {
    layout: 'border',
    items: [{
        region: 'north',
        margins: 5,
        height: 100,
        xtype: 'container',
        html: 'Logo Here'
    },  mainMenu, contentPanel]
});
```

How it works...

Ext JS allows us to nest all layout types within one another as deeply as we like. This allows us to create complex layouts.

When the browser window, or a component that contains children, is resized; new items added or existing items removed, the framework will automatically recalculate each child layout recursively, until each level has been computed. This means that, once configured, the layouts will always remain up-to-date.

This behavior is accomplished by executing the `doLayout()` method which triggers this recalculation process. We should never call this method manually within our application code as the framework calls it whenever it is required.

See also

▶ See all of the previous recipes in this chapter for details of each layout used.

▶ The *Constructing a complex form layout* recipe in *Chapter 5, Loading, Submitting, and Validating Forms*, which makes use of a variety of layouts.

4

UI Building Blocks—Trees, Panels, and Data Views

In this chapter, we will cover:

- ▸ Loading a tree's nodes from the server
- ▸ Sorting Tree nodes
- ▸ Dragging-and-dropping nodes within a tree
- ▸ Using a tree as a menu to load content into another panel
- ▸ Docking items to a panel's edges
- ▸ Displaying a simple form in a window
- ▸ Creating a tabbed layout with tooltips
- ▸ Manipulating a tab panel's TabBar
- ▸ Executing inline JavaScript in an XTemplate to customize appearance
- ▸ Creating `Ext.XTemplate` member functions
- ▸ Adding logic to XTemplates
- ▸ Formatting dates within an XTemplate
- ▸ Creating a DataView and binding it to a data store
- ▸ Displaying a detailed window after clicking on a Data View node

Introduction

Creating and manipulating the basic components that Ext JS provides is fundamental to producing a rich application. In this chapter, we will cover three fundamental Ext JS UI components and explore how to configure and control them within your applications.

We will start by exploring the `Ext.tree.Panel` class and demonstrate how to populate a tree with server-side data. From there we will delve into manipulating the tree component through filtering and sorting, and then by dragging-and-dropping individual nodes. Finally, we will show you how to incorporate a tree into a more real-life scenario by using it as a menu and loading another panel following node clicks.

The `Ext.panel.Panel` class will be focused on next where we will discover how to configure its headers, dock items to its edges, and to create tab panels. We will then go on to look at ways in which these tab panels can be customized with things like tooltips, icons, and tab positions.

Before moving onto the `Ext.view.View` component. We will talk about XTemplates, which allow us to create dynamic HTML very easily. We will discuss various features of the `Ext.XTemplate` class and how to use it.

This will lead us nicely into the `Ext.view.View` class, which makes heavy use of XTemplates, and is used to bind a data store to a presentation generator. We will also look into handling events on a View and how to integrate custom plugins to enrich our users' experience.

Loading a tree's nodes from the server

Creating a tree in your user interface is achieved using a Tree Panel. This recipe gives you the knowledge required to create and configure a Tree Panel and load JSON data asynchronously from your server to the tree. The final tree will look like the following screenshot:

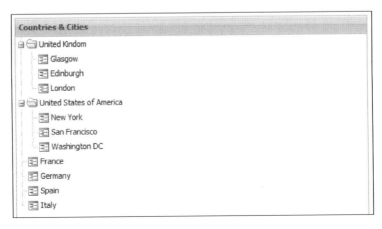

Getting ready

Make sure you have a web server installed and running on your development computer. For the purposes of this demonstration, your web server will need to serve JSON files. If your server is not capable, add a MIME type for JSON (application/json).

How to do it...

1. Start by defining an `Ext.data.TreeStore` to load our data into:

```
var store = Ext.create('Ext.data.TreeStore', {
    proxy: {
        type: 'ajax',
        url: 'treeData.json'
    },
    root: {
        text: 'Countries',
        expanded: true
    }
});
```

2. The `treeData.json` file that we are loading from contains a simple array of data, some of these objects contain nested data that will form our tree structure. A sample can be seen as follows:

```
[{
    "text": "United Kindom",
    "children": [{
        "text": "Glasgow",
        "leaf": true
    }, {
        "text": "Edinburgh",
        "leaf": true
    }, {
        "text": "London",
        "leaf": true
    }],
    "leaf": false
},
{
    "text": "France",
    "leaf": true
}
...
]
```

3. Create the Tree Panel and render it to the document's body.

```
Ext.create('Ext.tree.Panel', {
    title: 'Countries &amp; Cities',
    width: 500,
    height: 300,
    store: store,
    rootVisible: false,
    renderTo: Ext.getBody(),
    style: 'margin: 50px'
});
```

How it works...

The `Ext.tree.Panel` class holds the configuration required for the tree. The simple tree demonstrated in this recipe is bound to a TreeStore.

 All Tree Panel's must be bound to an `Ext.data.TreeStore` instance.

The `Ext.data.TreeStore` is used to load nodes into the tree and by default, if no other Model is provided, uses an implicit Model that implements the `Ext.data.NodeInterface` class, which provides a range of methods for working with the data in your tree.

This store has a `proxy` and a `root` defined. As we are working with server-side data the proxy's `type` is configured as `ajax`. The `url` is the location of the remote data (in this case `treeData.json`).

The `root` contains the root node—`Countries` for this dataset. As we want the child data that's loaded to be visible immediately, we set `expanded: true`. We've also set `rootVisible: false` in the Tree Panel which hides `Countries` from view, but still shows its children.

The data in our `treeData.json` file contains a JSON object for each tree node. The `text` property is displayed in the tree for each node. The `leaf` property indicates whether or not the node has any children. By setting this to `false`, the node will not be expandable. Finally, the `children` property contains an array of nodes, defined in the same way, which are displayed as children of the parent node.

See also

▶ You may be interested in visiting *Chapter 7, Working with the Ext JS Data Package*, to learn more about the framework's data package.

▶ The next three recipes in this chapter, which explore the TreePanel in further detail.

Sorting tree nodes

Sorting the data that's asynchronously loaded to a tree is straight-forward with Ext JS. This recipe, demonstrates how to sort a tree's data on the client-side.

How to do it...

1. Create a store with the `sorters` configuration option defined with an object specifying `property` and `direction` values:

```
var store = Ext.create('Ext.data.TreeStore', {
    proxy: {
        type: 'ajax',
        url: 'treeData.json'
    },
    root: {
        text: 'Countries',
        expanded: true
    },
    sorters: [{
        property: 'text',
        direction: 'ASC' //for descending change to 'DESC'
    }]
});
```

2. Create a tree to load the sorted data to.

```
Ext.create('Ext.tree.Panel', {
    title: 'Countries',
    width: 500,
    height: 200,
    store: store,
    rootVisible: false,
    renderTo: Ext.getBody(),
    style: 'margin: 50px'
});
```

How it works...

The sorting in this example is carried out by an `Ext.util.Sorter` that's defined in the `sorters` property of the TreeStore. The `Sorter` requires either a `property` or `sorterFn` option.

The sorter is configured with a `property`, which is the name of the field that we would like to sort by. The `direction` property sets the sorting direction for the sorter. This will default to ASC (ascending) if it's omitted from the `Sorter` configuration.

There's more...

Sorting data on the client side can be enhanced further with:

Complex and custom sorting

It's possible to customize the sorter and make complex comparisons by removing the `property` configuration and replacing it with the `sorterFn` option and assigning it a function that performs our sorting comparisons. The arguments of `sorterFn` are the two objects being compared and it should return:

▶ `-1` if *objectOne is less than objectTwo*

▶ `0` if *objectOne is equal to objectTwo*

▶ `1` if *objectOne is greater than objectTwo*

A simple example of this can be written to sort our list of countries by the length of their name which isn't possible using a simple property sort. We start by defining our `sorter` function, which we will compare two countries names and output the correct value either `-1`, `0`, or `1`:

```
var nameLengthSorter = function(objectOne, objectTwo){

    var objectOneLength = objectOne.get('text').length,
        objectTwoLength= objectTwo.get('text').length;

    if(objectOneLength=== objectTwoLength){
        return 0;
    } else if(objectOneLength<objectTwoLength){
        return -1;
    } else {
        return 1;
    }
};
```

We could combine this `if-else` block into a single line by using a ternary `if` statement and save some space:

```
return (objectOneLength === objectTwoLength) ? 0 : (objectOneLength <
objectTwoLength? -1 : 1);
```

Next, we apply this sorter to our store by replacing the `property` config with the `sorterFn` option and assigning it a reference to our new sorter function.

```
...
    sorters: [{
        sorterFn: nameLengthSorter,
        direction: 'ASC' //for descending change to 'DESC'
    }
...
```

Our new sorted tree can be seen in the following screenshot:

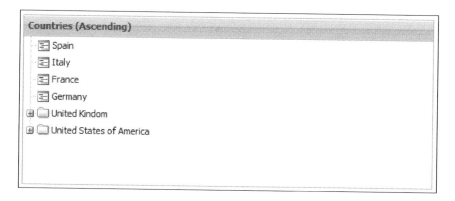

Sorting by multiple fields

It's possible to sort by multiple fields. If we added an extra field to the JSON called `continent`, we could sort by country name and continent as shown as follows:

```
...
    sorters: [{
        property: 'text',
        direction: 'ASC'
    }, {
        property: 'continent',
        direction: 'DESC'
    }]
...
```

Sorting on demand

We've demonstrated how to sort the data as the TreeStore is loaded. However, you may wish to add a button or toggle to allow users to sort the data on demand. `Ext.data.TreeStore` provides a `sort` method for this very purpose.

We could add a button to the page and sort the data when the button is pressed using the store's `sort` method:

```
Ext.create('Ext.Button', {
    text: 'Sort Tree',
    renderTo: Ext.getBody(),
    handler: function() {
        //this will toggle ASC & DESC automatically for you.
        store.sort('text');

        //or we can force a direction like so:
        store.sort('text', 'DESC');
    }
});
```

See also

▶ The previous recipe which introduces the Tree Panel.

▶ The recipe *Loading data into a Store from a server*, in *Chapter 7*, for more information on stores.

Dragging-and-dropping nodes within a tree

Dragging-and-dropping nodes within a tree or between trees can help make your application more interactive for your users. Ext JS has built-in drag-and-drop nodes making it easy for developers to add this functionality. Here, we will learn how to drag nodes from one tree to another.

How to do it...

1. Create a store and define some dummy inline data for the first tree:

```
var storeForTreeA = Ext.create('Ext.data.TreeStore', {
    root: {
        expanded: true,
        children: [{
            text: "Item 1",
            leaf: true
        },{
            text: "Item 2",
            leaf: true
        },{
            text: "Item 3",
            leaf: true
        },{
```

```
            text: "Item 4",
            leaf: true
        }]
    }
});
```

2. Create a tree and add the `Ext.tree.plugin.TreeViewDragDrop` plugin:

```
var treeA = Ext.create('Ext.tree.Panel', {
    title: 'Tree One (drag from here)',
    store: storeForTreeA,
    width: 500,
    height: 200,
    viewConfig: {
        plugins: {
            ptype: 'treeviewdragdrop'
        }
    },
    renderTo: Ext.getBody(),
    style: 'margin: 50px'
});
```

3. Define a second store for the second tree:

```
var storeForTreeB = Ext.create('Ext.data.TreeStore', {
    root: {
        expanded: true,
        children: [{
            text: "Item 5",
            leaf: true
        }]
    }
});
```

4. Add a second tree, also with the `Ext.tree.plugin.TreeViewDragDrop` plugin defined:

```
var treeB = Ext.create('Ext.tree.Panel', {
    title: 'Tree Two (drop here)',
    width: 500,
    height: 200,
    store: storeForTreeB,
    viewConfig: {
        plugins: {
            ptype: 'treeviewdragdrop',
            enableDrop: true,
            enableDrag: false,
```

```
                    allowContainerDrop: true
          }
      },
      renderTo: Ext.getBody(),
      style: 'margin: 50px'
  });
```

5. Now, try clicking-and-dragging nodes from the first tree and dropping them into the second.

How it works...

The drag/drop functionality is provided by the `Ext.tree.plugin.TreeViewDragDrop` class which is packaged with the framework. This functionality is included as a plugin so it can be separated from the main tree code and leverages the flexible plugin system provided by the library.

This plugin provides the functionality to the `Ext.tree.View` instance that is encapsulated by the Tree Panel. Therefore, it is defined in the `viewConfig` property of the Tree Panel.

The `TreeViewDragDrop` plugin can be configured with a number of options. In this example, the second tree has the following configuration set:

► `enableDrop: true` sets the tree to accept drop gestures

► `enableDrag: false` stops the users from dragging nodes within/from this TreeView

► `allowContainerDrop: true` allows the user to drop anywhere in the tree's container

As a TreePanel must be bound to a TreeStore, this example only works if two TreeStores are defined (one for each TreePanel). As the user drags a node from the first tree to the second the node is removed from the first store and inserted (at the correct position) into the second store.

See also

► The first recipe in this chapter *Loading a tree's nodes from the server* for an introduction to using a Tree Panel.

► For a more advanced look at plugins, we recommend reading the recipe *Advanced functionality with plugins*, in *Chapter 12*.

Using a tree as a menu to load content into another panel

Having your application perform an action when the user clicks a node in a tree can be done by listening for the events raised by the `Ext.tree.Panel` class.

This recipe gives some insight on how to listen for these events, have them interact with a second panel, and have it create a new tab in it. For the purposes of this demonstration, the new tab we create will have its HTML property set to the text from the node's record. It would be straight-forward to extend this example for adding more complex components to your TabPanel.

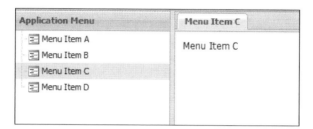

How to do it...

1. Define a TreeStore with some example nodes for the tree:

```
var store = Ext.create('Ext.data.TreeStore', {
    root : {
        expanded :true,
        children : [ {
            text : "Menu Item A",
            leaf :true
        }, {
            text : "Menu Item B",
            leaf :true
        }, {
            text : "Menu Item C",
            leaf :true
        }, {
            text : "Menu Item D",
            leaf :true
        }]
    }
});
```

2. Create a tree for the west region with the logic to create new tabs when the node is clicked:

```
var westPanel = Ext.create('Ext.tree.Panel', {
    title : 'Application Menu',
    region : 'west',
    margins : '0 5 0 0',
    width : 200,
    store : store,
    rootVisible :false,
    listeners : {
        itemclick : function(tree, record, item, index, e,
options) {

                var nodeText = record.data.text,
                    tabPanel = viewport.items.get(1),
                    tabBar = tabPanel.getTabBar(),
                    tabIndex;

                for ( vari = 0; i<tabBar.items.length; i++) {
                    if (tabBar.items.get(i).getText() === nodeText) {
                        tabIndex = i;
                    }
                }

                if (Ext.isEmpty(tabIndex)) {
                    tabPanel.add({
                        title :record.data.text,
                        bodyPadding : 10,
                        html :record.data.text
                    });

                    tabIndex = tabPanel.items.length - 1;
                }

                tabPanel.setActiveTab(tabIndex);
        }
    }
});
```

3. Add a BorderLayout to the Viewport with a TabPanel in the center region and our tree in the west:

```
var viewport = Ext.create('Ext.container.Viewport', {
    layout : 'border',
    items : [westPanel, {
        xtype : 'tabpanel',
```

```
            region : 'center'
        }]
    });
```

How it works...

The Viewport has a BorderLayout with a west region (for the TreePanel) and a center region (for the TabPanel).

As with the previous three recipes, the TreePanel must be bound to a TreeStore which we have defined with some static data.

The focus of this recipe is listening for the `itemclick` event on the TreePanel. When the user clicks on a node in the tree the `itemclick` event is fired passing the following parameters to its handler functions:

- `this : Ext.view.View`
- `record : Ext.data.Model`
- `item : HTMLElement`
- `index : Number`
- `e: Ext.EventObject`
- `options : Object`

The logic in the `itemclick` function has two outcomes:

- If the tab already exists then set it as the active tab
- If the tab doesn't exist then add it to the TabPanel and set it as the active tab

Firstly, we get the `text` field value from the record, the TabPanel, and TabBar components from the center region. We also create a local variable that will hold the tab index of our existing tab. We'll need these later on:

```
var nodeText = record.data.text,
    tabPanel = viewport.items.get(1),
    tabBar = tabPanel.getTabBar(),
    tabIndex;
```

The `for` loop iterates through all the tabs in the TabBar to determine if a tab for the node already exists (based on the Tab's title). If it does, our `tabIndex` variable is set to the index in the TabBar's `items` collection:

```
for(var i = 0; i < tabBar.items.length; i++) {
    if (tabBar.items.get(i).getText() === nodeText) {
        tabIndex = i;
    }
}
```

Having looped through the tabs, we now know whether the tab exists or not. If `tabIndex` is empty (null, undefined, and so on) then we'll add a new tab using the TabPanel's add method. Here we specify the `config` options for the tab's panel. The `tabIndex` is then set to the index of the last item added to the `items` collection:

```
if(Ext.isEmpty(tabIndex)) {
    tabPanel.add({
        title: nodeText,
        bodyPadding: 10,
        html: nodeText
    });

    tabIndex = tabPanel.items.length - 1;
}
```

Finally, we call the `setActiveTab` method, passing it the index of the tab we wish to activate for our user:

```
tabPanel.setActiveTab(tabIndex);
```

See also

- ▶ If you're not fully up to speed with trees yet it may be worth reading the first recipe in the chapter, *Loading a Tree's nodes from the server.*

- ▶ We've listened for the `itemclick` event on the tree in this example. If you want to know more about handling events the recipes *Handling Events on Elements and Components* in *Chapter 2, Manipulating the Dom, Handling Events, and Making AJAX Requests*, may be useful.

- ▶ TabPanels are discussed in more detail later in this chapter. The recipe *Creating a tabbed layout with tooltips*, is particularly a good place to start.

Docking items to panels' edges

This recipe demonstrates how to dock items to the edges of a panel. We will show this by adding a toolbar to a panel's edges.

How to do it...

1. Create a panel and render it to the document's body:

```
Ext.create('Ext.panel.Panel', {
    title: 'Panel Header',
    width: 500,
    height: 200,
```

```
        bodyPadding: 10,
        html: 'Panel Content',
        renderTo: Ext.getBody(),
        style: 'margin: 50px'
    });
```

2. Dock a toolbar to the top of the panel:

```
Ext.create('Ext.panel.Panel', {
        title: 'Panel Header',
        width: 500,
        height: 200,
        bodyPadding: 10,
        html: 'Panel Content',
        dockedItems: [{
            xtype: 'toolbar',
            dock: 'top',
            items: [{
                xtype: 'button',
                text: 'Click me'
            }, '->', 'Docked toolbar at the top']
        }],
        renderTo: Ext.getBody(),
        style: 'margin: 50px'
    });
```

 When creating a toolbar, any component configuration added to the items array without an xtype will default to being a button.

3. Add another item to the dockedItems collection. This time dock it to the bottom of the panel:

```
Ext.create('Ext.panel.Panel', {
        title: 'Panel Header',
        width: 500,
        height: 200,
        bodyPadding: 10,
        html: 'Panel Content',
        dockedItems: [{
            xtype: 'toolbar',
            dock: 'top',
            items: [{
                text: 'Click me'
            }, '->', 'Docked toolbar at the top']
        }, {
            xtype: 'toolbar',
            dock: 'bottom',
            items: [{
```

```
        xtype: 'button',
         text: 'Click me'
    }, '->', 'Docked toolbar at the bottom']
  }],
  renderTo: Ext.getBody(),
  style: 'margin: 50px'
});
```

The string `->` in our `items` array is automatically converted into an instance of the `Ext.toolbar.Fill` class, which is a simple component with a flex of 1. This forces all the toolbar items after it to the right side of the toolbar. Other useful toolbar shortcuts that can be included in its items array are `-`, which will create an `Ext.toolbar.Separator` instance that displays a vertical separator line, and (a space), which equates to an `Ext.toolbar.Spacer` instance that adds a space between components.

4. Add a footer bar to the panel using the `fbar` config option. The footer bar appears beneath the panel:

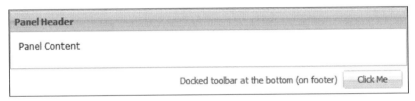

```
Ext.create('Ext.panel.Panel', {
    title: 'Panel Header',
    width: 500,
    height: 200,
    bodyPadding: 10,
    html: 'Panel Content',
    fbar: ['Docked toolbar at the bottom (on footer)', {
        xtype: 'button',
        text: 'Click Me'
    }],
    renderTo: Ext.getBody(),
    style: 'margin: 50px'
});
```

5. Ext JS provides further shortcuts for adding items to the left, right, top, and bottom of a panel:

```
Ext.create('Ext.panel.Panel', {
    title: 'Panel Header',
    width: 500,
    height: 200,
    bodyPadding: 10,
    html: 'Panel Content',
    lbar: ['lbar'],
    rbar: ['rbar'],
    tbar: ['tbar'],
    bbar: ['bbar'],
    renderTo: Ext.getBody(),
    style: 'margin: 50px'
});
```

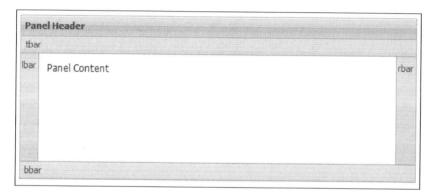

How it works...

In steps 2 and 3 the toolbar is defined in the panel's `dockedItems` collection. We specify where the item will be docked using the `dock` config option which takes the following values: `'left'`, `'right'`, `'top'`, or `'bottom'`. Step three demonstrates how it's possible to define multiple items in the `dockedItems` collection and specify a different position for each.

The `fbar` config option highlighted in step 4 shows that it's possible to dock a toolbar to a panel's bottom edge conveniently, without having to specify it in the `dockedItems` collection. It creates a docked item for you that is docked to the bottom with the `ui` config option set to `'footer'`.

The final step shows four other convenient methods provided in the framework for quickly specifying docked items on all sides of a panel.

There's more...

It's also possible to add `dockeditems` to your Panels at runtime, which means you can dynamically specify the dockedItems depending on specified criteria.

```
var panel = Ext.create('Ext.panel.Panel', {
    title: 'Panel Header',
    width: 500,
    height: 200,
    bodyPadding: 10,
    html: 'Panel Content',
    renderTo: Ext.getBody()
});

panel.addDocked({
    dock: 'top',
    xtype: 'toolbar',
    items: [{
        text: 'button'
    }]
});
```

The `addDocked` method simply adds the docked item to the container. You must not forget to configure your component with the `dock` config option (`'left'`, `'right'`, `'top'` or `'bottom'`) to ensure the component is docked in the correct position.

Displaying a simple form in a window

Most websites and applications make use of windows and forms on a regular basis. Here you'll learn the basics for creating a simple form and window with Ext JS and combining the two to display the form to the user.

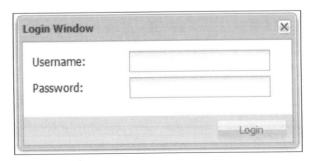

How to do it...

1. Start by creating a simple form with two fields and a button.

```
var form = Ext.create('Ext.form.Panel', {
    bodyPadding: 10,
    border: false,
    defaultType: 'textfield',
    items: [{
        fieldLabel: 'Username',
        name: 'username',
        allowBlank: false
    }, {
        fieldLabel: 'Password',
        name: 'password',
        inputType: 'password',
        allowBlank: false
    }],
    buttons: [{
        text: 'Login',
        formBind: true,
        disabled: true,
        handler: function(){
            alert('Login Button Pressed');
        }
    }]
});
```

2. Create an `Ext.window.Window` with the form in its `items` collection and display it to the user using the `show` method:

```
Ext.create('Ext.window.Window', {
    title: 'Login Window',
    height: 140,
    width: 300,
    layout: 'fit',
    items: [form]
}).show();
```

How it works...

There are two main components in this recipe, the form, and the window. As you can see from the code above it's very straight-forward creating and configuring both.

This recipe doesn't demonstrate how to populate or submit the form. The next chapter holds all the information you require to make the form actually work.

Firstly, we create an `Ext.form.Panel`. This will contain the configuration for the form. The form fields are specified in the panel's `items` collection. Setting `defaultType: 'textfield'` saves us from having to specify `xtype: 'textfield'` on each item. The benefits of `defaultType` are really seen when you have a large form with lots of similar fields.

Although the Password field is a `textfield` remember to set `inputType: 'password'` to ensure the password isn't displayed.

The `buttons` collection contains our form's buttons. In this example we've set `formBind: true`. This ensures the button remains disabled until the form is valid.

Each field has `allowBlank: false` configured, making the field required before the form validates. Additionally, to ensure the button starts inactive `disabled: true` must be set on the button.

Step two shows how to create a window with Ext JS. The form is added to the window's `items` collection. Finally, to display the window we call the `show` method.

See also

> ▶ Forms and form fields are covered in greater depth over the next two chapters. The recipe *Constructing a complex form layout* in *Chapter 5* may be particularly useful.

Creating a tabbed layout with tooltips

Creating a tabbed layout and adding tooltips to the tabs is straight-forward with Ext JS 4. In this recipe we will show you how to create a tab panel with multiple tabs, add tooltip text, and have the framework display the text as you hover over a tab.

How to do it...

1. Initialize the global QuickTipManager instance. We need this for the tooltips to be displayed:

    ```
    Ext.tip.QuickTipManager.init();
    ```

2. Create an `Ext.tab.Panel` with two tabs (added to the Panel's `items` collection) and render it to the document's body:

    ```
    Ext.create('Ext.tab.Panel', {
    ```

```
        width: 500,
        height: 200,
        style: 'margin: 50px',
        renderTo: Ext.getBody(),
        items: [{
            title: 'Tab One'
        }, {
            title: 'Tab Two'
        }]
    });
```

3. In tab two add a tooltip to the `tabConfig` config option. `tabConfig` takes configuration options that are applied to the Panel's `Ext.tab.Tab` instance:

```
    Ext.create('Ext.tab.Panel', {
        width: 500,
        height: 200,
        style: 'margin: 50px',
        renderTo: Ext.getBody(),
        items: [{
            title: 'Tab One'
        }, {
            title: 'Tab Two',
            tabConfig: {
                tooltip: 'Tab Two Tooltip Text'
            }
        }]
    });
```

4. Customize the tooltip with configuration options from `Ext.tip.QuickTip` class:

```
    Ext.create('Ext.tab.Panel', {
        width: 500,
        height: 200,
        style: 'margin: 50px',
        renderTo: Ext.getBody(),
        items: [{
            title: 'Tab One'
        }, {
            title: 'Tab Two',
            tabConfig: {
                tooltip: 'Tab Two Tooltip Text'
            }
        }, {
            title: 'Tab Three',
            tabConfig: {
                tooltip: {
                    title: 'Tooltip Header',
```

```
                    text: 'Tab Three Tooltip Text'
                }
            }
        }]
    });
```

Tab One	Tab Two	Tab Three	

Tooltip Header
Tab Three Tooltip Text

How it works...

Creating a tab panel in Ext JS is done using the `Ext.tab.Panel` class. Each tab is defined in the panel's `items` collection and has an associated `Ext.tab.Tab` instance created automatically, which represents the tab element that allows it to be activated.

In step three, we add the `tabConfig` config option to the second tab. Inside the `tabConfig` object we can specify configuration for the `Ext.tab.Tab` class. From here we've added a `tooltip` with a string value. Step 4 shows how it's possible to customize a tooltip by assigning an object literal with configuration from the `Ext.tip.QuickTip` class.

Don't forget to initialize the `QuickTipManager` instance otherwise your tooltips won't appear. This is done by calling `Ext.tip.QuickTipManager.init();` at the start of your code (as seen in step one).

See also

▶ The next recipe, which covers techniques on how to manipulate a TabBar.

Manipulating a tab panel's TabBar

A tab panel's TabBar is the area at the top of its content, which displays a button or tab for each of the child panels within it. By clicking on these tabs the relevant panel is displayed.

These tabs can be extensively customized, and in this recipe, we will discuss how to achieve the following:

- ▸ Configure a tab with an icon
- ▸ Dynamically switch icons
- ▸ Set tabs' widths
- ▸ Change the position of the tab bar
- ▸ Show and hide tabs on the fly

How to do it...

To start with we will create a basic Ext.tab.Panel with three child panels. We will use this as the base for all our examples:

```
var tabPanel = Ext.create('Ext.tab.Panel', {
    width: 500,
    height: 200,
    style: 'margin: 50px',
    renderTo: Ext.getBody(),
    items: [{
        title: 'Tab One',
        html: 'This is Tab One'
    }, {
        title: 'Tab Two - has a very, very long and silly title',
        html: 'This is Tab Two'
    }, {
        title: 'Tab Three',
        html: 'This is Tab Three'
    }]
});
```

Configure a tab with an icon

We will now add an icon to the first tab by creating a CSS class, with the icon defined as a background image, and applying it to the tab by using the tabConfig configuration option:

```
<style type="text/css">
    .icon-refresh {
        background-image: url('refresh.png');
        background-repeat: no-repeat;
    }
</style>

...

{
    title: 'Tab One',
```

```
tabConfig: {
    cls: 'x-btn-text-icon',
    iconCls: 'icon-refresh'
},
html: 'This is Tab One'
}
...
```

The result of this can be seen as follows:

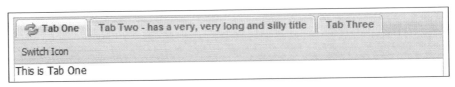

Dynamically switch icons

Although we have specified this refresh icon at configuration time, we can also change it at runtime by using the `setIconCls` method of the Tab component. We can access a panel tab by using its `tab` property. We will demonstrate this by adding a button to the tab panel's `tbar` that switches the icon class to another. In the following code snippet `tabPanelIcon` contains the original tab panel's instance:

```
tbar: [{
    text: 'Switch Icon',
    handler: function(){
        tabPanelIcon.items.get(0).tab.setIconCls('icon-tick');
    }
}]
```

Set tabs' widths

Ext JS gives us the option to control the minimum and maximum width of any tab in a tab panel's tab bar. We can do this by using the `minTabWidth` and `maxTabWidth` config options on the tab panel itself:

```
...
minTabWidth: 100,
maxTabWidth: 200
...
```

We are also able to specify the absolute width of individual tabs by defining the width option within the panel's `tabConfig` property:

```
...
tabConfig: {
    width: 150
}
...
```

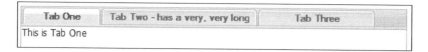

We can see in the screenshot that the first tab has its width constrained by the `minTabWidth` option. The second is constrained by the `maxTabWidth` value, which means some of its title is cut off. The third is set by the explicit value given.

Change the position of the tab bar

It is possible to reposition the tab bar to the bottom of the tab panel rather than having it at the top. This is very simple to accomplish by using the `tabPosition` config option of the `Ext.tab.Panel` class, and providing it with a value of `bottom` or `top`:

```
. . .
tabPosition: 'bottom'
. . .
```

Show and hide tabs on the fly

One new feature of the Ext JS 4's tab panel is that we are able to show and hide tabs on the fly. We can do this simply by calling the `show`, `hide`, or `setVisible` method on the child panels' Tab component.

We will demonstrate this by adding a button that toggles the visibility of the second tab:

```
tbar: [{
    text: 'Toggle Tab Two',
    handler: function(){
        var tab = tabPanelVisibility.items.get(1).tab;

        tab.setVisible(!tab.isVisible());
    }
}]
```

The second tab is hidden from view as shown in the following screenshot:

How it works...

When a panel is added to a tab panel it has an `Ext.tab.Tab` instance created to represent it in the tab bar. This class extends the `Ext.button.Button` class and gives us access to a selection of the properties and methods from this class. The `Ext.tab.Tab`'s instance is accessible through the panel's `tab` property as we have seen in our examples.

We can configure the `Ext.tab.Tab` by defining the `tabConfig` option in the panel's definition. This object is automatically applied to the `Ext.tab.Tab` instance when it is created and so through this, we can configure it how we need.

Executing inline JavaScript to in an XTemplate customize appearance

Within an `Ext.XTemplate`'s HTML we are able to include small pieces of JavaScript that will be executed when the template is processed. This feature is extremely useful for adding things such as, conditional formatting, simple member manipulation, or formatting.

In this recipe, we are going to demonstrate how to include some inline JavaScript within an `Ext.XTemplate`, in order to format our output dynamically based on the data's values.

The example that we will use is a simple bug list. We will use inline JavaScript code to color each row based on the severity of the bug.

How to do it...

1. We start by defining an array of bugs that we will use in our template (we have only shown one to demonstrate the structure):

```
var bugData = [{
    id: 1,
    title: 'Bug 1',
    description: 'Bug 1 Description',
    status: 'In Progress',
    severity: 1
}
...
]
```

2. Next, we create our template, containing a simple HTML table, to display our bug details. We then use `overwrite` method of the `Ext.XTemplate` to insert the generated HTML into the document's body element, replacing any HTML already there:

```
var tpl = new Ext.XTemplate(
```

```
            '<table>',
                '<tr>',
                    '<td>Title</td>',
                    '<td>Description</td>',
                    '<td>Severity</td>',
                '</tr>',
                '<tpl for=".">',
                    '<tr>',
                        '<td>{title}</td>',
                        '<td>{description}</td>',
                        '<td>{severity}</td>',
                    '</tr>',
                '</tpl>',
            '</table>');

    tpl.overwrite(Ext.getBody(), bugData);
```

3. We now add a background style to the status cell and add some inline JavaScript to either color the background green when the status is complete or transparent when it isn't:

```
var tpl = new Ext.XTemplate(
        '<table>',
            '<tr>',
                '<td>Title</td>',
                '<td>Description</td>',
                '<td>Severity</td>',
            '</tr>',
            '<tpl for=".">',
                '<tr>',
                    '<td style="background-color: {[values.status
=== "Complete" ? "green" : "transparent"]};">{title}</td>',
                    '<td>{description}</td>',
                    '<td>{severity}</td>',
                '</tr>',
            '</tpl>',
        '</table>');

    tpl.overwrite(Ext.getBody(), bugData);
```

How it works...

The Ext.XTemplate class evaluates anything within the tags {[...]} as JavaScript code and executes it within the scope of the template itself (see the next recipe, _Creating Ext.XTemplate member functions_, for more details).

In our example we use a simple ternary `if` statement to decide what color to use depending on the `status` property's value. We access the current data object and its properties through the `values` keyword which references the current object.

There's more...

As well as the `values` object there are several other variables that can be used to access helpful bits of information within an XTemplate:

- `parent`: the current data object's parent object. For example, if we were looping through an array the `parent` variable would refer to the data object that contains the array as a property
- `xindex`: when inside a loop, this variable contains the current (1-based) index
- `xcount`: when inside a loop, this variable contains the total number of items in the array that is being iterated over

See also

- The next recipe, to discover how to work with member functions in `Ext.XTemplates`.
- The recipe, *Adding logic to Ext.XTemplates*, for other methods of customizing the Ext.XTemplate.

Creating Ext.XTemplate member functions

`Ext.XTemplates` can be configured to contain functions and properties that are enclosed within the scope of the template itself. These functions can be used to encapsulate presentation logic, formatting, and other simple template data processing.

We are going to demonstrate how these functions can be included in an XTemplate's definition and how to access them within our template's code.

We will do this by building upon the example that we created in the previous recipe. Our goal is to highlight each of the rows that are deemed by our manager as high priority, in our situation this means any bug with a `severity` rating of 4 or 5.

How to do it...

1. We begin by creating our sample data and our basic `Ext.XTemplate` in the same way as we did in the previous recipe:

```
var bugData = [{
    id: 1,
    title: 'Bug 1',
```

```
            description: 'Bug 1 Description',
            status: 'In Progress',
            severity: 1
    }
    ...
    ];

    var tpl = new Ext.XTemplate(
        '<table>',
            '<tr>',
                '<td>Title</td>',
                '<td>Description</td>',
                '<td>Severity</td>',
            '</tr>',
            '<tpl for=".">',
                '<tr>',
                    '<td style="background-color: {[values.status ===
"Complete" ? "green" : "transparent"]};">{title}</td>',
                    '<td>{description}</td>',
                    '<td>{severity}</td>',
                '</tr>',
            '</tpl>',
        '</table>');

    tpl.overwrite(Ext.getBody(), bugData);
```

2. Next, we define a configuration object containing a simple function called
    isHighPriority, which accepts one argument called severity. We then
    include this object as the final parameter of our XTemplate's constructor call:

```
    var tpl = new Ext.XTemplate(
        '<table>',
            '<tr>',
                '<td>Title</td>',
                '<td>Description</td>',
                '<td>Severity</td>',
            '</tr>',
            '<tpl for=".">',
                '<tr>',
                    '<td style="background-color: {[values.status ===
"Complete" ? "green" : "transparent"]};">{title}</td>',
                    '<td>{description}</td>',
                    '<td>{severity}</td>',
                '</tr>',
            '</tpl>',
        '</table>',
        {
```

```
        isHighPriority: function(severity){
            return severity > 3
        }
    }
);
```

```
tpl.overwrite(Ext.getBody(), bugData);
```

3. Finally, we use the `<tpl>` tag's `if` attribute, to call our function and add some style markup if it evaluates to true. In this situation, we will add a red border and pink background if the bug is deemed to be of a high priority:

```
var tpl = new Ext.XTemplate('<table>',
    '<table>',
        '<tr>',
            '<td>Title</td>',
            '<td>Description</td>',
            '<td>Severity</td>',
        '</tr>',
        '<tpl for=".">',
            '<tr <tpl if="this.isHighPriority(values.
severity)">style="background-color: pink; border: 2px solid
#FF0000;"</tpl>>',
                '<td style="background-color: {[values.status ===
"Complete" ? "green" : "transparent"]};">{title}</td>',
                '<td>{description}</td>',
                '<td>{severity}</td>',
            '</tr>',
        '</tpl>',
    '</table>',
    {
        isHighPriority: function(severity){
            return severity > 3
        }
    }
);
```

```
tpl.overwrite(Ext.getBody(), bugData);
```

4. We are also able to call our member functions within the inline JavaScript that we spoke of in our last recipe, as those code snippets are executed in the scope of the XTemplate. Our example could be rewritten as:

```
{[this.isHighPriority(values.severity) ? "style="background-color:
pink; border: 2px solid #FF0000; " :""]}
```

How it works...

If we pass an object to the constructor of `Ext.XTemplate`'s (at any position) it is applied to the XTemplate's definition, in a similar manner to defining your own custom methods when extending a class.

By applying these configuration options the methods can be executed anywhere in the template from within `<tpl>` tags or in inline code blocks.

> Properties can also be defined in this configuration object. These can come in use when state is required to be preserved while a template is generated.

There's more...

Another valuable use of member functions is in formatting values before they are presented. If we were to consider using a member function to format the description of a bug, only the first ten characters would be displayed as shown in the following code:

```
// function defined in the constructor's config object
formatDescription: function(description){
    return description.substring(0, 10);
}

// code within your template
{[this.formatDescription(values.description)]}
```

This approach is perfectly valid and will function perfectly. However, Ext JS provides us with a clever short-hand syntax for achieving this goal:

```
{description:this.formatDescription}
```

When parsing this code, the XTemplate knows to execute the `formatDescription` method and pass the specified field (in this case the `description`) into it as its first parameter.

If your function accepts additional parameters, such as a length to decide how many characters to show, they can be added to the code in the following way:

```
// function defined in the constructor's config object
formatDescription: function(description, numberOfChars){
    return description.substring(0, numberOfChars);
}

// code within your template
{description:this.formatDescription(10)}
```

The field's value is always passed to the function as its first parameter, with the extra values following after it.

Adding logic to Ext.XTemplates

When presenting data, it is important to be able to include logic to allow different markup to be created depending on the data given to it.

Ext JS' Ext.XTemplate provides that functionality in an easy to use way, which we shall explore in this recipe.

We will show this functionality by adding an additional column to our bug table from our previous two recipes, to display the owner of the bug. If that owner is the same as the current user (which we will define as a member property) then we will display *Me* otherwise we will display the owner's name.

Getting ready

We will base this recipe heavily on the examples created in the previous two recipes. So make sure you have a look at them and remind yourself what we did!

How to do it...

1. We will start by adding an `owner` property to each of our bug data objects and a `currentUser` property to our XTemplate's configuration object.

```
var bugData = [{
    title: 'Bug 1',
    description: 'Bug 1 Description',
    status: 'In Progress',
    severity: 1,
    owner: 'Bob'
}
...
];

{
    // member property added to the XTemplate'sconfig object
    currentUser: 'Bob'
}
```

2. Next, we add the extra owner column to our markup and add the first condition for displaying the owner. Initially, we will tell the template to display the word *Me* when the `owner` property matches the template's `currentUser` property:

```
. . .
'<td>',
    '<tpl if="owner == this.currentUser">Me</tpl>',
'</td>',
. . .
```

3. Finally, we add the `else` statement to display the plain owner name, if it didn't match the `currentUser`'s value:

```
. . .
'<td>',
    '<tpl if="owner === this.currentUser">',
        'Me',
    '<tplelse>',
        '{owner}',
    '</tpl>',
'</td>',
. . .
```

How it works...

We can perform logic using the `<tpl if="condition"></tpl>` tags, which will output the content of the tags if the condition inside the `if` attribute evaluates to true.

We can also build up an if/else construct by adding further `tpl` tags with the `else` keyword within it. We do this in Step 3 to output the owner's name, if it isn't the current user's name. The else's tpl tag comes within the initial if's closing tpl tag and simply has the attribute `else` inside it.

We can add further `else-if` blocks by adding additional `tpl` tags in exactly the same way as earlier but include an `elseif` attribute and add another condition as its value. For example, `<tpl elseif="owner === \'Everyone\'">Me*</tpl>` would display `Me*` if the owner was set to `Everyone`.

There's more...

We're not limited to just the use of an if/else statement. We could have coded this recipe with a switch statement:

```
...
'<td>',
    '<tplswitch="owner">',
        '<tplcase="this.currentUser">',
            'Me',
        '<tpldefault>',
            '{owner}',
    '</tpl>',
'</td>',
...
```

Formatting dates within an Ext.XTemplate

Dates are one of the most common data types that need formatting before being displayed to the user. This is no different when creating Ext.XTemplates for use in plain components or more complex components such as Data Views.

This recipe will describe the best way to perform this formatting within an Ext.XTemplate.

How to do it...

1. First, we will create a simple Ext.XTemplate and render it to the document's body, applying a simple data object, containing a date:

    ```
    var data = {
        date: '5/8/1986 12:30:00'
    };

    var tpl = new Ext.XTemplate('{date}');

    tpl.overwrite(Ext.getBody(), data); // outputs '5/8/1986 12:30:00'
    ```

2. We then use the date function, passing it a formatting string to format the date property:

    ```
    var tpl = new Ext.XTemplate('{date:date("Y-m-d")}');

    tpl.overwrite(Ext.getBody(), data); // outputs '1986-08-05'
    ```

3. We can also use the globally defined patterns that we used in *Chapter 2, Manipulating the Dom, Handling Events, and Making AJAX Requests,* by concatenating them into the XTemplate's HTML string.

```
var tpl = new Ext.XTemplate('{date:date("' + Ext.Date.patterns.
LongDate + '")} ');

tpl.overwrite(Ext.getBody(), data); // outputs 'Tuesday, August
05, 1986'
```

How it works...

We discussed adding and using member functions within `Ext.XTemplates` in a previous recipe and you will notice this technique uses identical syntax. The framework provides us with a built-in member function called date, which, just like in the previous recipe, passes the date value into the function as parameter one and returns it in the specified format from parameter two.

We simply have to pass it a valid formatting string and the function will output the formatted string.

See also

▶ The recipe, *Parsing, formatting, and manipulating dates* in *Chapter 2, Manipulating the Dom, Handling Events, and Making AJAX Requests,* for a more detailed introduction to working with dates.

Creating a DataView bound to a data store

DataViews are a very useful component that allow us to render markup that is bound to an `Ext.data.Store` instance. This means that the View renders a defined template for each of the Model instances within the store and will automatically react to changes made to the store, and its data, by refreshing the rendered markup to reflect these changes.

By using this approach we can concentrate on manipulating data without needing to worry about how that data is presented because the framework takes care of it for us.

In this recipe, we will create a simple store containing data about software bugs and bind it to a data view that will display each of the bugs. We will then demonstrate how changes to the underlying data are automatically reflected in the data view's rendered markup.

How to do it...

1. We start by creating a simple `Ext.data.Model` to represent our bug data. This Model contains five fields—`id`, `title`, `description`, `severity`, and `status`:

```
Ext.define('Bug', {
    extend: 'Ext.data.Model',
    fields: ['title', 'description', 'status', 'severity']
});
```

2. Now that we have a Model, we can create an `Ext.data.Store` that will encompass a collection of bug Models and give it an array of bugs to be populated with:

```
var bugData = [{
    id: 1,
    title: 'Bug 1',
    description: 'Bug 1 Description',
    status: 'In Progress',
    severity: 1
}
...
]; // only one item shown for brevity

var bugStore = new Ext.data.Store({
    model: 'Bug',
    data: bugData
});
```

3. Our next step is to define our Data View, which will be an instance of the `Ext.view.View` class. This attaches our previously defined store to it and defines the markup that will be generated for each Model:

```
var dataview = Ext.create('Ext.view.View', {
    store: bugStore,
    tpl: '<tpl for=".">' +
            '<div class="bug-wrapper">' +
                '<span class="title">{title}</span>' +
                '<span class="severity severity-
{severity}">{severity}</span>' +
                '<span class="description">{description}</span>'
+
                '<span class="status {[values.status.
toLowerCase().replace(" ", "-")]}">{status}</span>' +
            '</div>' +
        '</tpl>',
    itemSelector: 'div.bug-wrapper',
    emptyText: 'Woo hoo! No Bugs Found!',
    deferEmptyText: false
});
```

4. Now that we have our Data View defined, we can add it to a wrapping panel that will render it to our document's body:

```
var panel = Ext.create('Ext.panel.Panel', {
    renderTo: Ext.getBody(),
    title: 'Creating a DataView bound to a data Store',
    height: 500,
    width: 580,
    layout: 'fit',
    style: 'margin: 50;',
    items: [dataview]
});
```

5. At the moment, if you run this code, our data will look pretty horrible! We can sort this by adding some simple CSS styles targeting the HTML contained in the `tpl` tag just as we would in a normal HTML page:

```
<style type="text/css">
    div.bug-wrapper
    {
        float: left;
        width: 150px;
        height: 150px;
        background-color: #eee;
        margin: 20px;
        border: 2px solid #eee;
    }

    div.bug-wrapper.x-item-selected
    {
        border: 2px solid #000;
    }

    div.bug-wrapperspan.title
    {
        font-size: 1.2em;
        font-weight: bold;
        text-align: center;
        display: block;
    }

    div.bug-wrapperspan.severity
    {
        display: block;
        width: 80%;
        height: 50px;
        color: white;
        font-weight: bold;
        font-size: 3em;
        text-align: center;
```

```
        margin: 10px 10%;
    }

    div.bug-wrapper span.severity.severity-1 {background-color:
green;}
    div.bug-wrapper span.severity.severity-2 {background-color:
yellow;}
    div.bug-wrapper span.severity.severity-3 {background-color:
orange;}
    div.bug-wrapper span.severity.severity-4 {background-color:
pink;}
    div.bug-wrapper span.severity.severity-5 {background-color:
red;}

    div.bug-wrapperspan.description
    {
        padding: 5px;
        display: block;
        text-align: center;
    }

    div.bug-wrapperspan.status
    {
        display: block;
        width: 60%;
        margin: 10px 20%;
        padding: 3px;
        text-align: center;
        color: white;
        font-weight: bold;
    }

    div.bug-wrapperspan.status.open{background-color: green;}
    div.bug-wrapper span.status.in-progress {background-color:
yellow;}
    div.bug-wrapperspan.status.complete{background-color: black;}
</style>
```

6. Although not beautiful, this is a lot better. Finally, we can demonstrate the brilliance of Data Views and the benefit of using them to display data contained in a store. We will add some buttons that will sort, filter, and update the store and we will see how the View redraws itself immediately. We do this by adding the following code to the wrapping panel:

```
..
tbar: [{
    xtype: 'combo',
    name: 'status',
```

```
                    width: 200,
                    labelWidth: 100,
                    fieldLabel: 'Severity Filter',
                    store: ['1', '2', '3', '4', '5'],
                    queryMode: 'local',
                    listeners: {
                        select: function(combo, value, options){
                            dataview.getStore().clearFilter(); // remove current
filters
                            dataview.getStore().filter('severity', combo.
getValue());
                        }
                    }
                }, '-', {
                    text: 'Sort by Severity',
                    handler: function(){
                        dataview.getStore().sort('severity', 'DESC');
                    }
                }, {
                    text: 'Open all Bugs',
                    handler: function(){
                        dataview.getStore().each(function(model){
                            model.set('status', 'Open');
                            model.commit();
                        }, this); }
                }, '->', {
                    text: 'Clear Filter',
                    handler: function(){
                        dataview.getStore().clearFilter();
                    }
                }]
            ...
```

The following screenshot shows our final DataView with its CSS styles applied and toolbar buttons along the top:

How it works...

The `Ext.view.View` works by rendering a node based on the defined template (within the `tpl` config option) for each of the store's Models. The View then binds to the store's change events (add, remove, data changed, and so on) and, when fired, refreshes the markup displayed.

We can see this happening with the addition of the store manipulations in Step 5. We have only performed a simple sort, filter, or update on the store and the view is automatically updated to reflect this without any prompting from us.

See also

▶ The data package is explored in further detail in *Chapter 7, Working with the Ext JS Data Package*. The recipes *Modeling a data object and loading data into a store from a server*, are particularly relevant to this example.

Displaying a detailed window after clicking a DataView node

In almost every web application, we will want to allow the user to select some data and edit it. Data Views expose a variety of events on each of the rendered nodes and by using these we can give the user the opportunity to interact with the View and perform any number of actions.

This recipe, will build on our previous bugs example and will add new functionality; presenting the user with a simple form, allowing them to change, and save the data stored about a specific bug. We will display this form after a single-click on a node and populate the form with that particular node's data.

Getting ready

We will be building on top of the previous DataView recipe so you may want to look back and quickly refresh your memory.

How to do it...

1. We start by creating an instance of `Ext.form.Panel` containing four form fields, one for each of the bug's data members. The form contains a text field for the bug's title, a text area for its description, a number field to define the bug's severity, and a combo box to allow the status to be changed:

    ```
    var editForm = Ext.create('Ext.form.Panel', {
        border: false,
    ```

```
    items: [{
        xtype: 'textfield',
        name: 'title',
        width: 300,
        fieldLabel: 'Title'
    }, {
        xtype: 'textarea',
        name: 'description',
        width: 300,
        height: 100,
        fieldLabel: 'Description'
    }, {
        xtype: 'numberfield',
        name: 'severity',
        width: 300,
        fieldLabel: 'Severity',
        value: 1,
        minValue: 1,
        maxValue: 5
    }, {
        xtype: 'combo',
        name: 'status',
        width: 300,
        fieldLabel: 'Status',
        store: ['Open', 'In Progress', 'Complete'],
        queryMode: 'local'
    }]
});
```

2. We then create an `Ext.window.Window` instance and add the `editForm` component to its `items` collection. This window will be shown when a node is clicked and hidden again after saving. Notice that we have left the save button's handler blank. We will revisit this at the end and add the necessary code:

```
var win = new Ext.window.Window({
    height: 250,
    width: 500,
    title: 'Edit Bug',
    modal: true,
    items: [editForm],
    closeAction: 'hide',
    buttons: [{
        text: 'Save',
        handler: function(){
            // save logic here
        }
    }]
});
```

3. Now that we have our form ready, we can attach an event handler to the `itemclick` event of the DataView (stored in the `dataview` variable). When the item (or node) is clicked we populate the `editForm` with the clicked node's record using the `loadRecord` method and then show the window (shown in the following screenshot). This code can be added anywhere in our `onReady` function after the DataView has been instantiated:

```
dataview.on({
    itemclick: function(view, record, item, index, e, opts){

        // populate the form with the clicked record
        editForm.loadRecord(record);

        win.show();
    }
});
```

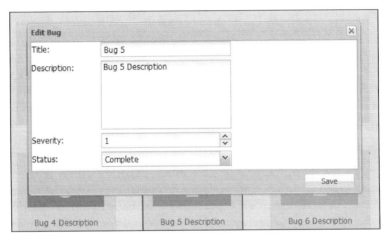

4. Finally, we implement the Save button's handler code. This code basically updates the bug record that we initially clicked on (that is, the one that is selected) and then closes the window:

```
handler: function(){
    // save data
    var selectedRecord = dataview.selModel.getSelection()[0];

    selectedRecord.set(editForm.getValues());

    // refilter
    dataview.getStore().filter();

    win.close();
}
```

How it works...

The DataView's `itemclick` event is fired whenever a single-click is made on any of the rendered nodes. The handlers for this event are passed various useful parameters, such as the record associated with the clicked node, the HTML element of the node, and the index of it.

 Remember we discussed event delegation in *Chapter 2*? The `Ext.view.View` class is a prime example of that concept in action. It uses the defined `itemSelector` config option to pick out the events on its nodes and fire its own custom events back to us.

By using these parameters we are able to use the `loadRecord` method of `Ext.form.Panel`, which takes a Model instance (or record) and matches its fields with the corresponding form fields in the panel. This relationship is based on each form field's `name` property.

When saving the edited values (Step 4) we retrieve the record that is currently selected in the DataView by accessing its selection model (through the `selModel` property) and subsequently the `getSelection` method. Once this has been retrieved we can use its `set` method, which accepts a JavaScript object of name/value pairs, among other formats, to update it with the edit form's values.

There's more...

DataViews expose a huge number of other useful events that we can bind to and have our application react appropriately. We will describe a couple of the most popular here. For a full list of events and their parameters check out the online documentation.

itemcontextmenu

This event fires when an item is right-clicked by the user. This event could be used to create and display a menu with various actions.

itemdblclick

When an item is double-clicked this event is fired.

selectionchange

This is a very useful event that fires whenever the DataView's selected node(s) changes. We could, for example, listen for this event in order to maintain a status bar containing a count of the selected items, similar to Windows Explorer.

See also

- If you want to know more about handling events, the recipe *Handling events on elements and components* in *Chapter 2*, may be useful.

- Forms and form fields are covered in greater depth over the next two chapters. The recipe *Constructing a complex form layout*, in *Chapter 5, Loading, Submitting, and Validating Forms,* is a good place to start.

5
Loading, Submitting, and Validating Forms

In this chapter, we will cover the following topics:

- ▶ Constructing a complex form layout
- ▶ Populating your form with data
- ▶ Submitting your form's data
- ▶ Validating form fields with VTypes
- ▶ Creating custom VTypes
- ▶ Uploading files to the server
- ▶ Handling exceptions and callbacks

Introduction

This chapter introduces forms in Ext JS 4. We begin by creating a support ticket form in the first recipe. To get the most out of this chapter you should be aware that this form is used by a number of recipes throughout the chapter.

Instead of focussing on how to configure specific fields, we demonstrate more generic tasks for working with forms. Specifically, these are populating forms, submitting forms, performing client-side validation, and handling callbacks/exceptions.

Constructing a complex form layout

In the previous releases of Ext JS, complicated form layouts were quite difficult to achieve. This was due to the nature of the `FormLayout`, which was required to display labels and error messages correctly, and how it had to be combined with other nested layouts.

Ext JS 4 takes a different approach and utilizes the `Ext.form.Labelable` mixin, which allows form fields to be decorated with labels and error messages without requiring a specific layout to be applied to the container. This means we can combine all of the layout types the framework has to offer (which are discussed in detail in *Chapter 3, Laying Out your Components*) without having to overnest components in order to satisfy the form field's layout requirements.

We will describe how to create a complex form using multiple nested layouts and demonstrate how easy it is to get a form to look exactly as we want. Our example will take the structure of a **Support Ticket Request** form and, once we are finished, it will look like the following screenshot:

How to do it...

1. We start this recipe by creating a simple form panel that will contain all of the layout containers and their fields:

```
var formPanel = Ext.create('Ext.form.Panel', {
    title: 'Support Ticket Request',
    width: 650,
    height: 500,
    renderTo: Ext.getBody(),
    style: 'margin: 50px',
    items: []
});
```

2. Now, we will create our first set of fields—the `FirstName` and `LastName` fields. These will be wrapped in an `Ext.container.Container` component, which is given an `hbox` layout so our fields appear next to each other on one line:

```
var formPanel = Ext.create('Ext.form.Panel', {
    title: 'Support Ticket Request',
    width: 650,
    height: 500,
    renderTo: Ext.getBody(),
    style: 'margin: 50px',
    items: [{
        xtype: 'container',
        layout: 'hbox',
        items: [{
            xtype: 'textfield',
            fieldLabel: 'First Name',
            name: 'FirstName',
            labelAlign: 'top',
            cls: 'field-margin',
            flex: 1
        }, {
            xtype: 'textfield',
            fieldLabel: 'Last Name',
            name: 'LastName',
            labelAlign: 'top',
            cls: 'field-margin',
            flex: 1
        }]
    }]
});
```

3. We have added a CSS class (`field-margin`) to each field, to provide some spacing between them. We can now add this style inside `<style>` tags in the head of our document:

```
<style type="text/css">
    .field-margin {
        margin: 10px;
    }
</style>
```

4. Next, we create a container with a column layout to position our e-mail address and telephone number fields. We nest our telephone number fields in an `Ext.form.FieldContainer` class, which we will discuss later in the recipe:

```
items: [

...

{
    xtype: 'container',
    layout: 'column',
    items: [{
        xtype: 'textfield',
        fieldLabel: 'Email Address',
        name: 'EmailAddress',
        labelAlign: 'top',
        cls: 'field-margin',
        columnWidth: 0.6
    }, {
        xtype: 'fieldcontainer',
        layout: 'hbox',
        fieldLabel: 'Tel. Number',
        labelAlign: 'top',
        cls: 'field-margin',
        columnWidth: 0.4,
        items: [{
            xtype: 'textfield',
            name: 'TelNumberCode',
            style: 'margin-right: 5px;',
            flex: 2
        }, {
            xtype: 'textfield',
            name: 'TelNumber',
            flex: 4
        }]
    }]
}

...

]
```

5. The text area and checkbox group are created and laid out in a similar way to the previous sets, by using an `hbox` layout:

```
items: [

...

{
    xtype: 'container',
    layout: 'hbox',
    items: [{
        xtype: 'textarea',
        fieldLabel: 'Request Details',
        name: 'RequestDetails',
        labelAlign: 'top',
        cls: 'field-margin',
        height: 250,
        flex: 2
    }, {
        xtype: 'checkboxgroup',
        name: 'RequestType',
        fieldLabel: 'Request Type',
        labelAlign: 'top',
        columns: 1,
        cls: 'field-margin',
        vertical: true,
        items: [{
            boxLabel: 'Type 1',
            name: 'type1',
            inputValue: '1'
        }, {
            boxLabel: 'Type 2',
            name: 'type2',
            inputValue: '2'
        }, {
            boxLabel: 'Type 3',
            name: 'type3',
            inputValue: '3'
        }, {
            boxLabel: 'Type 4',
            name: 'type4',
            inputValue: '4'
        }, {
            boxLabel: 'Type 5',
            name: 'type5',
            inputValue: '5'
        }, {
```

```
            boxLabel: 'Type 6',
            name: 'type6',
            inputValue: '6'
        }],
        flex: 1
    }]
}
...
]
```

6. Finally, we add the last field, which is a file upload field, to allow users to provide attachments:

```
items: [
...
{
    xtype: 'filefield',
    cls: 'field-margin',
    fieldLabel: 'Attachment',
    width: 300
}
...
]
```

How it works...

All Ext JS form fields inherit from the base `Ext.Component` class and so can be included in all of the framework's layouts. For this reason, we can include form fields as children of containers with layouts (such as `hbox` and `column` layouts) and their position and size will be calculated accordingly.

 Upgrade Tip: Ext JS 4 does not have a `form` layout meaning a level of nesting can be removed and the form fields' labels will still be displayed correctly by just specifying the `fieldLabel` config.

The `Ext.form.FieldContainer` class used in step 4 is a special component that allows us to combine multiple fields into a single container, which also implements the `Ext.form.Labelable` mixin. This allows the container itself to display its own label that applies to all of its child fields while also giving us the opportunity to configure a layout for its child components.

- The recipe explaining mixins found in *Chapter 1, Classes, Object-Oriented Principles, and Structuring your Application.*

- You may also find *Chapter 3, Laying Out your Components* useful, which explains how each of the layouts used here work, in particular those about the `hbox` and `column` layouts.

- For more details about how to use form fields and elements take a look at *Chapter 6, Using and Configuring Form Fields.*

Populating your form with data

After creating our beautifully crafted and user-friendly form we will inevitably need to populate it with some data so users can edit it. Ext JS makes this easy, and this recipe will demonstrate four simple ways of achieving it.

We will start by explaining how to populate the form on a field-by-field basis, then move on to ways of populating the entire form at once. We will also cover populating it from a simple object, a Model instance, and a remote server call.

Getting ready

We will be using the form created in this chapter's first recipe as our base for this section, and many of the subsequent recipes in this chapter, so please look back if you are not familiar with it.

All the code we will write in this recipe should be placed under the definition of this form panel.

You will also require a working web server for the *There's More* example, which loads data from an external file.

How to do it...

We'll demonstrate how to populate an entire form's fields in bulk and also how to populate them individually.

Populating individual fields

1. We will start by grabbing a reference to the first name field using the `items` property's `get` method. The `items` property contains an instance of `Ext.util.MixedCollection`, which holds a reference to each of the container's child components. We use its `get` method to retrieve the component at the specified index:

```
var firstNameField = formPanel.items.get(0).items.get(0);
```

2. Next, we use the `setValue` method of the field to populate it:

```
firstNameField.setValue('Joe');
```

Populating the entire form

1. To populate the entire form, we must create a data object containing a value for each field. The property names of this object will be mapped to the corresponding form field by the field's `name` property. For example, the `FirstName` property of our `requestData` object will be mapped to a form field with a `name` property value of `FirstName`:

```
var requestData = {
    FirstName: 'Joe',
    LastName: 'Bloggs',
    EmailAddress: 'info@swarmonline.com',
    TelNumberCode: '0777',
    TelNumber: '7777777',
    RequestDetails: 'This is some Request Detail body text',
    RequestType: {
        type1: true,
        type2: false,
        type3: false,
        type4: true,
        type5: true,
        type6: false
    }
};
```

2. We then call the `setValues` method of the form panel's `Ext.form.Basic` instance, accessed through the `getForm` method, passing it our `requestData` variable:

```
formPanel.getForm().setValues(requestData);
```

How it works...

Each field contains a method called `setValue`, which updates the field's value with the value that is passed in. We can see this in action in the first part of the *How to do it* section.

A form panel contains an internal instance of the `Ext.form.Basic` class (accessible through the `getForm` method), which provides all of the validation, submission, loading, and general field management that is required by a form.

This class contains a `setValues` method, which can be used to populate all of the fields that are managed by the basic form class. This method works by simply iterating through all of the fields it contains and calling their respective `setValue` methods.

This method accepts either a simple data object, as in our example, whose properties are mapped to fields based on the field's `name` property. Alternatively, an array of objects can be supplied, containing `id` and `value` properties, with the `id` mapping to the field's `name` property. The following code snippet demonstrates this usage:

```
formPanel.getForm().setValues([{id: 'FirstName', value: 'Joe'}]);
```

There's more...

Further to the two previously discussed methods there are two others that we will demonstrate here.

Populating a form from a Model instance

Being able to populate a form directly from a Model instance is extremely useful and is very simple to achieve. This allows us to easily translate our data structures into a form without having to manually map it to each field.

We initially define a Model and create an instance of it (using the data object we used earlier in the recipe):

```
Ext.define('Request', {
    extend: 'Ext.data.Model',
    fields: [
        'FirstName',
        'LastName',
        'EmailAddress',
        'TelNumberCode',
        'TelNumber',
        'RequestDetails',
        'RequestType'
    ]
});

var requestModel = Ext.create('Request', requestData);
```

Following this we call the `loadRecord` method of the `Ext.form.Basic` class and supply the Model instance as its only parameter. This will populate the form, mapping each Model field to its corresponding form field based on the name:

```
formPanel.getForm().loadRecord(requestModel);
```

Populating a form directly from the server

It is also possible to load a form's data directly from the server through an AJAX call.

Firstly, we define a JSON file, containing our request data, which will be loaded by the form:

```
{
    "success": true,
    "data": {
        "FirstName": "Joe",
        "LastName": "Bloggs",
        "EmailAddress": "info@swarmonline.com",
        "TelNumberCode": "0777",
        "TelNumber": "7777777",
        "RequestDetails": "This is some Request Detail body text",
        "RequestType": {
            "type1": true,
            "type2": false,
            "type3": false,
            "type4": true,
            "type5": true,
            "type6": false
        }
    }
}
```

Notice the format of the data: we must provide a `success` property to indicate that the load was successful and put our form data inside a `data` property.

Next we use the basic form's `load` method and provide it with a configuration object containing a `url` property pointing to our JSON file:

```
formPanel.getForm().load({
    url: 'requestDetails.json'
});
```

This method automatically performs an AJAX request to the specified URL and populates the form's fields with the data that was retrieved. This is all that is required to successfully load the JSON data into the form.

The basic form's `load` method accepts similar configuration options to a regular AJAX request, which are discussed in the _Loading Data through AJAX_ recipe, in _Chapter 2_.

See also

▸ The previous recipe, which shows how to create the form we have used in this recipe's examples.

▸ The recipes explaining the `Ext.data` package, which include details of Models.

▸ To learn about submitting forms see the next recipe in this chapter.

Submitting your form's data

Having taken care of populating the form it's now time to look at sending newly added or edited data back to the server. As with form population you'll learn just how easy this is with the Ext JS framework.

There are two parts to this example. Firstly, we will submit data using the options of the basic form that wraps the form panel. The second example will demonstrate binding the form to a Model and saving our data.

Getting ready

We will be using the form created in the first recipe as our base for this section, so refer to the _Constructing a complex form layout_ recipe, if you are not familiar with it.

How to do it...

1. Add a function to submit the form:

```
var submitForm = function(){
    formPanel.getForm().submit({
        url: 'submit.php'
    });
};
```

2. Add a button to the form that calls the `submitForm` function:

```
var formPanel = Ext.create('Ext.form.Panel', {
    ...
    buttons: [{
        text: 'Submit Form',
        handler: submitForm
    }],
    items: [
        ...
    ]
});
```

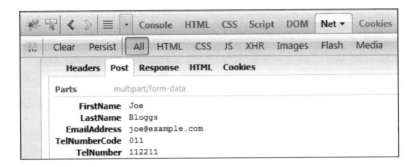

How it works...

As we learned in the previous recipe, a form panel contains an internal instance of the `Ext.form.Basic` class (accessible through the `getForm` method).

The `submit` method in `Ext.form.Basic` is a shortcut to the `Ext.form.action.Submit` action. This class handles the form submission for us. All we are required to do is provide it with a URL and it will handle the rest.

 It's also possible to define the URL in the configuration for the `Ext.form.Panel`.

Before submitting, it must first gather the data from the form. The `Ext.form.Basic` class contains a `getValues` method, which is used to gather the data values for each form field. It does this by iterating through all fields in the form making a call to their respective `getValue` methods.

There's more...

The previous recipe demonstrated how to populate the form from a Model instance. Here we will take it a step further and use the same Model instance to submit the form as well.

Submitting a form from a Model instance

1. Extend the Model with a proxy and load the data into the form:

```
Ext.define('Request', {
    extend: 'Ext.data.Model',

    fields: ['FirstName', 'LastName', 'EmailAddress',
    'TelNumberCode', 'TelNumber', 'RequestDetails', 'RequestType'],
    proxy: {
        type: 'ajax',
        api: {
            create: 'addTicketRequest.php',
            update: 'updateTicketRequest.php'
        },
        reader: {
            type: 'json'
        }
    }
});

var requestModel = Ext.create('Request', {
    FirstName: 'Joe',
    LastName: 'Bloggs',
    EmailAddress: 'info@swarmonline.com'
});

formPanel.getForm().loadRecord(requestModel);
```

2. Change the submitForm function to get the Model instance, update the record with the form data, and save the record to the server:

```
var submitForm = function(){
    var record = formPanel.getForm().getRecord();
    formPanel.getForm().updateRecord(record);
    record.save();
};
```

See Also

▸ The previous recipe which shows how to create the form we have used in this recipe's examples.

▸ The basic form's submit method accepts similar configuration options as a regular AJAX request which are discussed in the _Loading data through AJAX_ recipe, in _Chapter 2_.

▸ To learn about loading forms see the previous recipe in this chapter.

Validating form fields with VTypes

In addition to form fields' built-in validation (such as `allowBlank` and `minLength`), we can apply more advanced and more extensible validation by using VTypes. A VType (contained in the `Ext.form.field.VTypes` singleton) can be applied to a field and its validation logic will be executed as part of the field's periodic validation routine.

A VType encapsulates a validation function, an error message (which will be displayed if the validation fails), and a regular expression mask to prevent any undesired characters from being entered into the field.

This recipe will explain how to apply a VType to the e-mail address field in our example form, so that only properly formatted e-mail addresses are deemed valid and an error will be displayed if it doesn't conform to this pattern.

How to do it...

1. We will start by defining our form and its fields. We will be using our example form that was created in the first recipe of this chapter as our base.

2. Now that we have a form we can add the `vtype` configuration option to our e-mail address field:

    ```
    {
        xtype: 'textfield',
        fieldLabel: 'Email Address',
        name: 'EmailAddress',
        labelAlign: 'top',
        cls: 'field-margin',
        columnWidth: 0.6,
        vtype: 'email'
    }
    ```

3. That is all we have to do to add e-mail address validation to a field. We can see the results in the following screenshot, with an incorrectly formatted e-mail address on the left and a valid one on the right:

How it works...

When a field is validated it runs through various checks. When a VType is defined the associated validation routine is executed and will flag the field invalid or not .

As previously mentioned, each VType has an error message coupled with it, which is displayed if it is found to be invalid, and a mask expression which prevents unwanted characters being entered.

Unfortunately, only one VType can be applied to a field and so, if multiple checks are required, a custom hybrid may need to be created. See the next recipe for details on how to do this.

There's more...

Along with the e-mail VType, the framework provides three other VTypes that can be applied straight out of the box. These are:

- ▶ **alpha**: this restricts the field to only alphabetic characters
- ▶ **alphnum**: this VType allows only alphanumeric characters
- ▶ **url**: this ensures that the value is a valid URL

See also

- ▶ See the next recipe that demonstrates how to create your own custom VTypes.
- ▶ The recipe about displaying validation alerts to the user later in this chapter.

Creating custom VTypes

We have seen in the previous recipe how to use VTypes to apply more advanced validation to our form's fields. The built-in VTypes provided by the framework are excellent but we will often want to create custom implementations to impose more complex and domain specific validation to a field.

We will walkthrough creating a custom VType to be applied to our telephone number field to ensure it is in the format that a telephone number should be.

Although our telephone number field is split into two (the first field for the area code and the second for the rest of the number), for this example we will combine them so our VType is more comprehensive.

For this example, we will be validating a very simple, strict telephone number format of `"0777-777-7777"`.

How to do it...

1. We start by defining our VType's structure. This consists of a simple object literal with three properties. A function called `telNumber` and two strings called `telNumberText` (which will contain the error message text) and `telNumberMask` (which holds a regex to restrict the characters allowed to be entered into the field) respectively.

```
var telNumberVType = {
    telNumber: function(val, field){
        // function executed when field is validated
        // return true when field's value (val) is valid
        return true;
    },

    telNumberText: 'Your Telephone Number must only include
numbers and hyphens.',

    telNumberMask: /[\d\-]/
};
```

2. Next we define the regular expression that we will use to validate the field's value. We add this as a variable to the `telNumber` function:

```
telNumber: function(val, field){
    var telNumberRegex = /^\d{4}\-\d{3}\-\d{4}$/;

    return true;
}
```

3. Once this has been done we can add the logic to this `telNumber` function that will decide whether the field's current value is valid. This is a simple call to the regular expression string's `test` method, which returns true if the value matches or false if it doesn't:

```
telNumber: function(val, field){
    var telNumberRegex = /^\d{4}\-\d{3}\-\d{4}$/;

    return telNumberRegex.test(val);
}
```

4. The final step to defining our new VType is to apply it to the `Ext.form.field.VTypes` singleton, which is where all of the VTypes are located and where our field's validation routine will go to get its definition:

```
Ext.apply(Ext.form.field.VTypes, telNumberVType);
```

5. Now that our VType has been defined and registered with the framework, we can apply it to the field by using the `vtype` configuration option. The result can be seen in the following screenshot:

```
{
    xtype: 'textfield',
    name: 'TelNumber',
    flex: 4,

    vtype: 'telNumber'
}
```

How it works...

A VType consists of three parts:

- The validity checking function
- The validation error text
- A keystroke filtering mask (optional)

VTypes rely heavily on naming conventions so they can be executed dynamically within a field's validation routine. This means that each of these three parts must follow the standard convention. The validation function's name will become the name used to reference the VType and form the prefix for the other two properties. In our example, this name was `telNumber`, which can be seen referencing the VType in Step 5.

The error text property is then named with the VType's name prefixing the word `Text` (that is, `telNumberText`). Similarly, the filtering mask is the VType's name followed by the word `Mask` (that is, `telNumberMask`).

The final step to create our VType is to merge it into the `Ext.form.field.VTypes` singleton allowing it to be accessed dynamically during validation. The `Ext.apply` function does this by merging the VType's three properties into the `Ext.form.field.VTypes` class instance.

When the field is validated, and a `vtype` is defined, the VType's validation function is executed with the current value of the field and a reference to the field itself being passed in.

If the function returns true then all is well and the routine moves on. However, if it evaluates to false the VType's `Text` property is retrieved and pushed onto the `errors` array. This message is then displayed to the user as our screenshot shown earlier.

This process can be seen in the code snippet as follows, taken directly from the framework:

```
if (vtype) {
    if(!vtypes[vtype](value, me)){
        errors.push(me.vtypeText || vtypes[vtype +'Text']);
    }
}
```

There's more...

It is often necessary to validate fields based on the values of other fields as well as their own. We will demonstrate this by creating a simple VType for validating that a confirm password field's value matches the value entered in an initial password field. We start by creating our VType structure as we did before:

```
Ext.apply(Ext.form.field.VTypes, {
    password: function(val, field){
        return false;
    },

    passwordText: 'Your Passwords do not match.'
});
```

We then complete the validation logic. We use the field's up method to get a reference to its parent form. Using that reference, we get the values for all of the form's fields by using the getValues method:

```
password: function(val, field){
    var parentForm = field.up('form'); // get parent form

    // get the form's values
    var formValues = parentForm.getValues();
    return false;
}
```

The next step is to get the first password field's value. We do this by using an extra property (firstPasswordFieldName) that we will specify when we add our VType to the confirm password field. This property will contain the name of the initial password field (in this example Password). We can then compare the confirm password's value with the retrieved value and return the outcome:

```
password: function(val, field){
    var parentForm = field.up('form'); // get parent form

    // get the form's values
```

```
    var formValues = parentForm.getValues();

    // get the value from the configured 'First Password' field
    var firstPasswordValue = formValues[field.firstPasswordFieldName];

    // return true if they match
    return val === firstPasswordValue;
}
```

The VType is added to the confirm password field in exactly the same way as before but we must include the extra `firstPasswordFieldName` option to link the fields together:

```
{
    xtype: 'textfield',
    fieldLabel: 'Confirm Password',
    name: 'ConfirmPassword',
    labelAlign: 'top',
    cls: 'field-margin',
    flex: 1,

    vtype: 'password',
    firstPasswordFieldName: 'Password'
}
```

See also

▸ For an introduction to VTypes see the previous recipe.

▸ The recipe titled *Displaying validation alerts to the user,* in this chapter.

Uploading files to the server

Uploading files is very straightforward with Ext JS 4. This recipe will demonstrate how to create a basic file upload form and send the data to your server:

Getting Ready

This recipe requires the use of a web server for accepting the uploaded file. A PHP file is provided to handle the file upload; however, you can integrate this Ext JS code with any server-side technology you wish.

How to do it...

1. Create a simple form panel.

```
Ext.create('Ext.form.Panel', {
    title: 'Document Upload',
    width: 400,
    bodyPadding: 10,
    renderTo: Ext.getBody(),
    style: 'margin: 50px',
    items: [],
    buttons: []
});
```

2. In the panel's `items` collection add a file field:

```
Ext.create('Ext.form.Panel', {
    ...
    items: [{
        xtype: 'filefield',
        name: 'document',
        fieldLabel: 'Document',
        msgTarget: 'side',
        allowBlank: false,
        anchor: '100%'
    }],
    buttons: []
});
```

3. Add a button to the panel's `buttons` collection to handle the form submission:

```
Ext.create('Ext.form.Panel', {
    ...
    buttons: [{
        text: 'Upload Document',
        handler: function(){
            var form = this.up('form').getForm();
            if (form.isValid()) {
                form.submit({
                    url: 'upload.php',
                    waitMsg: 'Uploading...'
```

```
            });
        }
    }
}]
});
```

How it works...

Your server-side code should handle these form submissions in the same way they would handle a regular HTML file upload form. You should not have to do anything special to make your server-side code compatible with Ext JS.

The example works by defining an `Ext.form.field.File`(xtype: `'filefield'`), which takes care of the styling and the button for selecting local files.

The form submission handler works the same way as any other form submission; however, behind the scenes the framework tweaks how the form is submitted to the server.

A form with a file upload field is not submitted using an `XMLHttpRequest` object—instead the framework creates and submits a temporary hidden `<form>` element whose target is referenced to a temporary hidden `<iframe>`. The request header's `Content-Type` is set to `multipart/form`. When the upload is finished and the server has responded, the temporary form and `<iframe>` are removed.

A fake `XMLHttpRequest` object is then created containing a `responseText` property (populated from the contents of the `<iframe>`) to ensure that event handlers and callbacks work as if we were submitting the form using AJAX.

If your server is responding to the client with JSON, you must ensure that the response `Content-Type` header is `text/html`.

There's more...

It's possible to customize your `Ext.form.field.File`. Some useful config options are highlighted as follows:

buttonOnly: Boolean

Setting `buttonOnly: true` removes the visible text field from the file field.

buttonText: String

If you wish to change the text in the button from the default of "Browse..." it's possible to do so by setting the `buttonText` config option.

buttonConfig: Object

Changing the entire configuration of the button is done by defining a standard `Ext.button.Button` config object in the `buttonConfig` option. Anything defined in the `buttonText` config option will be ignored if you use this.

See also

 ▶   The recipe covering form submission earlier in this chapter.

Handling exception and callbacks

This recipe demonstrates how to handle callbacks when loading and submitting forms. This is particularly useful for two reasons:

 ▶   You may wish to carry our further processing once the form has been submitted (for example, display a thank you message to the user)

 ▶   In the unfortunate event when the submission fails, it's good to be ready and inform the user something has gone wrong and perhaps perform extra processing

The recipe shows you what to do in the following circumstances:

 ▶   The server responds informing you the submission was successful

 ▶   The server responds with an unusual status code (for example, `404`, `500`, and so on)

 ▶   The server responds informing you the submission was unsuccessful (for example, there was a problem processing the data)

 ▶   The form is unable to load data because the server has sent an empty `data` property

 ▶   The form is unable to submit data because the framework has deemed the values in the form to be invalid

Getting ready

The following recipe requires you to submit values to a server. An example `submit.php` file has been provided. However, please ensure you have a web server for serving this file.

How to do it...

1. Start by creating a simple form panel:

```
var formPanel = Ext.create('Ext.form.Panel', {
    title: 'Form',
    width: 300,
    bodyPadding: 10,
    renderTo: Ext.getBody(),
    style: 'margin: 50px',
    items: [],
    buttons: []
});
```

2. Add a field to the form and set `allowBlank` to `false`:

```
var formPanel = Ext.create('Ext.form.Panel', {
    ...
    items: [{
        xtype: 'textfield',
        fieldLabel: 'Text field',
        name: 'field',
        allowBlank: false
    }],
    buttons: []
});
```

3. Add a button to handle the forms submission and add `success` and `failure` handlers to the `submit` method's only parameter:

```
var formPanel = Ext.create('Ext.form.Panel', {
...
buttons: [{
    text: 'Submit',
    handler: function(){
        formPanel.getForm().submit({
            url: 'submit.php',
            success: function(form, action){
                Ext.Msg.alert('Success', action.result.message);
            },
            failure: function(form, action){
                if (action.failureType === Ext.form.action.Action.
CLIENT_INVALID) {
                    Ext.Msg.alert('CLIENT_INVALID', 'Something
has been missed. Please check and try again.');
                }
```

```
                    if (action.failureType === Ext.form.action.Action.
    CONNECT_FAILURE) {
                        Ext.Msg.alert('CONNECT_FAILURE', 'Status: ' +
    action.response.status + ': ' + action.response.statusText);
                    }
                    if (action.failureType === Ext.form.action.Action.
    SERVER_INVALID) {
                        Ext.Msg.alert('SERVER_INVALID', action.result.
    message);
                    }
                }
            });
        }
    }]
    });
```

3. When you run the code, watch for the different `failureTypes` or the success callback:

   ❑ `CLIENT_INVALID` is fired when there is no value in the text field.

   ❑ The success callback is fired when the server returns `true` in the `success` property.

   ❑ Switch the response in `submit.php` file and watch for `SERVER_INVALID` `failureType`. This is fired when the `success` property is set to `false`.

   ❑ Finally, edit `url: 'submit.php'` to `url: 'unknown.php'` and `CONNECT_FAILURE` will be fired.

How it works...

The `Ext.form.action.Submit` and `Ext.form.action.Load` classes both have a `failure` and `success` function. One of these two functions will be called depending on the outcome of the action.

The `success` callback is called when the action is successful and the `success` property is `true`.

The `failure` callback, on the other hand, can be extended to look for specific reasons why the failure occurred (for example, there was an internal server error, the form did not pass client-side validation, and so on). This is done by looking at the `failureType` property of the `action` parameter.

`Ext.form.action.Action` has four `failureType` static properties: `CLIENT_INVALID`, `SERVER_INVALID`, `CONNECT_FAILURE`, and `LOAD_FAILURE`, which can be used to compare with what has been returned by the server.

There's more...

A number of additional options are described as follows:

Handling form population failures

The `Ext.form.action.Action.LOAD_FAILURE` static property can be used in the `failure` callback when loading data into your form. The `LOAD_FAILURE` is returned as the `action` parameter's `failureType` when the `success` property is `false` or the `data` property contains no fields. The following code shows how this failure type can be caught inside the `failure` callback function:

```
failure: function(form, action){
    ...
    if(action.failureType == Ext.form.action.Action.LOAD_FAILURE){
        Ext.Msg.alert('LOAD_FAILURE', action.result.message);
    }
    ...
}
```

An alternative to CLIENT_INVALID

The `isValid` method in `Ext.form.Basic` is an alternative method for handling client-side validation before the form is submitted. `isValid` will return true when client-side validation passes:

```
handler: function(){
    if (formPanel.getForm().isValid()) {
        formPanel.getForm().submit({
            url: 'submit.php'
        });
    }
}
```

See also

▶   The recipes *Submitting your form's data* and *Populating your form with data,* in this chapter.

6
Using and Configuring Form Fields

In this chapter, we will cover:

- ▶ Displaying radio buttons in columns
- ▶ Populating CheckboxGroups
- ▶ Dynamically generate a CheckboxGroup from JSON
- ▶ Setting up available date ranges in Date fields
- ▶ Loading and parsing Dates into a Date field
- ▶ Entering numbers with a Spinner field
- ▶ Sliding values using a Slider field
- ▶ Loading server side data into a combobox
- ▶ Autocompleting a combobox's value
- ▶ Rendering the results in a combobox
- ▶ Rich editing with an HTML field
- ▶ Creating repeatable form fields and fieldsets
- ▶ Combining form fields

Introduction

Forms make up a huge part of most web applications and are a fundamental part of how users interact with the web. This chapter will focus on how we configure and use Ext JS 4's built-in form fields and features to make our forms hone for a perfect user experience.

We will cover various form fields and move up from configuring the fields using their built-in features to customizing the layout and display of these fields to create a form that creates a smooth and seamless user experience.

Displaying radio buttons in columns

Displaying radio buttons in columns is an easy task with Ext JS 4. This recipe aims to demonstrate how to render your radio buttons in columns both horizontally and vertically.

How to do it...

1. Create a RadioGroup using the default layout:

```
var radioGroupAutoLayout = Ext.create('Ext.form.Panel', {
    title: 'Radio Group Columns',
    width: 500,
    autoHeight: true,
    bodyPadding: 10,
    items: [{
        xtype: 'radiogroup',
        fieldLabel: 'Gender',
        items: [{
            boxLabel: 'Male',
            name: 'gender',
            inputValue: 'male'
        }, {
            boxLabel: 'Female',
            name: 'gender',
            inputValue: 'female'
        }]
    }],
    renderTo: Ext.getBody(),
    style: 'margin: 50px'
});
```

2. Create a RadioGroup with columns arranged horizontally:

```
var radioGroupMultiColumn = Ext.create('Ext.form.Panel', {
    title: 'Radio Group Columns (horizontal)',
    width: 500,
    autoHeight: true,
    bodyPadding: 10,
```

```
        items: [{
            xtype: 'radiogroup',
            columns: 3,
            items: [{
                boxLabel: 'Option 1',
                name: 'option',
                inputValue: 1
            }, {
                boxLabel: 'Option 2',
                name: 'option',
                inputValue: 2
            }, {
                boxLabel: 'Option 3',
                name: 'option',
                inputValue: 3
            }, {
                boxLabel: 'Option 4',
                name: 'option',
                inputValue: 4
            }, {
                boxLabel: 'Option 5',
                name: 'option',
                inputValue: 5
            }, {
                boxLabel: 'Option 6',
                name: 'option',
                inputValue: 6
            }]
        }],
        renderTo: Ext.getBody(),
        style: 'margin: 50px'
    });
```

3. Create a RadioGroup with columns arranged vertically:

```
var radioGroupVerticalColumn = Ext.create('Ext.form.Panel', {
    title: 'Radio Group Columns (vertical)',
    width: 500,
```

```
            autoHeight: true,
            bodyPadding: 10,
            items: [{
                xtype: 'radiogroup',
                columns: 3,
                vertical: true,
                items: [{
                    boxLabel: 'Extra Small',
                    name: 'size',
                    inputValue: 'xs'
                }, {
                    boxLabel: 'Small',
                    name: 'size',
                    inputValue: 's'
                }, {
                    boxLabel: 'Medium',
                    name: 'size',
                    inputValue: 'm'
                }, {
                    boxLabel: 'Large',
                    name: 'size',
                    inputValue: 'l'
                }, {
                    boxLabel: 'Extra Large',
                    name: 'size',
                    inputValue: 'xl'
                }, {
                    boxLabel: 'Extra Extra Large',
                    name: 'size',
                    inputValue: 'xxl'
                }]
            }],
            renderTo: Ext.getBody(),
            style: 'margin: 50px'
        });
```

4. Create a RadioGroup with custom columns:

```
var radioGroupCustomColumn = Ext.create('Ext.form.Panel', {
    title: 'Radio Group Columns',
    width: 500,
    autoHeight: true,
    bodyPadding: 10,
    items: [{
        xtype: 'radiogroup',
        layout: 'column',
        defaultType: 'container',
        items: [{
            columnWidth: 0.5,
            items: [{
                xtype: 'component',
                html: 'Drink',
                cls: 'x-form-check-group-label'
            }, {
                xtype: 'radiofield',
                boxLabel: 'Beer',
                name: 'drink',
                inputValue: 'beer'
            }, {
                xtype: 'radiofield',
                boxLabel: 'Wine',
                name: 'drink',
                inputValue: 'wine'
            }]
        }, {
            columnWidth: 0.5,
            items: [{
                xtype: 'component',
                html: 'Food',
                cls: 'x-form-check-group-label'
            }, {
                xtype: 'radiofield',
                boxLabel: 'Pizza',
                name: 'food',
                inputValue: 'pizza'
            }, {
                xtype: 'radiofield',
                boxLabel: 'Burger',
                name: 'food',
                inputValue: 'burger'
```

```
                    }]
                }]
            }],
            renderTo: Ext.getBody(),
            style: 'margin: 50px'
        });
```

Radio Group Columns	
Drink	Food
○ Beer	○ Pizza
○ Wine	○ Burger

How it works...

The `Ext.form.RadioGroup` is an extension of `Ext.form.FieldContainer` and provides the layout we need for arranging radio buttons into columns.

The first example highlights the default behaviour of the RadioGroup, which is to render all radio buttons on one row (one per column). The radio buttons will be evenly distributed across the row.

The second and third example shows how you can specify the number of columns for the RadioGroup. As we created six radio buttons and three columns the framework automatically distributes the radio buttons over two rows.

The difference between the second and third example is `vertical: true`. Setting this config option makes the framework fill a column at a time before moving onto the next. Instead of rendering the second item in the top-middle space, it's rendered in the bottom left.

The final example demonstrates how to set the RadioGroups's layout and set custom columns. The `columnWidth` for both columns is `0.5` (50 percent) but depending on your form it's easy to change this (or set a fixed width for a column).

The column headings are made with an `Ext.Component` that has the class `x-form-check-group-label`. This class provides a bottom border, padding, and margins so the HTML of the component is in keeping with the RadioGroup.

See Also

▶ The next recipe about CheckboxGroups, which has many common characteristics.

Populating CheckboxGroups

CheckboxGroups are very similar to RadioGroups but allows a user to select as many options as they want. Populating these CheckBoxGroups is notoriously difficult because mapping a dataset to the group can be done in various ways and depends on the dataset's structure.

This recipe will demonstrate how to overcome these difficulties and various ways of populating a CheckboxGroup:

How to do it...

1. We will start by creating a form containing a CheckboxGroup listing some technologies that will form the base of our examples. We will then add this group to a Form Panel:

```
var checkboxGroup = new Ext.form.CheckboxGroup({
    columns: 2,
    fieldLabel: 'Technologies',
    name: 'technologies',
    style: {
        padding: '5px 10px 5px 10px'
    },
    items: [{
        xtype: 'checkbox',
        boxLabel: 'JavaScript',
        name: 'technologies',
        inputValue: 'javascript'
    }, {
        xtype: 'checkbox',
        boxLabel: 'C#',
        name: 'technologies',
        inputValue: 'c#'
    }, {
        xtype: 'checkbox',
```

```
            boxLabel: 'HTML',
            name: 'technologies',
            inputValue: 'html'
    }, {
            xtype: 'checkbox',
            boxLabel: 'SQL',
            name: 'technologies',
            inputValue: 'sql'
    }, {
            xtype: 'checkbox',
            boxLabel: 'Python',
            name: 'technologies',
            inputValue: 'python'
    }, {
            xtype: 'checkbox',
            boxLabel: 'CSS',
            name: 'technologies',
            inputValue: 'css'
    }]
});

var formPanel = new Ext.form.Panel({
    renderTo: Ext.getBody(),

    title: 'Technologies',

    tbar: [{
        text: 'Submit',
        handler: function(){
            console.log(formPanel.getValues());
        }
    }],

    items: [checkboxGroup]
});
```

2. We can now call the CheckboxGroup's `setValue` method to pre-check some of the checkboxes:

```
checkboxGroup.setValue({
  technologies: ['javascript', 'css']
});
```

 You can make a checkbox checked by default, by configuring it with `checked: true`.

How it works...

In our example you will notice that each of the checkboxes' `name` property matches that of the CheckboxGroup. As in traditional HTML, by giving multiple fields the same name they will, when submitted, be combined into an array. When this is the case the `inputValue` is the property that is used to differentiate the fields. This then becomes the value that must be passed to the `setValue` method to tell the framework which of the child checkboxes to check.

As mentioned, the output from this situation is an array of values which means that our i nput to the `setValue` method must also be an array of values, with each value mapping to a checkbox's `inputValue` property. If the value can be mapped to a checkbox then that box is checked, otherwise it is unchecked.

There's more...

There are a number of ways, in addition to the one just outlined, of populating checkboxes. To demonstrate these we will take our initial form code and modify it so that not all of the checkboxes share the same technologies name as the parent CheckboxGroup. We will also remove the `inputValue` configuration from the HTML and SQL checkboxes:

```
var checkboxGroup = new Ext.form.CheckboxGroup({
    columns: 2,
    fieldLabel: 'Technologies',
    name: 'technologies',
    style: {
        padding: '5px 10px 5px 10px'
    },
    items: [{
        xtype: 'checkbox',
        boxLabel: 'JavaScript',
        name: 'javascript',
        inputValue: 'javascript'
    }, {
        xtype: 'checkbox',
        boxLabel: 'C#',
        name: 'c#',
        inputValue: 'c#'
    }, {
        xtype: 'checkbox',
        boxLabel: 'HTML',
        name: 'html'
    }, {
```

```
            xtype: 'checkbox',
            boxLabel: 'SQL',
            name: 'sql'
        }, {
            xtype: 'checkbox',
            boxLabel: 'Python',
            name: 'technologies',
            inputValue: 'python'
        }, {
            xtype: 'checkbox',
            boxLabel: 'CSS',
            name: 'technologies',
            inputValue: 'css'
        }]
    });

    var formPanel = new Ext.form.Panel({
        renderTo: Ext.getBody(),

        title: 'Technologies',

        tbar: [{
            text: 'Submit',
            handler: function(){
                console.log(formPanel.getValues());
            }
        }],

        items: [checkboxGroup]
    });
```

When a checkbox has an `inputValue` property, such as our JavaScript checkbox, we can use this to check it by passing in a name/value pair made up of the field's name and its `inputValue` to the `setValue` method:

```
    checkboxGroup.setValue({
        javascript: 'javascript'
    });
```

Equally, we can pass in a Boolean value instead of the string `'javascript'` in this example and this will check/uncheck the box accordingly:

```
    checkboxGroup.setValue({
        javascript: true
    });
```

When a checkbox does not have an `inputValue`, such as the HTML checkbox in our example, then a Boolean must be used to indicate its checked status.

Finally, all of these techniques can be combined into one single `setValue` call if there is a mixture of checkbox configurations. The following code will check the HTML, JavaScript, CSS, and Python checkboxes, leaving the rest unchecked:

```
checkboxGroup.setValue({
    javascript: 'javascript',
    html: true,
    technologies: ['css', 'python']
});
```

See also

▶ The recipe explaining how to *Displaying radio buttons in columns*, which can also be applied to CheckBoxGroups.

▶ The *Populating your form with data* recipe in the previous chapter.

Dynamically generate a CheckboxGroup from JSON

When creating real-world applications with Ext JS, it is often the case that we don't know how forms and UI elements are going to look at design time and so must be generated at runtime, based on data stored in a database.

In the previous chapter we looked at dynamically creating components from configurations loaded directly from the server. In this recipe, we will go into more detail by looking at how to create checkbox groups which are often required to be generated from lists of possible values stored in a database.

Imagine you are creating a social networking website and are creating an area where users can send a message to one or more of their friends by ticking a checkbox beside their name to include them in the recipients list. Obviously the number of friends and who they are will be different for each user and will also change over time.

This is a prime example of where this technique will be needed. We will demonstrate it in this recipe. We will load a list of friends through an AJAX call and create an appropriate number of checkboxes based on the result.

How to do it...

1. Back in *Chapter 1*, we demonstrated how to extend Ext JS components to create your own custom components. Using this technique we will create a simple form with a title and a send button which will log the form's current values to the console. We will then instantiate this component which will be rendered to the document's body:

```
Ext.define('Ext.ux.MessagePanel', {

    extend: 'Ext.form.Panel',

    initComponent: function(){
        Ext.apply(this, {
            renderTo: Ext.getBody(),
            title: 'Message',

            tbar: [{
                text: 'Send',
                handler: function(){
                    console.log(this.getValues());
                },
                scope: this
            }],

            items: []
        });
```

```
            this.callParent(arguments);
        }
    });
    var messagePanel = new Ext.ux.MessagePanel();
```

2. Before we start coding the guts of the recipe, we will create a simple JSON file that will be the target of our AJAX call. It will contain a simple list of names, IDs, and selected flags. A snippet is shown as follows:

```
{
    "success": true,
    "recipients": [{
        "fullName": "Stuart Ashworth",
        "userID": 1,
        "selected": true // check the generated CheckBox
    }, {
        "fullName": "Andrew Duncan",
        "userID": 2,
        "selected": false
    }
    ...
    ]
}
```

3. Our next step, is to create an AJAX call that will load our JSON file and then use it to create our form. We start by creating a `loadCheckboxes` method as part of the class we defined in step 1. This will make our AJAX call and output the response to the console so that we can see what's happening:

```
loadCheckboxes: function() {

    Ext.Ajax.request({
        url: 'recipients.json',
        success: function(response) {
            console.log(response);
        },
        scope: this
    });
}
```

4. We can now call this method just after our `callParent` call in the `initComponent` method so the data loading process starts as soon as possible:

```
this.loadCheckboxes();
```

5. At the moment, after our AJAX call has received its response all we do is log its output. We will now replace this placeholder method and create an `onLoad` method that will process this response and start to create our checkboxes. Initially we will define our `onLoad` method to decode the JSON `response` and check whether it was successful.

```
onLoad: function(response){
    var jsonResponse = Ext.decode(response.responseText);

    if (jsonResponse.success) {
        // success
    }
}
```

6. We can then wire this method up to the AJAX request's `success` handler that we defined in the previous step:

```
Ext.Ajax.request({
    url: 'recipients.json',
    success: this.onLoad,
    scope: this
});
```

7. Now we get to the important part where we create our checkbox group. All we must do is, after the `onLoad` method's success check, define the configuration for the group and pass it as a parameter to the form's `add` method:

```
var checkboxGroup = {
    xtype: 'checkboxgroup',
    columns: 2,
    fieldLabel: 'Recipients',
    name: 'recipients',
    style: {
        padding: '10px'
    },
    items: []
};
this.add(checkboxGroup);
```

8. We can now see our empty checkbox group in our form, so our final step is to use our loaded data to create its checkboxes. We do this by looping around the elements in the `recipients` array and pushing a checkbox configuration onto the `items` array of `checkboxGroup`. We do this before calling the form's `add` method:

```
var i, len = jsonResponse.recipients.length, recipient;
for (i = 0; i < len; i++) {
    recipient = jsonResponse.recipients[i];
```

```
checkboxGroup.items.push({
    xtype: 'checkbox',
    boxLabel: recipient.fullName,
    name: 'recipients',
    inputValue: recipient.userID,
    checked: recipient.selected
});
}
```

9. Now that our form is complete we can see what would be posted back to the server through a submit action by clicking the **Send** button. The following screenshot shows how the checkboxes get combined into a single parameter named `recipients` containing an array of `userID`:

recipients	[1, 3, 5]
0	1
1	3
2	5

How it works...

The code we have created works very well by creating JavaScript configuration objects that the Ext JS framework will parse when passed to a container's `add` method. This technique shows the flexibility and convenience of the `xtype` system and why it is important to get to grips with it early on in your Ext JS learning.

When dealing with checkboxes and CheckboxGroups it's crucial to name your items consistently so, when it comes to form submission and population, they are combined into a single parameter. In our example, we want to have our server deal with a single array of `userID` that our message will be sent to which is why the CheckboxGroup and all the checkboxes share the same name.

If we had named each checkbox by the `userID` that it represents then we would have multiple name/value pairs being sent to the server (see the following screenshot). While this is ok for static types, it would be very difficult for the server to parse this data when the number and variety of recipients is always changing.

1	1
3	3
5	5

There's more...

With a situation similar to the one we have explored previously, it's possible that the number of checkboxes could grow to large numbers. If a user wanted to send a message to all of their friends then that equates to a lot of checkbox clicking. This is a tedious task and so we will demonstrate how to implement a **Check /Uncheck All** button to make our users' lives easier:

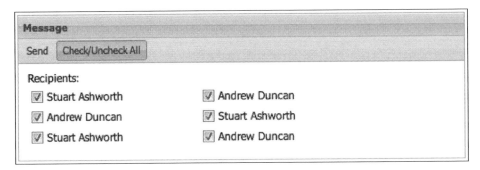

We start by creating a second button on the top toolbar with the `enableToggle` configuration option set to `true`. This will make the button into a toggle button, which will toggle between a pressed state and a non-pressed state:

```
{
    text: 'Check/Uncheck All',
    enableToggle: true
}
```

We will now implement the logic that clicking on this button will follow. We use the button's `toggleHandler`, which is a shortcut to binding a listener to the `toggle` event, to attach a function that will execute when the button is toggled. This function accepts two parameters—a reference to the button and a Boolean determining if the button is in a pressed state or not:

```
{
    text: 'Check/Uncheck All',
    enableToggle: true,
    toggleHandler: function(button, pressed){
    },
    scope: this
}
```

We must now loop through each checkbox within the CheckBoxGroup and set the value of it to the value contained in the `pressed` variable:

```
this.items.get(0).items.each(function(checkbox){
    checkbox.setValue(pressed);
}, this);
```

See also

▸ The two recipes before this explaining RadioGroups and CheckboxGroups in more detail.

▸ The recipe in _Chapter 5, Loading, Submitting, and Validating Forms_, demonstrating how to dynamically create forms from JSON data.

Setting up available date ranges in Date fields

When using Date fields we will often want to restrict the dates that a user can pick from.

In this recipe we will explain how to configure a Date field to only have a specific range of dates available for selection and how to extend this functionality with advanced date disabling.

How to do it...

1. First of all we create a very simple Date field and render it to the document's body.

```
Ext.create('Ext.form.field.Date', {
    fieldLabel: 'Pick a Date',

    value: new Date(2011, 7, 8),

    renderTo: Ext.getBody()
});
```

2. We can now introduce the `minValue` and `maxValue` configuration options to restrict the available dates.

```
Ext.create('Ext.form.field.Date', {
    fieldLabel: 'Pick a Date',

    minValue: new Date(2011, 7, 5),
    maxValue: new Date(2011, 7, 17),

    renderTo: Ext.getBody()
});
```

How it works...

When defined, the `minValue` and `maxValue` are used to disable any dates later than the `maxValue` or earlier than the `minValue`. These values are inclusive and so, in our example, we are still able to select the 5th and 17th of August 2011.

 Useful tip: Months in JavaScript are zero based, so 7 is August.

The following screenshot is the result of our date restrictions in Step 2 and shows the unavailable dates greyed out:

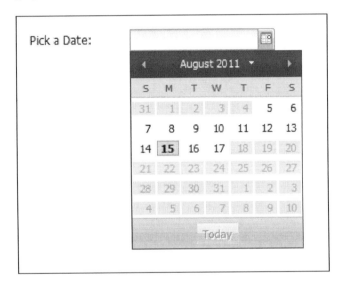

There's more...

As well as allowing one specific range of dates, Ext JS allows us to be more specific and disable dates individually and by using regular expressions. This section will focus on examples of how to achieve this.

Disabling specific dates

The Date field's `disabledDates` config option can be used to define an array of specific dates that will be unavailable for selection by the user. The date strings specified in this array must follow the format defined by the Date field, either by its configured format or its default (m/d/y).

The following code shows how to disable the 8th, 10th, and 12th of August 2011 using the standard British date format:

```
Ext.create('Ext.form.field.Date', {
    fieldLabel: 'Pick a Date',

    format: 'd/m/Y',
    disabledDates: ['08/08/2011', '10/08/2011', '12/08/2011'],

    renderTo: Ext.getBody()
});
```

Disabling specific days

It is also possible to disable all dates that fall on a particular day of the week. The disabledDays configuration option accepts an array of numbers representing days of the week, with 0 representing Sunday and 6, Saturday, that will be disabled.

The following example shows how to disable all Mondays, Wednesdays, and Fridays within the Date field:

```
Ext.create('Ext.form.field.Date', {
    fieldLabel: 'Pick a Date',

    disabledDays: [1, 3, 5],

    renderTo: Ext.getBody()
});
```

Advanced Date Disabling with Regular Expressions

In addition to accepting explicit date values, the disabledDates configuration can also contain regular expressions which will be matched to the dates that are currently on display and, if they are matched, are disabled.

We will not go into details about how to construct regular expressions (as that is a book in itself!) but we will demonstrate a couple of examples of putting this technique to use. The following example disables the first date in every month in every year:

```
// disable first of every month
Ext.create('Ext.form.field.Date', {
    fieldLabel: 'Pick a Date',

    format: 'd/m/Y',
    disabledDates: ['^01'],

    renderTo: Ext.getBody()
});
```

This following `disabledDates` configuration will disable the entire months of August and September every year:

```
disabledDates: ['../08/..', '../09/..']
```

Finally, this config disables dates between 10 and 19 of each month:

```
disabledDates: ['^1.']
```

 If your date format includes any reserved regular expression characters then they must be escaped.

See Also

▸   The next recipe that explains how to load and parse dates with the Date field.

Loading and parsing Dates into a Date field

Dates are notoriously difficult to work with, especially when dealing with multiple and non-standard formats. This recipe will explore how to set the value of a date picker and how to use it in combination with different date formats.

How to do it...

1. We start by creating a simple Date Picker:

    ```
    var dateField = Ext.create('Ext.form.field.Date', {
        fieldLabel: 'Pick a Date',
        renderTo: Ext.getBody()
    });
    ```

2. Now we can use the Date Picker's `setValue` method to give it a value. We will use British date formatting in this example with our date formatted as dd/mm/yyyy.

    ```
    dateField.setValue('31/01/2011');
    ```

3. After running this code we see that the field doesn't understand the format and so does not display or select a value.

4. To solve this problem we can specify the format that the date picker expects the values being passed to the `setValue` method are in. We do this by using the `format` configuration option.

    ```
    var dateField = Ext.create('Ext.form.field.Date', {
        fieldLabel: 'Pick a Date',
        renderTo: Ext.getBody(),
    ```

```
        format: 'd/m/Y'
    });
    dateField.setValue('31/01/2011');
```

5. When we run this code we see that our date field contains the correct value.

How it works...

When we try to set the value of a date field, the field parses that value into a proper date object. By default the field uses the standard American date format of mm/dd/yyyy, which is why our initial attempt in step 2, displayed the incorrect value. By explicitly specifying a date format the field can then interpret the value as we expect it to.

 The `format` config option also controls how the date is displayed to the user after being selected.

There's more...

It is possible to specify multiple formats that are valid for a particular date field. This can come in handy when you are not in control of how users enter dates and so the field can be flexible enough to accommodate different formats.

We can demonstrate this by passing a date formatted with hyphens instead of slashes to the field's `setValue` method:

```
    dateField.setValue('31-01-2011');
```

This results in the same outcome as we just saw in step 2 because the field isn't able to understand that the date is in dd-mm-yyyy format.

This is easy to rectify by making use of the `altFormats` configuration option which accepts a string of alternative date formats, separated by a pipe character (|). We can demonstrate this in action by setting `altFormats` to accept the date we passed above and see it display properly:

```
var dateField = Ext.create('Ext.form.field.Date', {
    fieldLabel: 'Pick a Date',
    renderTo: Ext.getBody(),

    format: 'd/m/Y',
    altFormats: 'd-m-Y|dmY'
});
//Both are valid.
dateField.setValue('31-01-2011');
dateField.setValue('31012011');
```

Our date field now understands the format we are giving it and displays the correct value to the user.

See also

▶ The previous recipe on using a Date field and setting date ranges.

▶ The recipe *Populating your form with data* in *Chapter 5, Loading, Submitting, and Validating Forms,* for more information on how to remotely load data into your form.

Entering numbers with a Spinner field

In this recipe, we will demonstrate how to use Ext JS' number field to enter numbers. The number field is an extended Spinner field and provides enhanced functionality to the user with very simple configuration.

The Spinner allows users to increase/decrease values by using the arrow buttons, the arrow keys on the keyboard, or by rotating the mouse wheel. Of course, it's also possible to turn these options off:

How to do it...

1. Create a form panel:

```
var formPanel = Ext.create('Ext.form.Panel', {
    title: 'Spinner Field Example',
    width: 350,
    height: 100,
    bodyPadding: 10,
    defaults: {
        labelWidth: 150
    },
    items: [],
    renderTo: Ext.getBody(),
    style: 'margin: 50px'
});
```

2. Add a number field to the form panel's items collection:

```
var formPanel = Ext.create('Ext.form.Panel', {
    ...
    items: [{
        xtype: 'numberfield',
        fieldLabel: 'Card Expiry Date',
        minValue: 2011,
        maxValue: 2020
    }],
    ...
});
```

3. Create a second number field and customize it with extra configuration:

```
var formPanel = Ext.create('Ext.form.Panel', {
    ...
    items: [{
        xtype: 'numberfield',
        fieldLabel: 'Card Expiry Date',
        minValue: 2011,
        maxValue: 2020
    }, {
        xtype: 'numberfield',
        fieldLabel: 'Weight (KG)',
        minValue: -100,
        maxValue: 100,
        allowDecimals: true, //Default behaviour
        decimalPrecision: 1,
        step: 0.5
    }],
    ...
});
```

How it works...

The number field behaves the same as a text field with a number of additional features. The field has built-in filtering for values that are not numeric.

In Ext JS 4 the number field extends the `Ext.form.field.Spinner` class that provides a set of up and down spinner buttons to the field.

The `minValue` and `maxValue` config options allow us to define a range of valid values for the field. Should the user attempt to enter a value that is outside the boundaries, the field will not validate.

The second example demonstrates three extra config options: `allowDecimals`, `decimalPrecision`, and `step`:

- ▸ `allowDecimals` determines whether the field should be capable of taking decimal digits. Setting `allowDecimals: false` ensures that the field will only accept whole numbers.

- ▸ `decimalPrecision` gives you the ability to define how precise you require the number to be. In our example, we accept numbers with one digit to the right of the decimal point.

- ▸ `step` is used to determine how much the value of the field is increased or decreased when the spinner is invoked. The example of `step: 0.5` ensures that the increment is `0.5` when the user moves up or down the values.

There's More...

By default, the number field provides the Spinner functionality, however, it's possible to turn this off. The `hideTrigger`, `keyNavEnabled`, and `mouseWheelEnabled` configuration can be set accordingly:

```
var formPanel = Ext.create('Ext.form.Panel', {
    ...
    items: [{
        xtype: 'numberfield',
        fieldLabel: 'Card Expiry Date',
        minValue: 2011,
        maxValue: 2020,
        hideTrigger: true,
        keyNavEnabled: false,
        mouseWheelEnabled: false
    }],
    ...
});
```

This example will create a text field with the pre-configured validation required for a number field but render it without the spinner buttons or the keyboard arrows/mouse wheel listeners.

See Also

- ▸ As an alternative to the Spinner field you could try the Slider field which is discussed in the next recipe.

Sliding values using a Slider field

Ext JS `Ext.slider` package provides a simple way for allowing users to enter numeric values and value ranges. This recipe will look at configuring this component to allow single and multiple values, as well as demonstrating how we can react to a user changing these values.

How to do it...

1. We start by instantiating the `Ext.slider.Single` class, a subclass of `Ext.slider.Multi`, and giving it a width, a label, and rendering it to the body of our document:

    ```
    Ext.create('Ext.slider.Single', {
        fieldLabel: 'Maximum Price',

        width: 400,
        renderTo: Ext.getBody()
    });
    ```

2. We now provide the field with a default value and some constraints as to what value can be chosen. This is done by using the `value`, `minValue`, and `maxValue` configuration options respectively:

    ```
    Ext.create('Ext.slider.Single', {
        fieldLabel: 'Maximum Price',
        value: 100,
        minValue: 0,
        maxValue: 500,
        width: 400,
        renderTo: Ext.getBody()
    });
    ```

3. Finally, we restrict the user even further by configuring an increment value that specifies by how much the slider's value changes as the thumb is dragged:

    ```
    Ext.create('Ext.slider.Single', {
        fieldLabel: 'Maximum Price',
        value: 100,
        minValue: 0,
        maxValue: 500,
        increment: 10,
        width: 400,
        renderTo: Ext.getBody()
    });
    ```

How it works...

The `Ext.slider.Single` class inherits from the `Ext.form.field.Base` class and so inherits all of the features of form fields, such as labels and values, as well as being a `Component` class and therefore, able to be added as a child to any container and be included in layouts.

When created with basic configuration, as in step 1, the Slider acquires default values for `value`, `minValue`, `maxValue`, and `increment`. This produces a Slider ranging from `0` to `100` and giving an incremental change of `1`.

 By default a tip will be displayed when you drag the slider. If you don't want to show tips you can turn them off by configuring the slider with `useTips: false`.

There's more...

So far we have described how to create a Slider allowing a user to select a single value. We are now going to demonstrate how to allow a Slider to contain multiple thumbs to define value ranges. We will also discuss how to react to the dragging of a slider's thumbs by listening to the `drag` event.

Defining Multiple Thumbs

1. First we create a very basic slider as we did in the first examples but by using the `Ext.slider.Multi` class instead of the `Ext.slider.Single` class:

```
var priceRangeSlider = Ext.create('Ext.slider.Multi', {
    fieldLabel: 'Price Range',
    minValue: 0,
    maxValue: 500,
    increment: 10,
    width: 400,
    renderTo: Ext.getBody()
});
```

2. Next, we define the starting values of our slider's thumbs. We do this by passing an array of values to the `values` config option. The slider class will create a thumb for each element in the array and place it on the slider at its appropriate numeric position:

```
var priceRangeSlider = Ext.create('Ext.slider.Multi', {
    fieldLabel: 'Price Range',
    values: [100, 200],
    minValue: 0,
    maxValue: 500,
```

```
        increment: 10,

        width: 400,
        renderTo: Ext.getBody()
    });
```

 If we require more thumbs we can simply add another item to the `values` array or, at runtime, use the `addThumb` method.

Reacting to a thumb being dragged

We will start from where we had left off earlier with the simple multi-thumb slider.

1. We must first create a component that we will use to display the current values of the slider and which will get updated as the thumbs are moved. This component has a simple template and a starting value to match the slider's (this could be set dynamically on creation):

    ```
    var valueDisplayComponent = Ext.create('Ext.Component', {
        tpl: 'Current Price Range: &pound;{min} - &pound;{max}',
        data: {min: 100, max: 200},
        renderTo: Ext.getBody()
    });
    ```

2. Now, we add a listener to the slider's `drag` event, which is fired when a thumb is moved to a new value. In this listener function, we gather the values of the slider using the `getValues` method and update the display component using its `update` method:

    ```
    var priceRangeSlider = Ext.create('Ext.slider.Multi', {
        ...
        listeners: {
            drag: function(slider, e, opts){
                // get the slider's thumbs' values
                var vals = slider.getValues();

                // update the display container
                valueDisplayContainer.update({
                    min: vals[0],
                    max: vals[1]
                });
            }
        }
        ...
    });
    ```

> The `getValues` method returns an array containing each thumb's value. The ordering of this mirrors the order that the values were defined in the configuration.

See Also

▶ For a simpler way of gathering a numeric value see the recipe discussing the Spinner field earlier in this chapter.

Loading server side data into a combobox

A combobox's selection list can be loaded from locally defined data (in JavaScript) or remotely from a web server. This recipe provides an introduction on how to load JSON data from a server into the combobox's selection list.

Getting ready

The following recipe requires you to interact with a web server. Please ensure you have a running web server for serving the `users.json` file. The file should contain:

```
{
    "success": true,
    "users": [{
        "fullName": "Joe Bloggs",
        "userID": 1
    }, {
        "fullName": "John Smith",
        "userID": 2
    }]
}
```

How to do it...

1. Start by defining a model.

```
Ext.define('User', {
    extend: 'Ext.data.Model',
    fields: [{
        type: 'string',
        name: 'fullName'
    }, {
```

```
            type: 'int',
            name: 'userID'
    }]
});
```

2. Create an `Ext.data.Store` that is linked to the `User` model:

```
var store = Ext.create('Ext.data.Store', {
    model: 'User',
    proxy: {
        type: 'ajax',
        url: 'users.json',
        reader: {
            type: 'json',
            root: 'users'
        }
    }
});
```

3. Create a form panel with a `ComboBox` and bind it to the store we created above:

```
var formPanel = Ext.create('Ext.form.Panel', {
    title: 'ComboBox with server side data example',
    width: 350,
    autoHeight: true,
    bodyPadding: 10,
    items: [{
        xtype: 'combobox',
        fieldLabel: 'Select User',
        displayField: 'fullName',
        valueField: 'userID',
        store: store,
        queryMode: 'remote', //default behavior
        forceSelection: true,
        anchor: '100%'
    }],
    renderTo: Ext.getBody(),
    style: 'margin: 50px'
});
```

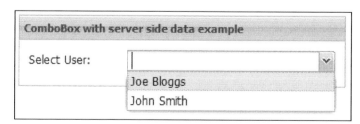

How it works...

The combobox's selection list is populated using an `Ext.data.Store`. To make the combobox retrieve data from the server, we have defined, in this case, a remote store with an AJAX proxy.

When the user clicks on the trigger field of the combobox for the first time, the store makes a call to the server and turns the returned data into a collection of Model instances that are then loaded into the store.

The `displayField` config option is used to determine which of our model's fields we wish to present to the user (in this case, the `fullName` field) and the `valueField` is used for setting the hidden data value that represents the value selected by the user. When we eventually submit the form the value submitted is the `userID`.

The config option `forceSelection: true` ensures that the user is only able to select and submit the combobox from the predefined list of options and isn't allowed to type in their own value.

Finally, it's worth noting that the `queryMode: 'remote'` option tells the framework to load the store dynamically when the field is triggered. By default, the `queryMode` for a combobox is `'remote'`, however, if you do not want to load remote data it is recommended this option is set to `'local'` for increased responsiveness.

See also

▸ Learn how to add auto-complete to your comboboxes in the next recipe.

▸ The next chapter, which explains the data package in further detail.

Autocompleting a combobox's value

ComboBoxes are a very handy control to use when creating a form, giving the user a convenient list of values you want them to choose from. However, these lists grow very long and the convenience starts to shrink as they are forced to trawl through a lengthy list of options.

Ext JS has provided us with the ability to allow comboboxes to autocomplete and select an option as we type, so we can find the correct value faster. This recipe will demonstrate how to set up this functionality.

How to do it...

1. Our first step is to create an `Ext.data.Store`, which we will bind to our combobox to give it its list of values. Our example will display a list of car manufacturers:

```
var carManufacturersStore = Ext.create('Ext.data.Store', {
    fields: ['name'],
    data: [{
        name: 'Aston Martin'
    }, {
        name: 'Bentley'
    }, {
        name: 'Daimler'
    }, {
        name: 'Jaguar'
    }, {
        name: 'Lagonda'
    }, {
        name: 'Land Rover'
    }, {
        name: 'Lotus'
    }, {
        name: 'McLaren'
    }, {
        name: 'Morgan'
    }, {
        name: 'Rolls-Royce'
    }]
});
```

2. We then create a very simple combobox bound to this store and rendered to the document's body:

```
Ext.create('Ext.form.ComboBox', {
    fieldLabel: 'Car Manufacturer',
    store: carManufacturersStore,
    queryMode: 'local',
    displayField: 'name',
    valueField: 'name',

    renderTo: Ext.getBody()
});
```

3. Now, we configure the combobox to find the nearest match after the user has started typing, and set the value of the combobox's text field. We do this by adding the `typeAhead` configuration option:

```
Ext.create('Ext.form.ComboBox', {
        fieldLabel: 'Car Manufacturer',
        store: carManufacturersStore,
        queryMode: 'local',
        displayField: 'name',
        valueField: 'name',

        typeAhead: true,

        renderTo: Ext.getBody()
});
```

4. The following screenshot shows the result of using this simple configuration option:

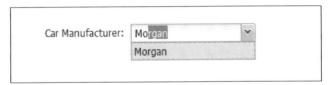

How it works...

When we set `typeAhead` to `true`, the combobox performs some extra processing when a query is run that filters the drop-down list. The routine uses the store's `findRecord` method to retrieve the first matching record, comparing the entered value and the record's `displayField`. It then changes the field's value to the complete entry and highlights the text that wasn't entered by the user.

The natural functionality of the browser then takes over as the user continues typing and so replacing the highlighted, autocompleted text.

There's more...

The `Ext.form.field.ComboBox` class offers various other useful configuration options that complement the autocomplete setup. We will now look at making the autocomplete process more responsive and how to remove the trigger button to make the combobox more like a text field with a lookup.

Increasing autocomplete response time

The combobox component has a `typeAheadDelay` configuration option that accepts a numeric value defining the number of milliseconds before the auto-completed text is displayed in the text field. By setting this to a lower number your application will appear quicker and more responsive:

```
Ext.create('Ext.form.ComboBox', {
    fieldLabel: 'Car Manufacturer',
    store: carManufacturers,
    queryMode: 'local',
    displayField: 'name',
    valueField: 'name',

    typeAhead: true,
    typeAheadDelay: 100,

    renderTo: Ext.getBody()
});
```

Defining the minimum characters before autocompleting

By default, when using a `queryMode` of local, the minimum number of characters that a user must enter before the field is autocompleted is `0`. However, this may not always be desirable so it can be configured using the `minChars` option, which accepts a numeric value.

Removing the combobox's trigger button

ComboBoxes can have their trigger button (the down arrow on the right hand side) hidden if required. This is particularly useful when using the autocomplete options as you may wish the field to become more of an assisted TextField rather than a combobox.

This can be achieved by setting the `hideTrigger` option to true.

```
Ext.create('Ext.form.ComboBox', {
    fieldLabel: 'Car Manufacturer',
    store: carManufacturers,
    queryMode: 'local',
    displayField: 'name',
    valueField: 'name',

    typeAhead: true,
    typeAheadDelay: 100,
    hideTrigger: true,

    renderTo: Ext.getBody()
});
```

▶ See the previous recipe about loading comboboxes' values from a server.

▶ To read more about stores and models, take a look at the next chapter, which focuses on the Ext.data package.

Rendering the results in a combobox

By default, the ComboBox component provides a neatly presented list of options for a user to choose from based on the value in the displayField giving the same experience as the HTML <select> tag.

However, there are occasions when we may wish to present more to the user or customize the styling of the results. This recipe aims to demonstrate how to tackle this problem and produce a combobox with a customized list of results.

How to do it...

1. Define an Issue Model:

```
Ext.define('Issue', {
    extend: 'Ext.data.Model',
    fields: ['id', 'raisedBy', 'title', 'body', 'status']
});
```

2. Create a store and add some data for local loading:

```
var store = Ext.create('Ext.data.Store', {
    model: 'Issue',
    data: [{
        id: 1,
        raisedBy: 'Joe',
        title: 'Registration Form Not Emailing User',
        body: 'The registration email is not being sent to users
upon regisration.',
        status: 'Open'
    }, {
        id: 2,
        raisedBy: 'John',
        title: 'Account Details Loading Issue',
        body: 'The account details page is not loading data from
the server.',
        status: 'Closed'
    }, {
        id: 3,
        raisedBy: 'Fred',
```

```
            title: 'Account Details Missing Email Field',
            body: 'The account details page is missing a field to
      allow the user to update their email address.',
            status: 'Open'
      }]
});
```

3. Add the combobox to a form panel and customize the combo's list through `Ext.view.BoundList` (accessible through the `listConfig` config option):

```
var formPanel = Ext.create('Ext.form.Panel', {
    title: 'Custom ComboBox Results',
    width: 500,
    autoHeight: true,
    bodyPadding: 10,
    items: [{
        xtype: 'combobox',
        fieldLabel: 'Select Issue',
        displayField: 'title',
        store: store,
        queryMode: 'local',
        anchor: '100%',
        listConfig: {
            getInnerTpl: function(){
                return '<h3>{title} ({status})</h3>' +
                '<div class="reportedBy">Reported by
                {raisedBy}</div>' +
                '{body}';
            }
        }
    }],
    renderTo: Ext.getBody(),
    style: 'margin: 50px'
});
```

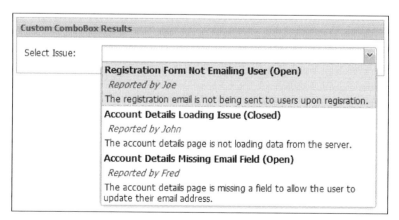

How it works...

The list component of `Ext.form.field.ComboBox` is an `Ext.view.BoundList`. The `BoundList` class is extended from the `Ext.view.View` (DataView) class and has been specifically written for the combobox. The DataView gives us a wealth of possibilities for customizing how the list is presented and how we work with the list.

To configure the DataView we use the `listConfig` config option in the `Ext.form.field.ComboBox` class. The configurable properties in the `listConfig` object are applied to the `BoundList`.

The example shows, in its list, a series of issues or support tickets. However, instead of simply displaying the issue title we are looking to show more information. Achieving this was done by:

- Defining the necessary fields in our `Issue` Model
- Creating a store for the combobox (with some predefined data for loading into the Model)
- Applying a custom template to the DataView through the combo's `listConfig` property

The custom template is applied by overriding the `BoundList` class' `getInnerTpl` method. By default, the `getInnerTpl` method returns the value of the combobox's `displayField`. The framework code is:

```
getInnerTpl: function(displayField) {
    return '{' + displayField + '}';
},
```

If we had set `displayField: 'title'` in the combo this method would have added `{title}` automatically to the list's `Ext.XTemplate` for us. However, by overriding this method in the `listConfig` configuration we are able to provide the `BoundList` with further fields and a layout of our choice.

See Also

- The last two recipes discussing loading and adding autocomplete to comboboxes.
- The recipes in Chapter 4, *UI Building Blocks—Trees, Panels, and Data Views*.

Rich editing with an HTML field

The framework provides a lightweight text editor for use in forms. The `Ext.form.field.HtmlEditor` enhances the user experiences giving them the capability to:

- Format text as bold, italics, or underlined
- Add links to content
- Change the font, font color, and font size
- Create ordered and unordered lists
- Left, center, or right align text

This recipe will explain how to use the HTML editor field in your form for a rich text editing experience.

How to do it...

1. Initialize the `QuickTipManager`:

   ```
   Ext.tip.QuickTipManager.init();
   ```

2. Create a narrow form panel and add an `HtmlEditor` field to the panel's `items` collection:

   ```
   var formPanelNarrow = Ext.create('Ext.form.Panel', {
       title: 'HTML Editor (narrow)',
       width: 350,
       height: 200,
       layout: 'fit',
       items: [{
           xtype: 'htmleditor'
       }],
       renderTo: Ext.getBody()
   });
   ```

3. Create a second form panel with the `HtmlEditor` but this time set the `width` to 600:

   ```
   var formPanelWide = Ext.create('Ext.form.Panel', {
       title: 'HTML Editor (wide)',
       width: 600,
       height: 200,
       layout: 'fit',
   ```

```
        items: [{
            xtype: 'htmleditor'
        }],
        renderTo: Ext.getBody()
    });
```

4. Create a third form panel with an HTML editor but customize the toolbar options as follows:

```
var formPanelCustomOptions = Ext.create('Ext.form.Panel', {
        title: 'HTML Editor (customising the toolbar)',
        width: 600,
        height: 200,
        layout: 'fit',
        items: [{
            xtype: 'htmleditor',
            enableSourceEdit: false,
            enableColors: false,
            enableLinks: false,
            fontFamilies: ["Arial", "Tahoma", "Verdana"]
        }],
        renderTo: Ext.getBody()
    });
```

How it works...

The reason we initialized the `Ext.tip.QuickTipManager` in Step 1 is because the toolbar buttons have predefined `buttonTips`, which will not display until the global `QuickTipManager` is initialized. For example, if you hover the mouse over the bold button the tip appears as shown as follows:

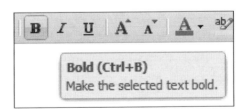

The first example of the `HtmlEditor` shows the editor in a form panel that is 350 pixels wide. In this instance the toolbar will automatically overflow the remaining toolbar buttons into a drop-down menu. This menu is accessible from the right pointing guillemet:

The second example, on the other hand, demonstrates the toolbar without overflow.

The final example shows how you can customize the toolbar buttons with the configuration options available in the Ext.form.field.HtmlEditor class. Setting the options enableSourceEdit, enableColors, and enableLinks to false turns off the source editing, text color editing, and the create link features respectively. The fontFamilies option accepts an array of font names that will be made available for users to select from:

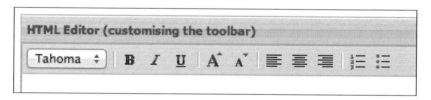

Creating repeatable form fields and fieldsets

It is sometimes necessary to gather repeating data from a user. For example, a booking form (for a hotel, restaurant, or attraction) sometimes requires the total number of guests and information about each individual. More often than not these questions are the same for each person.

This example will demonstrate how to create a form panel with a set of repeating questions. The repeated questions will be dynamically added to the form by pressing an **Add Another Guest** button. The fields will sit inside a FieldSet that has reference to the number of repeated items.

How to do it...

1. Start by creating a form panel and rendering it to the document's body:

```
var formPanel = Ext.create('Ext.form.Panel', {
    title: 'Reservation Form',
    width: 350,
    autoHeight: true,
    bodyPadding: 10,
    defaults: {
        labelWidth: 150
    },
    items: [],
    renderTo: Ext.getBody()
});
```

2. Add some fields to the form's items collection to capture name and Ticket Type for the first person:

```
var formPanel = Ext.create('Ext.form.Panel', {
    ...
    items: [{
        xtype: 'textfield',
        fieldLabel: 'Your Name',
        name: 'name'
    }, {
        xtype: 'radiogroup',
        fieldLabel: 'Ticket Type',
        items: [{
            boxLabel: 'Adult',
            name: 'type',
            inputValue: 'adult'
        }, {
            boxLabel: 'Child',
            name: 'type',
            inputValue: 'child'
        }]
    }],
    ...
});
```

3. Create our GuestFieldSet by extending the Ext.form.FieldSet class:

```
Ext.define('GuestFieldSet', {
    extend: 'Ext.form.FieldSet',
    alias: 'widget.GuestFieldSet',
```

```
    initComponent: function(){
        Ext.apply(this, {
            title: 'Guest ' + this.guestCount,
            collapible: true,
            defaultType: 'textfield',
            defaults: {
                anchor: '100%'
            },
            layout: 'anchor',
            items: [{
                fieldLabel: 'Guest ' + this.guestCount + ' Name',
                name: 'name-' + this.guestCount
            }, {
                xtype: 'radiogroup',
                fieldLabel: 'Ticket Type',
                items: [{
                    boxLabel: 'Adult',
                    name: 'type-' + this.guestCount,
                    inputValue: 'adult'
                }, {
                    boxLabel: 'Child',
                    name: 'type-' + this.guestCount,
                    inputValue: 'child'
                }]
            }]
        });
        this.callParent(arguments);
    }
});
```

4. Finally, add a button under the fields in the form panel to allow the user to add a second guest. The button's `handler` function contains the logic to add the additional fields:

```
var formPanel = Ext.create('Ext.form.Panel', {
    ...
    items: [{
        ...
    }, {
        xtype: 'button',
        text: 'Add Another Guest',
        margin: '0 0 5 0',
        handler: function(){
            guestCount = formPanel.items.length - 2;
            formPanel.add({
```

```
                    xtype: 'GuestFieldSet',
                    guestCount: guestCount
                });
            }
        }],
        ...
    });
```

How it works...

The button we added in step 3 is where the magic happens in this recipe. The button's handler function makes a call to the add method of Ext.form.Panel.

The add method is used for adding components to the end of the panel's items collection. In this instance our component is GuestFieldSet.

The GuestFieldSet class is an extension of the Ext.form.FieldSet class, which wraps our repeatable fields (guest name and ticket type). We are able to lazily instantiate this class because it has an alias configured—widget.GuestFieldSet. When we add the component we do so through the xtype configuration option, defined as GuestFieldSet (which is the alias for the class).

The guestCount variable is used for determining the number of fieldsets the user has added. This variable is used for two purposes in this example:

 ▶ To give the user a visual indication of which guest the FieldSet is referring to. This can be seen in the guest name fieldLabel and in the FieldSet's legend.

 ▶ To name the fields dynamically for each guest. When we submit the form with one guest, for example, the parameters passed will be:

   ❏ name

   ❏ type

   ❏ name-1 (guest one)

   ❏ type-1 (guest one)

Combining form fields

Every now and then we may want to group a set of related fields together and present them with one label. This example aims to show you how to make a form that combines three number fields (separated by hyphens) for gathering a UK banking sort code.

This will gather the three parts of the sort code as separate fields and present it in a user friendly manner to the user.

Getting ready

As this recipe is a form to collect a UK bank account number and sort code we have written a custom VType for the sort code. If you are not already familiar with how to write or use a VType you'll find the two recipes in Chapter 5, *Loading, Submitting, and Validating Forms*, useful. The code for this VType is shown as follows:

```
Ext.apply(Ext.form.field.VTypes, {
    SortCode: function(val){
     var sortCodeRegex = /^(([0-9][0-9])|(99))$/;
        return sortCodeRegex.test(val);
    },
    SortCodeText: 'Must be a numeric value between 00 and 99',
    SortCodeMask: /[\d]/i
});
```

How to do it...

1. Create a form panel:

```
var formPanel = Ext.create('Ext.form.Panel', {
    title: 'Combining Form Fields',
    width: 350,
    autoHeight: true,
    bodyPadding: 10,
    defaults: {
        anchor: '100%',
        labelWidth: 100
    },
    items: [],
    renderTo: Ext.getBody()
});
```

2. In the panel's `items` collection add a `FieldContainer` with an hbox layout:

```
var formPanel = Ext.create('Ext.form.Panel', {
    ...
    items: [{
        xtype: 'fieldcontainer',
        fieldLabel: 'Sort Code',
        combineErrors: true,
        layout: 'hbox',
        defaults: {
            hideLabel: true,
            vtype: 'SortCode'
        },
```

```
                    items: []
            }],
            ...
    });
```

3. In the `items` collection of `FieldContainer`, add the fields for gathering the Sort Code:

```
var formPanel = Ext.create('Ext.form.Panel', {
        ...
        items: [{
            ...
            items: [{
                xtype: 'textfield',
                name: 'sortcode1',
                allowBlank: false,
                flex: 1
            }, {
                xtype: 'displayfield',
                value: '-',
                margin: '0 0 0 3',
                width: 10
            }, {
                xtype: 'textfield',
                name: 'sortcode2',
                allowBlank: false,
                flex: 1
            }, {
                xtype: 'displayfield',
                value: '-',
                margin: '0 0 0 3',
                width: 10
            }, {
                xtype: 'textfield',
                name: 'sortcode3',
                allowBlank: false,
                flex: 1
            }]
        }],
        ...
    });
```

4. Finally, add a second field to the panel's `items` collection for gathering the account number:

```
var formPanel = Ext.create('Ext.form.Panel', {
    ...
    items: [{
        ...
    }, {
        xtype: 'numberfield',
        name: 'accountNumber',
        fieldLabel: 'Account Number',
        msgTarget: 'side',
        minValue: 10000000,
        maxValue: 99999999,
        hideTrigger: true,
        keyNavEnabled: false,
        mouseWheelEnabled: false,
        allowBlank: false
    }],
    ...
});
```

Combining Form Fields			
Sort Code:	80	- 00	- 00
Account Number:	10998855		

How it works...

The custom `VType` tests the value against a regular expression that expects two digits (between 0 and 9) in the field. We make reference to this VType in the form by setting the relevant fields with `vtype: 'SortCode'`.

To achieve the grouping effect for the sort code we put the three fields in a `FieldContainer`. The `Ext.form.FieldContainer` class is extended from the `Container` class with the added benefit of containing the `Labelable` mixin.

By defining an hbox layout on the `FieldContainer`, we are ensuring that the components are set out in columns. To ensure each field has the same width, the flex is set to the same for each (that is, 1). Over and above the three text fields we have added two display fields with hyphens to give the form the appearance of a sort code. The fixed width and margins ensure that they consume a minimal amount of space.

The config option `combineErrors: true` of `FieldContainer` ensures that when any of the fields are invalid the error messages are combined and presented to the user as a single error message.

See also

▶ *Chapter 5, Loading, Submitting, and Validating Forms*, contains a number of examples on how to use and write custom `VTypes`.

▶ The recipe on complex form layouts in *Chapter 5*, which uses a `FieldContainer`.

7
Working with the Ext JS Data Package

In this chapter, we will cover:

- ▸ Modeling a data object
- ▸ Loading and saving a Model using proxies
- ▸ Loading cross-domain data with a Store
- ▸ Associating Models and loading nested data
- ▸ Applying validation rules to Models' fields
- ▸ Grouping a Store's data
- ▸ Handling Store exceptions
- ▸ Saving and loading data with HTML5 local storage

Introduction

Ext JS 4 introduces a new comprehensive and extensive data package for modeling, storing, validating, and persisting your applications' data.

This chapter will cover the core topics to help you get a solid understanding of some of the components found in the `Ext.data` package. In particular, we will demonstrate Models, Stores, and proxies, and explain how each is used for working with your applications' structured data.

Modeling a data object

In previous versions of Ext JS, a data store's Ext.data.Record class would be defined implicitly based on the fields that were supplied on its creation. This approach meant that the data structures the application represented took a back seat, and it simply became a means to have a store hold your data.

In Ext JS 4, the Ext.data.Record has been superseded by the Ext.data.Model class, which acts in a very similar way but introduces a whole host of new capabilities and becomes a much more prominent part of an application's design. It introduces new concepts such as validation, proxies, and relationships, which we will discuss throughout this chapter.

The Ext.data.Model class is used to represent an entity within your application, be it a user, a vehicle, or a group of settings, and an instance of it contains the data relating to one of those entities. Data stores are simply made up of a collection of these Model instances and are manipulated by the store as required.

This recipe will demonstrate how to define a Model class to represent a Book and how we can create new instances of it.

How to do it...

1. As always we will start with a simple HTML page with the Ext JS 4 library referenced and add our code to the onReady function.

2. We start by using the Ext.define function to create a new class that extends the base Ext.data.Model class:

```
Ext.define('Book', {
    extend: 'Ext.data.Model'
});
```

3. We continue by defining the fields property and supplying it with an array of configuration objects. These objects will be used to create Ext.data.Field instances and define how the data will be made up:

```
Ext.define('Book', {
    extend: 'Ext.data.Model',
    fields: [{
        name: 'Title',
        type: 'string'
    }, {
        name: 'Publisher',
        type: 'string'
    }, {
        name: 'ISBN',
```

```
        type: 'string'
    }, {
        name: 'PublishDate',
        type: 'date',
        dateFormat: 'd-m-Y'
    }, {
        name: 'NumberOfPages',
        type: 'int'
    }, {
        name: 'Read',
        type: 'boolean'
    }]
});
```

> In our example we have defined each field with a `name` and `type`. By including the field `type` the framework will convert and store the data as a specified data type. It is also acceptable to supply the `fields` property with an array of strings, which will be automatically used as field names and given a data type of `auto`. This type means that no conversion will take place before the value is stored in the Model instance.

4. Now that we have defined our data Model we can create an instance of it containing data about this book in the same way that we would any other class:

```
var book = Ext.create('Book', {
    Title: 'Ext JS 4 CookBook',
    Publisher: 'Packt Publishing',
    ISBN: '978-1-849516-86-0',
    PublishDate: '01-01-2012',
    NumberOfPages: 300,
    Read: false
});
```

5. We are able to call any of the `Ext.data.Model` class methods on our book instance to retrieve or set its data:

```
console.log('Title: ' + book.get('Title'));
//outputs 'Title: Ext JS CookBook'

console.log('Publish Date: ' + book.get('PublishDate'));
 // outputs 'Publish Date: Sun Jan 01 2012 00:00:00 GMT+0000 (GMT
Standard Time)'

console.log('Read: ' + book.get('Read'));
// outputs 'Read: false'
book.set('Read', true);

console.log('Read: ' + book.get('Read'));
// outputs 'Read: true'
```

How it works...

Creating a new Model is identical to extending any other Ext JS class or component and so follows exactly the same pattern. The `Ext.define` method will define our class and resolve any namespaces that we include.

The `fields` property is where the main focus is placed as this defines the structure of our data. We can supply this property with an array of configuration objects containing config options of the `Ext.data.Field` class, a simple array of strings, or a combination of both.

By specifying a `type` for each field, the field's value will be parsed into this type before it is stored. For example, by specifying the `type` as `'date'` the loaded value will be parsed into a real date object.

As with any class definition it can be instantiated using the `Ext.create` method. When using this with Models, the configuration passed as the second parameter is used as the model data and mapped to the model's fields.

There's more...

A Model and its fields can be configured in various ways, which we will look at here.

Setting the Model's uniquely identifying property

Models support the notion of having a unique property. This can be used to navigate to a particular Model instance when it is part of a collection, that is, in a Store. This acts as a primary key would in a database.

By default, this is set to the `id` field but can be customized as required by your data structure by specifying the `idProperty` configuration option. In our example, we could set our `ISBN` field as the `ID` field using the following code:

```
Ext.define('Book', {
    extend: 'Ext.data.Model',

    idProperty: 'ISBN',

    fields: [{
        name: 'Title',
        type: 'string'
    }, {
        name: 'Publisher',
        type: 'string'
    }, {
        name: 'ISBN',
        type: 'string'
    }, {
```

```
        name: 'PublishDate',
        type: 'date',
        dateFormat: 'd-m-Y'
    }, {
        name: 'NumberOfPages',
        type: 'int'
    }, {
        name: 'Read',
        type: 'boolean'
    }]
});
```

Parsing date fields correctly

When including date fields in your Models you may need to explicitly tell the model what format the dates being loaded in will have. This is important to remember if your dates are going to be in non-standard formats. It is very easy to achieve this by including the `dateFormat` configuration option in the field's definition. This string will then be used in conjunction with the `Ext.Date.parse` method when the field's data is loaded:

```
fields: [
...
{
        name: 'PublishDate',
        type: 'date',
        dateFormat: 'd-m-Y'
}
...
]
```

Processing a field's data before loading

A field's value can be manipulated very easily before it is loaded into a Model instance by using the `convert` option when defining the field. This option accepts a function that takes two parameters—the field's value and the Model instance as it stands.

 The model instance passed into this function might not be complete depending on the order that the reader has parsed the fields. If you need to perform processing based on other fields, you must make sure that the field order is correct to ensure the field's value exists.

This function can perform any necessary manipulation to the field's value and return it to have the Model store the changed value.

An example of this can be seen as follows, where we define a `convert` function to pre-pend the Book's ISBN number to its Title:

```
...
{
    name: 'Title',
    type: 'string',
    convert: function(v, record){
            return record.get('ISBN') + ' :: ' + v;
    }
}
...
```

See also

> ▸ See the recipe titled *Associating Models and loading nested data* to learn about how to define relationships between Models.

> ▸ The *Loading and saving a Model using proxies* recipe, which explains how to link model's to a server.

> ▸ Learn about how to validate a Model's fields in the *Applying Validation Rules to Models' Fields* recipe.

Loading and saving a Model using proxies

Another huge advantage of the new `Ext.data.Model` class is that it is capable of saving and loading its own data without having to be attached to a data store.

This means that we can create new data objects anywhere within our code and easily send them to the defined URL to be saved by the server. This results in much less code and duplication, which is always a good thing!

This recipe will show this piece of functionality in action, building on our Book model that was used in previous recipe.

Getting ready

This recipe requires a running web server. There are four PHP files (which are supplied) that will be used for loading data into our Model.

How to do it...

1. We start by defining our Model. We will use the Book model used in the previous recipe but will update it by adding an extra field called BookID and assign this as the idProperty:

```
Ext.define('Book', {
        extend: 'Ext.data.Model',
        idProperty: 'BookID',
        fields: [{
                name: 'BookID',
                type: 'int'
        }, {
                name: 'Title',
                type: 'string'
        }, {
                name: 'Publisher',
                type: 'string'
        }, {
                name: 'ISBN',
                type: 'string'
        }, {
                name: 'PublishDate',
                type: 'date',
                dateFormat: 'd-m-Y'
        }, {
                name: 'NumberOfPages',
                type: 'int'
        }, {
                name: 'Read',
                type: 'boolean'
        }],
        validations: [{
                type: 'length',
                field: 'Title',
                min: 1
        }, {
                type: 'presence',
                field: 'Publisher'
        }]
});
```

2. Our next task is to define the Model's proxy. This will define how the Model will load or save itself when asked to. We will use a simple AJAX proxy with a URL defined for each of the four CRUD (Create, Read, Update, Delete) actions:

```
. . .
proxy: {
  type: 'ajax',
  api: {
    read: 'bookRead.php',
    create: 'bookCreate.php',
    update: 'bookUpdate.php',
    destroy: 'bookDestroy.php'
  }
}
```

3. Now that we have a Proxy set up we can use the Book's static `load` method to call the server and fetch a Book's data based on the ID passed in, as in our first example. As the call is asynchronous we use a callback function to simply log the loaded model instance once the AJAX call is complete:

```
Book.load(1, {
  callback: function(book, operation){
    console.log(book);
  }
});
```

4. If we manually create a new Book model instance, and include a `BookID` in its data, we can call the `save` method and see the `bookUpdate.php` file being called, with the Book's data being posted to it:

```
var book = Ext.create('Book', {
    BookID: 1,
    Title: 'Ext JS 4 CookBook',
    Publisher: 'Packt Publishing',
    ISBN: '978-1-849516-86-0',
    PublishDate: '01-01-2012',
    NumberOfPages: 300,
    Read: false
});
book.save();
```

5. Similarly, if we create a Book without a BookID and call the `save` method, the `bookCreate.php` file with be called with the Book's data passed to it.

```
var book = Ext.create('Book', {
    Title: 'Ext JS 4 CookBook',
    Publisher: 'Packt Publishing',
    ISBN: '978-1-849516-86-0',
    PublishDate: '01-01-2012',
```

```
        NumberOfPages: 300,
        Read: false
    });
    book.save();
```

6. Finally, we can delete a Book record by calling the `destroy` method of the Book instance, which will cause an AJAX call to be made to the configured `destroy` URL:

```
var book = Ext.create('Book', {
    BookID: 1,
    Title: 'Ext JS 4 CookBook',
    Publisher: 'Packt Publishing',
    ISBN: '978-1-849516-86-0',
    PublishDate: '01-01-2012',
    NumberOfPages: 300,
    Read: false
});
book.destroy();
```

How it works...

A Proxy takes care of the interaction between our application and an external data source. They come in several varieties but the most common is the AJAX proxy, which allows data to be saved through an AJAX call to a web server, and this is the one we have used in this example.

The `type` configuration tells the Model what type of proxy we require, and will be used to internally instantiate the `Ext.data.proxy.Ajax` class.

The `api` option is used to define the URLs that the Proxy will use to carry out each of the CRUD operations. It is equally possible to specify a single `url` configuration that will be used for all of the operations. In our case, we have a PHP file to handle each action.

Now that we have the interaction setup, we are able to start using them to load and save data.

Each Model class has a static `load` method, which is used to retrieve a Model instance from its defined data source. It accepts an ID as its first parameter and a configuration object, which is applied to the request's options, as its second. The ID we specify is included in the AJAX call and used on the server to retrieve the correct record. You can see the AJAX call in the following screenshot:

⊟ GET	/bookRead.php?_dc=1317403500331&id=1 200 OK 115ms
Params Headers Response HTML JSON Cookies	

```
_dc  1317403500331
 id  1
```

> The _dc parameter is also supplied, and is used for cache busting.

As this is an AJAX call, the results must be consumed in a `callback` function that will be executed when the request is complete.

The key to the next operation is the presence of the BookID, which was defined as the Model's ID property. This property is used to decide which CRUD operation is needed to save the current Model.

If a BookID is present then it is assumed the Model already exists on the server and so an update is carried out. Similarly, if the BookID is missing then the Model will be saved using the create URL and will expect its new BookID to be returned after the create request was successful.

The delete operation is a special case and uses its own method called `destroy`. When called, this will immediately make the proxy carry out its destroy routine, in this case, a call to the server with the details of the record being deleted, as seen here:

See also

- ▸ The previous recipe, *Loading and saving a Model using proxies.*
- ▸ Learn about defining relationships between Models and loading nested data in this chapter's recipe, *Associating Models and loading nested data.*

Loading cross-domain data with a Store

Now that we have a Model, the next step is to load some data into it for use throughout our applications. An `Ext.data.Store` is an ideal way of doing this. It has all the features we require to load and save data and can be linked with a proxy to determine how we may wish to do this (for example, through AJAX, JSONP, and so on)

This recipe will demonstrate how to load data that originates from a different domain directly into your application using JSONP. We are going to use Flickr's API feeds for our cross-domain data.

 JSONP is a method for making cross-domain AJAX requests.

How to do it...

1. Start by defining a model to define the data we are loading:

```
Ext.define('Flickr', {
    extend: 'Ext.data.Model',

    fields: [{
      name: 'title',
      type: 'string'
    }, {
      name: 'link',
      type: 'string'
    }]
});
```

2. Create a store with a JSONP proxy:

```
var JSONPStore = Ext.create('Ext.data.Store', {
    model: 'Flickr',
    proxy: {
        type: 'jsonp',
        url:
'http://api.flickr.com/services/feeds/photos_public.gne',
        callbackKey: 'jsoncallback',
        extraParams: {
            tags: 'swan',
            tagmode: 'any',
            format: 'json'
        }
    },
    reader: {
        type: 'json',
        root: 'items'
    }
});
```

3. Load data into the Store by calling the store's `load` method:

```
JSONPStore.load();
```

4. Finally, once the load has finished check to make sure that the data has loaded correctly by returning the first record from the Model:

```
JSONPStore.on('load', function(){
    var record = JSONPStore.getAt(0);
    console.log(record.data.title + ' ' + record.data.link);
}, this);
```

How it works...

The JSONP proxy allows us to load cross-domain data directly into our app. This could, for example, save you from having to process the remote data on your server before serving it to the client. There are two main tasks that the framework undertakes to load data successfully:

- ▶ A temporary `<script>` tag is inserted in the DOM
- ▶ A temporary callback function is created, which is called as a result of the request

The proxy inserts a `<script>` tag into the DOM to make the request using the `createScript` method of the `Ext.data.JsonP` class:

```
createScript: function(url, params) {
    var script = document.createElement('script');
    script.setAttribute("src", Ext.urlAppend(url, Ext.Object.
toQueryString(params)));
    script.setAttribute("async", true);
    script.setAttribute("type", "text/javascript");
    return script;
}
```

In our case this will return:

```
<script src="http://... &jsoncallback=Ext.data.JsonP.callback1"
async="true" type="text/javascript"></script>
```

The JSON returned by Flickr looks something like the following code snippet:

```
Ext.data.JsonP.callback1({
    "items": [{
        "title": "",
        "link": ""
    }]
})
```

When this data is returned it will automatically run the `Ext.data.JsonP.callback1` function passing the JSON in as a parameter. This is the temporary callback that the framework has made for us in order to load the data into the Model.

There's more...

You need to be careful when using JSONP as there are a few security risks to loading data in this way. Make sure you trust the source of the data as the script they return could, potentially, contain malicious JavaScript.

See also

- ▸ The first recipe of this chapter explaining how to define Models.
- ▸ The *Handling Store exceptions* recipe to learn about how to react to things going wrong.

Associating Models and loading nested data

Ext JS 4 provides a straight forward way for defining relationships between two or more Data Models. This book, for example has two authors, which can be expressed as a one-to-many relationship between a book and its authors with Model associations. The framework has support for three common relationships:

- ▸ One-to-many (`Ext.data.HasManyAssociation`)
- ▸ Many-to-one (`Ext.data.BelongsToAssociation`)
- ▸ Has-one (`Ext.data.association.HasOne`)

This recipe will provide a basic demonstration of linking two Models together and adding associated data to the second, associated, Model from an instance of the first Model. The last part of the recipe will explore loading nested data into these associated Models.

Getting ready

This recipe requires the use of a web server for serving the provided `books.json` file.

How to do it...

1. The first step in linking two Models together is to define them. Start by defining a `Book` model:

```
Ext.define('Book', {
    extend: 'Ext.data.Model',
    fields: [{
        name: 'Title',
        type: 'string'
    }, {
        name: 'Publisher',
        type: 'string'
    }, {
        name: 'ISBN',
        type: 'string'
    }, {
        name: 'PublishDate',
        type: 'date',
        dateFormat: 'd-m-Y'
    }, {
        name: 'NumberOfPages',
        type: 'int'
    }, {
        name: 'Read',
        type: 'boolean'
    }]
});
```

2. The second Model, `Author`, should be defined next:

```
Ext.define('Author', {
    extend: 'Ext.data.Model',
    fields: [{
        name: 'Title',
        type: 'string'
    }, {
        name: 'FirstName',
        type: 'string'
    }, {
        name: 'LastName',
        type: 'string'
    }, {
        name: 'book_id',
        type: 'int'
    }]
});
```

3. Add an association to the `Book` Model:

```
Ext.define('Book', {
    ...
    associations: [{
        type: 'hasMany',
        model: 'Author',
        name: 'authors'
    }]
});
```

 We could also have written this relationship as
`hasMany: ['Author']`

4. Now that we have defined the `Book` Model, we can create an instance of it containing some data about this book:

```
var book = Ext.create('Book', {
    Title: 'Ext JS 4 CookBook',
    Publisher: 'Packt Publishing',
    ISBN: '978-1-849516-86-0',
    PublishDate: '01-01-2012',
    NumberOfPages: 300,
    Read: false
});
```

5. Run the `book.authors()` function, which returns a Store for the authors:

```
var authors = book.authors();
```

6. Add two authors to the `Author` Store. These authors will be linked to the book through a foreign key `book_id`:

```
authors.add({
    Title: 'Mr',
    FirstName: 'Andrew',
    LastName: 'Duncan'
}, {
    Title: 'Mr',
    FirstName: 'Stuart',
    LastName: 'Ashworth'
});
```

7. Create a Store with a `Book` Model and load the provided `books.json` file:

```
var store = Ext.create('Ext.data.Store', {
    model: 'Book',
    autoLoad: true,
    proxy: {
        type: 'ajax',
        url: 'books.json'
    }
});
```

8. When the `load` event has been fired we will do some processing to ensure that the data has been loaded into its respective Models:

```
store.on('load', function(){
    var record = store.getAt(0);
    console.log(record);
    console.log(record.get('Title'));

    var authors = record.getAssociatedData();
    console.log(authors);

    var author = record.authors().getAt(0);
    console.log(author.get('FirstName'));
});
```

How it works...

The association between the two models is defined in the first model (`Book`). The `associations` array in this model contains configuration from the `Ext.data.HasManyAssociation` class. Here we have set the `type`, `model`, and `name`:

- `type` is either `hasMany`, `hasOne` or `belongsTo` depending on the association type
- `model` is the name of the model we wish to associate to
- `name` is the function name that will create the child Store

Now that we have defined the relationship the framework adds a new method to the parent Model. As we have set `name: 'authors'`, this method will be `authors`. When called, `authors` will return a Store instance, configured with the relationship's model type, and will be dynamically filtered to only contain associated data.

When we load the `books.json` file into the Store, the two Models are populated with data even though we have only specified the `Book` model to the Store. The load routine recognizes the array of author data in the `authors` property (based on the association's `name` configuration) as an association and so loads it into the `authors` child store. We can verify this by looking at the data in the Store.

At present you cannot send your associated/nested data back to the server. Each model has to be handled individually when syncing.

There's more...

The previous example has focused on looking at the `hasMany` association. The `belongsTo` association can be used in a very similar fashion. The following example will, once again, demonstrate an association between an author and a book. By using a `belongsTo` association, we are able to load the associated book model for that author:

1. Start by defining an `Author` Model. The `Author` Model will belong to the `Book` Model:

```
Ext.define('Author', {
    extend: 'Ext.data.Model',

    fields: [{
        name: 'Title',
        type: 'string'
    }, {
        name: 'FirstName',
        type: 'string'
    }, {
        name: 'LastName',
        type: 'string'
    }, {
        name: 'book_id',
        type: 'int'
    }],
    belongsTo: 'Book'
});
```

2. Next, define the second model, `Book`, with an AJAX proxy. We'll use this proxy later for loading data:

```
Ext.define('Book', {
    extend: 'Ext.data.Model',

    fields: [{
        name: 'Title',
        type: 'string'
    }],
```

```
        proxy: {
            type: 'ajax',
            url: 'books.json'
        }

    });
```

3. Create an instance of the `Author` model that includes a `book_id` in its data:

```
var author = Ext.create('Author', {
    Title: 'Mr',
    FirstName: 'Joe',
    LastName: 'Bloggs',
    book_id: 1
});
```

4. Call the `getBook` method (that's automatically created by the framework) to initiate a request to the server with the request parameter `id=1`:

```
author.getBook();
```

The authors associated data is loaded when we make a call to the `getBook` method. The `getBook` method is an automatically generated `get` method that loads data through the model's proxy.

When running the example, look at the network tab on your browser's Developer Tools. After the `getBook` method is called a request is made with the parameter `id: 1` to `books.json`. This request is made because we've assigned `book_id: 1` to our author.

Ext.data.association.HasOne

The HasOne association type allows us to link one model instance directly to another in a one-to-one relationship. We will now discuss how to use this association type, once again using our book and author example. In this example, we will assume that a book has one author.

We start by defining our Book model as we have done before, but we will add a new foreign key field that will link our Book and Author models together and define the HasOne association on the Book model.

```
Ext.define('Book', {
    extend: 'Ext.data.Model',
    fields: [
    ...
    {
        name: 'author_id',
        type: 'int'
    }],
```

```
        associations: [{
            type: 'hasOne',
            model: 'Author',
            name: 'author'
        }]
    });
```

Next, we define our Author model and give it a proxy that will be used to load the author data. In this case we will point it to a simple JSON file that contains a standard response with a `success` flag and a `rows` array containing a single Author:

```
Ext.define('Author', {
    extend: 'Ext.data.Model',

    fields: [{
        name: 'Title',
        type: 'string'
    }, {
        name: 'FirstName',
        type: 'string'
    }, {
        name: 'LastName',
        type: 'string'
    }],

    proxy: {
        type: 'ajax',
        url: 'author.json',
        reader: {
            type: 'json',
            root: 'rows'
        }
    }
});
```

The contents of the author's json in the `authors.json` file is:

```
{
    "success": true,
    "rows": [{
        "Title": "Mr",
        "FirstName": "Andrew",
        "LastName": "Duncan"
    }]
}
```

By defining a HasOne association between these two models, a new method is automatically created in the `Book` class called `getAuthor`. This method will use the author model's proxy and the foreign key defined (either explicitly defined by the `foreignKey` config or the default one which is "<association name>_id") to load the associated record.

We can use this method and a callback function to retrieve and then use the associated record as the following code demonstrates:

```
var book = Ext.create('Book', {
    Title: 'Ext JS 4 CookBook',
    Publisher: 'Packt Publishing',
    ISBN: '978-1-849516-86-0',
    PublishDate: '01-01-2012',
    NumberOfPages: 300,
    Read: false,
    author_id: 1
});

book.getAuthor(function(author, operation){
    console.log(author); // our new Author model instance
});
```

Once loaded the `getAuthor` method will return the associated record directly without the need for a callback.

See also

▸ For a detailed introduction to Models we recommend you read the first recipe in this chapter, *Modeling a data object*.

Applying validation rules to Models' fields

A huge advantage of the new data modeling class is that validation rules can be applied directly to the Model's fields. By centralizing the validation of data fields we are able to reduce code duplication and keep our application much more organized.

This recipe will cover how to define validation rules on each of our Model's fields and also how we can create our own validation rules.

How to do it...

1. We will start this recipe with the `Book` Model class we defined in the previous recipes:

```
Ext.define('Book', {
    extend: 'Ext.data.Model',

    fields: [{
        name: 'Title',
        type: 'string'
    }, {
        name: 'Publisher',
        type: 'string'
    }, {
        name: 'ISBN',
        type: 'string'
    }, {
        name: 'PublishDate',
        type: 'date',
        dateFormat: 'd-m-Y'
    }, {
        name: 'NumberOfPages',
        type: 'int'
    }, {
        name: 'Read',
        type: 'boolean'
    }]
});
```

2. Now we use the `validations` configuration to define a minimum length of `1` on the book's title and make the `Publisher` field mandatory:

```
Ext.define('Book', {
    extend: 'Ext.data.Model',

    fields: [{
        name: 'Title',
        type: 'string'
    }, {
        name: 'Publisher',
        type: 'string'
    }, {
        name: 'ISBN',
        type: 'string'
    }, {
```

```
            name: 'PublishDate',
            type: 'date',
            dateFormat: 'd-m-Y'
    }, {
            name: 'NumberOfPages',
            type: 'int'
    }, {
            name: 'Read',
            type: 'boolean'
    }],

    validations: [{
            type: 'length',
            field: 'Title',
            min: 1
    }, {
            type: 'presence',
            field: 'Publisher'
    }]
});
```

3. We can now demonstrate the validation being executed by using the `validate` method of the `Ext.data.Model` class. This method returns an `Ext.data.Errors` instance which contains any errors that were found based on the defined rules:

```
var book = Ext.create('Book', {
    Title: '', // invalid Title
    Publisher: 'Packt Publishing',
    ISBN: '978-1-849516-86-0',
    PublishDate: '01-01-2012',
    NumberOfPages: 300,
    Read: false
});
console.log(book.validate());

var book = Ext.create('Book', {
    Title: '', // invalid Title
    // missing Publisher
    ISBN: '978-1-849516-86-0',
    PublishDate: '01-01-2012',
    NumberOfPages: 300,
    Read: false
});
console.log(book.validate());
```

How it works...

The `validations` array that we populated in step 2 is processed and mapped to the methods and properties contained in the `Ext.data.validations` singleton.

The `field` property is used to link the validator to one of the `Ext.data.Field`s defined on the Model. This is a string value that corresponds to the field's name.

The `type` property determines which validation routine is to be applied to the specified field. This string relates to a method of the `Ext.data.validations` singleton.

Any other properties defined in these objects are passed to the validation method and can be used to customize the validation. In our example, we have defined the `min` property which is used to determine what an invalid string length is.

There's more...

A Model and its fields can be validated in various further ways that we will look at here.

Other built-in validators

There are a total of six built-in validators that can be applied to a Model's fields. In our previous example, we encountered two of them—presence and length. The other four are outlined as follows:

- ▸ `email`: validates that the field contains a valid e-mail address
- ▸ `exclusion`: accepts a `list` configuration containing an array of values and will return true if the field's value is not in the list
- ▸ `inclusion`: identical to exclusion but evaluates to true if the field's value is present in the `list` array
- ▸ `format`: accepts a `matcher` configuration option that should contain a regex for the field's value to be matched against

Creating a custom validator

Although the built-in validators cover the majority of cases, we may need to create our own custom validation routine for special fields. We will walk through how to create a validation routine to validate our `ISBN` field.

Before we begin we will define the rules that will make our ISBN valid (ISBN numbers are more complex than this but we'll use these simplified rules to demonstrate this technique):

- ▸ It must contain 13 digits
- ▸ It must be split into five sections by hyphens

The structure of our validation is similar to that of a `VType`—it has two parts that follow a specific naming convention so they can be referenced easily.

The first part is the validation method itself, whose name will be used to reference it in the `validations` array. This function accepts two parameters and must return a Boolean value. The first parameter contains the configuration object that was defined in the validations array. This can contain any extra properties that we might need to perform our validation, for example, a minimum length. The second parameter contains the actual value of the field that we are validating.

In addition to our validation method we must define an error message that will be used if the field is invalid. This property must be named in the same way as the method with the word `Message` appended to it (that is, if our validator was named `isbn`, our error message would be named `isbnMessage`).

Unfortunately, because the `Ext.data.validations` class is a singleton, we cannot use the usual `Ext.override` method to add new properties. Instead we shall simply define the new validation method and properties that we need on the class instance itself.

 All singleton classes in Ext JS are named with a lowercase first letter that allows them to be easily identifiable within the documentation and code base.

So, using this technique and following the naming guidelines, our ISBN validation will look like this:

```
Ext.data.validations.isbnMessage = 'is not a valid ISBN Number';
Ext.data.validations.isbn = function(config, value){
    return true;
};
```

We can now flesh out the validation function with some simple code to validate the ISBN number based on our defined rules:

```
Ext.data.validations.isbn = function(config, value){
    var valid = false;

    valid = value.length === 17; // 13 digits + 4 hyphens
    valid = valid && (value.split('-').length === 5); // contains 4
hyphens
    return valid;
};
```

Using our new validation is done by including the following configuration item in the `validations` array:

```
...
{
    type: 'isbn',
    field: 'ISBN'
}
...
```

Accessing error details

After executing a Model's `validate` method an instance of the `Ext.data.Errors` class is returned, which contains details of any validation errors that were found. This class extends the `Ext.util.MixedCollection` class and essentially contains a collection of error messages as a result of any failing validation routines. We can interrogate this class to find out if the Model is indeed valid by using the `isValid` method, which returns a Boolean value.

We are also able to get any validation errors for a particular field by calling the `getByField` method, which accepts the field's name as a parameter.

See also

▸ The first recipe of this chapter that demonstrates how to define a data model.

▸ The *Creating custom VTypes* recipe in *Chapter 5*, which explains how to define our own VTypes to validate form fields.

Grouping a Store's data

In Ext JS 3, data grouping was achieved by using the specialist GroupingStore. As a result, grouping data could not be done with more general Store classes. Fortunately, Ext JS 4 encapsulates this grouping functionality into the base Store class so groupings can now be defined on any Store.

We will delve into groupings with a simple example that loads some XML data taken from the Twitter API. We will then continue to demonstrate how to group by specific fields, examine the groupings' data, and manipulate these groupings on the fly.

We will then investigate how we can use these groupings to perform aggregate operations.

Getting ready

We will be loading our XML data through an AJAX call and so you must run these examples on a web server.

Unfortunately, the Twitter API doesn't handle JSONP calls when requesting XML data, so we will be loading the Twitter data manually and pasting it into a static XML file for use in our examples. Our data contains the latest Tweets referring to Sencha.

 You can hook this demo up to the live Twitter API using the JSON format and take advantage of the JSONP proxy if you wish.

How to do it...

1. We will start by examining the XML output of the Twitter API and identifying which fields we want and how it is structured. A sample of the data can be seen as follows (some data has been omitted to save space):

```
<entry>
    <published>
        Published Date
    </published>
    <title>
        Tweet Contents
    </title>
    <author>
        <name>
            Username
        </name>
    </author>
</entry>
```

2. Our first step is to define a Model that will contain our Twitter feed data. We will only map the useful fields that we included, which contain the user, the tweet itself, and the published date:

```
Ext.define('Tweet', {
    extend: 'Ext.data.Model',

    fields: [{
        name: 'user',
        mapping: 'author/name',
        type: 'string'
    }, {
```

```
            name: 'tweet',
            mapping: 'title',
            type: 'string'
        }, {
            name: 'published',
            type: 'date'
        }]
    });
```

3. We now create an `Ext.data.Store` that will be made up of Tweet models and have it load the Tweets with an AJAX proxy, pointing to our static `twitterData.xml` file:

```
var twitterStore = Ext.create('Ext.data.Store', {
    model: 'Tweet',
    proxy: {
        type: 'ajax',
        url: 'twitterData.xml',
        reader: {
            type: 'xml',
            record: 'entry'
        }
    }
});

twitterStore.load();
```

4. Now we can define how we would like to group the store's data. We will group it on the `user` field and, after it has loaded, we will log the grouped data to the console:

```
var twitterStore = Ext.create('Ext.data.Store', {
    model: 'Tweet',
    proxy: {
        type: 'ajax',
        url: 'data.xml',
        reader: {
            type: 'xml',
            record: 'entry'
        }
    },
    groupers: [{
        property: 'user'
    }]
});

twitterStore.load({
```

```
            callback: function(){
                console.log(twitterStore.getGroups());
            }
        });
```

The output of the previous code can be seen in the following screenshot :

▶ 0	Object { name="ExtJSBoy", children=[1] }
▶ 1	Object { name="ExigencyGrok39", children=[1] }
▶ 2	Object { name="Hwyl76", children=[2] }
▶ 3	Object { name="Labretifery25", children=[1] }
▶ 4	Object { name="Ubiquitous92", children=[1] }
▶ 5	Object { name="SherriffBevel18", children=[1] }
▶ 6	Object { name="SemanticsExpiate", children=[2] }
▶ 7	Object { name="ParticipleStammel", children=[5] }
▶ 8	Object { name="OracularTabard", children=[1] }

5. Finally, we will demonstrate how to group the Store at runtime using the `group` method. We will remove our `groupers` configuration and add a grouping on the `published` field:

```
var twitterStore = Ext.create('Ext.data.Store', {
    model: 'Tweet',
    proxy: {
        type: 'ajax',
        url: 'twitterData.xml',
        reader: {
            type: 'xml',
            record: 'entry'
        }
    }
});

twitterStore.load({
    callback: function(){
        twitterStore.group('published');

        console.log(twitterStore.getGroups());
    }
});
```

The output from the `getGroups` method can be seen as follows:

⊞ 0	Object {	name=Date, children=[1] }
⊞ 1	Object {	name=Date, children=[2] }
⊞ 2	Object {	name=Date, children=[1] }
⊞ 3	Object {	name=Date, children=[1] }
⊞ 4	Object {	name=Date, children=[1] }
⊞ 5	Object {	name=Date, children=[1] }
⊞ 6	Object {	name=Date, children=[1] }
⊞ 7	Object {	name=Date, children=[1] }
⊞ 8	Object {	name=Date, children=[1] }
⊞ 9	Object {	name=Date, children=[1] }
⊞ 10	Object {	name=Date, children=[1] }
⊞ 11	Object {	name=Date, children=[1] }
⊞ 12	Object {	name=Date, children=[1] }
⊞ 13	Object {	name=Date, children=[1] }

We can remove the defined groupings by calling the store's `clearGrouping` method. This will fire the `groupchange` event (which is also fired when groupings are added using the `group` method) allowing you to have your UI react accordingly.

How it works...

When you define the `groupers` configuration option the framework creates an `Ext.util.Grouper` object for each item in the array. This class is an extension of the `Ext.util.Sorter` class and works by adding a new sorter (that is, itself) to the beginning of the Store's `sorter` array, ensuring it is used first. Once the Store has been sorted, a call to the `getGroups` method can be made, making the Store process the records and collect each set of records whose grouped fields match.

Although the `groupers` configuration option can accept an array of definitions it is only capable of one level of grouping and so the first one is always used.

The Store's `group` method allows it to be grouped at runtime. It accepts a single parameter containing one of the Model's field names. When this is called, the current set of groupers is thrown away and the new one put in its place.

Extracting Records from XML

If you examine the `twitterData.xml` file, you will see that the data is not structured in the way we are used to with JSON data as there is no records array containing each set of data. To get around this, and allow the XML reader to find each record, we define the `record` option and set it to the element's name that contains the repeating record data.

Field Mapping

You may have noticed that the name of the Twitter user is nested within the `author` element but is still loaded into the model's `user` field. This is achieved by using the `mapping` configuration option, which allows us to define a path to the piece of data we want to fill the field with. In our example, we have used XML data and so this option uses an XPath expression to navigate down from the record's root to the correct node. If JSON data had been used, we would have used the object dot notation (for example, `author.name`) to achieve the same result.

There's more...

Being able to calculate aggregate values on a collection of data is very useful and allows us to easily provide summary data to users.

The `Ext.data.Store` class contains five aggregate methods allowing the minimum (`min`), maximum (`max`), `sum`, `count`, and `average` of a field's values to be calculated.

All of these methods, except `count`, take two parameters. The first contains the name of the field to be aggregated and the second a Boolean deciding if the aggregate should be calculated on a per group basis. The `count` method does not need the first parameter as it is not specific to a field and so only accepts a Boolean value.

The following example shows minimum and maximum published dates being calculated for our Twitter data:

```
twitterStore.min('published'); // returns a single Date
twitterStore.max('published'); // returns a single Date
twitterStore.min('Published', true); //returns an Object
```

To have the results returned on a per group you would simply pass `true` into each method, as seen in the third example, and the results would be returned as an object containing name/value pairs of the grouped value and the aggregate value.

See also

▸ The recipe *Loading and saving a Model using proxies*.

Handling Store exceptions

Unfortunately we cannot guarantee that the server will process our stores' requests correctly 100 percent of the time. When the server returns an error or fails to respond, it's useful to be ready to inform our users that something has not worked as expected and perhaps perform extra processing or tidying up. This recipe demonstrates how to handle proxy exceptions and present an error message to the user.

Getting ready

To demonstrate exception handling you will need to ensure that you have a running web server to host the example and serve the provided `error-response.json` file.

How to do it...

1. Define the Model that we will attempt to load data into:

```
Ext.define('Book', {
    extend: 'Ext.data.Model',

    fields: [{
        name: 'Title',
        type: 'string'
    }]
});
```

2. Add an AJAX Proxy to the Model, defining the `url` config option as `error-response.json`:

```
Ext.define('Book', {
    ...
    proxy: {
        type: 'ajax',
        url: 'error-response.json'
    }
});
```

3. Listen for the `exception` event on the AJAX proxy. The `exception` event will be fired should the server return an exception:

```
proxy: {
    ...
    listeners: {
        'exception': function(proxy, response, operation, eOpts){
        }
    }
}
```

4. Add logic to the function to change the behavior depending on the type of error.

```
'exception': function(proxy, response, operation, eOpts){
    if (response.status !== 200) {
        alert(response.status + ' ' + response.statusText);
    } else {
        var responseText = Ext.decode(response.responseText);
        alert(responseText.error);
    }
}
```

If the server responds with a 200 Status Code and the exception event has been fired then it is safe to assume that the responses `success` property is set to `false`. In this case, we will output the `error` value in the `responseText` property. However, should the server respond with another Status Code (for example, 404, 500...) then we will output the Status Code and Status Text.

How it works...

The AJAX proxy's superclass `Ext.data.proxy.Server` contains an `exception` event that is fired when the server responds with an error (that is, the `success` property is `false`) or an HTTP exception.

By listening for this event we can perform some additional processing on the response and, if desired, alert the user to the fact that there has been a problem. This is done in the `exception` event's handler.

The `response` parameter contains the response from the AJAX request. We can check the HTTP status code sent from the server by reading the `status` property (`response.status`) and get access to the text body of the response with the `responseText` property. As `error-response.json` returns JSON, we can decode this with the `Ext.decode()` method and work with the data that is returned.

 For a different outcome to the previous example try changing the name of the URL we are calling to a non-existent file or altering the `error-response.json` to return `"success": true`

There's more...

To help you get the most out of exception handling there are a couple of extra pieces of information that are worth noting.

Add a generic response handler to all AJAX proxies

If the way you wish to handle exceptions to requests made from an AJAX proxy remains fairly consistent throughout your application, you could write a generic exception handler. This piece of code will fire the `GenericReponseHandler` function when the `exception` event is fired from an AJAX proxy in your app. The magic happens in `Ext.util.Observable. observe(Ext.data.proxy.Ajax)`.

Here, the `observe` method allows us to centrally handle events fired on any instance of the `Ext.data.proxy.Ajax` class:

```
var GenericResponseHandler = function(proxy, response, operation,
eOpts){
    if (response.status !== 200) {
        alert(response.status + ' ' + response.statusText);
    }
    else {
        var responseText = Ext.decode(response.responseText);
        Ext.Msg.alert('Generic Response', responseText.error);
    }
};
Ext.util.Observable.observe(Ext.data.proxy.Ajax);
Ext.data.proxy.Ajax.on('exception', GenericResponseHandler);
```

Ext.data.proxy.Server's afterRequest method

The subclasses of `Ext.data.proxy.Server` inherit its `afterRequest` method which is called when the server's response is processed. You can override this method in your proxy instance to perform some extra logic after each request is made.

 The `afterRequest` is called regardless of the response from the server. You can use the success parameter that is passed in to determine the outcome of the response. This will help you customize the clean-up routine based on the response outcome.

See also

▸   The recipe explaining how to load and save models using proxies.

▸   The recipe about *App Wide Exception Handling* in *Chapter 12*.

Saving and loading data with HTML5 Local Storage

Ext JS 4 provides a new LocalStorageProxy (`Ext.data.proxy.LocalStorage`) which allows you to save data to the client's browser with the HTML5 localStorage API.

This recipe demonstrates how to use this proxy to save and retrieve your user's settings.

How to do it...

1. Start by defining the `UserSetting` model with the following fields. We are going to assign `userID` as the `idProperty` and you will see why this is important later.

> If we do not assign our own id field the `Ext.data.Model` will create one automatically for us called `id`.

```
Ext.define('UserSetting', {
    extend: 'Ext.data.Model',

    idProperty: 'userID',

    fields: [{
        name: 'userID',
        type: 'int'
    }, {
        name: 'fontSize',
        type: 'string'
    }, {
        name: 'theme',
        type: 'string'
    }, {
        name: 'language',
        type: 'string'
    }, {
        name: 'dateFormat',
        type: 'string'
    }]
});
```

2. Add a proxy to the `UserSetting` model, setting the proxy `type` to `localstorage`. We need to give the proxy a unique key prefix for storing items in localStorage. To do this set `id: 'user-settings'`.

```
Ext.define('UserSetting', {
    ...
    proxy: {
        type: 'localstorage',
        id: 'user-settings'
    }
});
```

3. Now create an instance of the `UserSetting` model and assign it to the `settings` variable.

```
var settings = Ext.create('UserSetting', {
    userID: 1,
    fontSize: 'medium',
    theme: 'default',
    language: 'en-gb',
    dateFormat: 'd/m/Y'
});
```

4. Call the `save` method on the model instance to persist the data to localStorage.

```
settings.save();
```

Having saved the model instance to localStorage we can see the values by looking at your browser's Developer Tools. As you can see the unique key prefix `user-settings` (set on the proxy) appears in the Key column. In addition to this a `-1` has appeared at the end of the `user-settings` Key in the first row. This value is the `userID` or `idProperty` set on the model. The second row contains an index of all `UserSetting` records stored in localStorage.

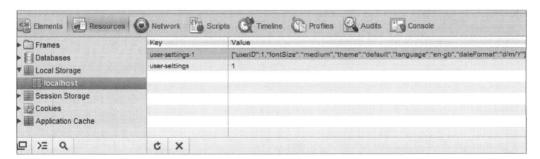

5. Having saved data to localStorage it is now time to retrieve it. Load the data by calling the `load` method on the `UserSetting` class. Pass in the `userID` to the first parameter and a `load` configuration object to the second parameter. Add a callback to the `load` configuration object to prove that we are able to retrieve the data.

```
UserSetting.load(1, {
    callback: function(model, operation){
        console.log(model.get('language'));
    }
});
```

How it works...

HTML5 Local Storage provides a method to store named key/value pairs locally on the browser. One particularly useful feature of Local Storage is persistent data. Even when the browser is closed the data will become accessible again when the user next visits your app.

 There are size restrictions to Local Storage, usually 5 or 10 megabytes.

Harnessing HTML5 Local Storage is done by using a `LocalStorageProxy`. The `LocalStorageProxy` performs two main tasks:

- Communication with the browser's Local Storage (retrieving/storing data)
- Serializing and de-serializing data

The second task is particularly helpful as it means we're not limited to working with simple key/value pairs. The `LocalStorageProxy` allows us to work with complex data objects as we would with other proxies.

 HTML5 Local Storage is not supported by all web browsers, notably Internet Explorer 6 and 7. Before using the `LocalStorageProxy` you will need to ensure support for the browser(s) you are targeting otherwise an error will be thrown.

See also

- The recipe *Loading and saving a Model using proxies*.

8
Displaying and Editing Tabular Data

In this chapter, we will cover:

- ▶ Displaying simple tabular data
- ▶ Editing grid data with a RowEditor
- ▶ Adding a paging toolbar for large datasets
- ▶ Dealing with large datasets with an infinite scrolling grid
- ▶ Dragging-and-dropping records between grids
- ▶ Creating a grouped grid
- ▶ Custom rendering of grid cells with template columns
- ▶ Creating summary rows aggregating the grid's data
- ▶ Displaying full-width row data with the RowBody feature
- ▶ Adding a context menu to grid rows
- ▶ Populating a form from a selected grid row
- ▶ Adding buttons to grid rows with action columns

Introduction

Displaying tabular data is a very common task in modern web applications and has made the `Ext.grid.Panel` one of the most popular and heavily used components in the framework. Sencha has worked hard on perfecting the performance and features of the data grid bundled with Ext JS 4.

This chapter will cover the basics of simple grids and move on to advanced topics, such as infinite scrolling and grouping. We will also demonstrate how to edit data easily, customize how we present the data, and link your grids with other Ext JS components.

Displaying simple tabular data

This recipe walks you through the steps required to display tabular data using a grid component in Ext JS 4. Grids allow us to display data and allow the user to interact with it through various plugins and features.

To demonstrate displaying simple tabular data, we will create a straightforward grid panel (with the `Ext.grid.Panel` class). The grid will display a list of invoices with the following columns:

- **Client**
- **Date**
- **Amount**
- **Status**

The final grid is shown in the following screenshot:

Client ▲	Date	Amount	Status	
Ace Outsourcin...	Sat Oct 08 2011...	500.5	Sent	
Acme Corporation	Sat Oct 08 2011...	1000	Viewed	
Acme Corporation	Sat Oct 08 2011...	380	Paid	
Global Interacti...	Sat Oct 08 2011...	200	Paid	

Chapter 8 - Grids

Getting ready

This recipe uses a generic `Ext.data.Store` and `Ext.data.Model`, which can be found in the `invoices-store.js` and `invoices-model.js` files, respectively. We have bundled these with the resources for this chapter.

How to do it...

1. Include the `invoices-model.js` file. This model will define the fields that we are expecting to load:

   ```
   <script type="text/javascript" src="invoices-model.js">
   </script>
   ```

The code that we are including is shown as follows:

```
Ext.define('Invoice', {
    extend: 'Ext.data.Model',
    fields: [{
        name: 'InvoiceID',
        type: 'string'
    }, {
        name: 'Client',
        type: 'string'
    }, {
        name: 'Description',
        type: 'string'
    }, {
        name: 'Date',
        type: 'date',
        dateFormat: 'c'
    }, {
        name: 'Amount',
        type: 'float'
    }, {
        name: 'Currency',
        type: 'string'
    }, {
        name: 'Status',
        type: 'string'
    }]
});
```

2. Include the `invoices-store.js` file. This will define the store for loading data into the grid:

```
<script type="text/javascript" src="invoices-store.js">
</script>
```

The code that we are including is shown as follows:

```
var invoiceStore = Ext.create('Ext.data.Store', {
  autoLoad: true,
  autoSync: true,
  model: 'Invoice',
  groupField: 'Client',
    proxy: {
        type: 'ajax',
        url: 'invoices.json',
        reader: {
```

```
                    type: 'json',
                    root: 'rows'
                },
                writer: {
                    type: 'json',
                    writeAllFields: false
                }
            }
        });
```

 We configure our store with `autoSync: true` for use in the next few recipes. By setting this to `true` the store will automatically send any changes to the server as soon as they are made.

3. Create a grid panel that is bound to our `invoiceStore` and render it to the document's body. We do this by instantiating the `Ext.grid.Panel` class. We also define our grid's columns that match the invoice model's data:

```
Ext.create('Ext.grid.Panel', {
    title: 'Chapter 8 - Grids',
    height: 300,
    width: 600,
    store: invoiceStore,
    columns: [{
        header: 'Client',
        dataIndex: 'Client'
    }, {
        header: 'Date',
        dataIndex: 'Date'
    }, {
        header: 'Amount',
        dataIndex: 'Amount'
    }, {
        header: 'Status',
        dataIndex: 'Status'
    }]
    renderTo: Ext.getBody()
});
```

How it works...

A **grid panel** is a data-bound component and is linked to an `Ext.data.Store` instance. In this case our `invoiceStore` is the data source used for rendering the grid rows. The grid will render a row for each of the Model instances contained in the data store.

Apart from the `store` option, `columns` is the only other configuration option needed to have a grid display a store's data. This option takes an array of `Ext.grid.column.Column` class configurations, namely including a `header`, which is displayed at the top of each column, and a `dataIndex`. This option maps to an `Ext.data.Field` that exists in the store's Model and indicates what data will be displayed in the column.

See also

▸ The previous chapter for a more detailed look at models and stores.

Editing grid data with a RowEditor

The grid panel has built-in features to allow users to amend data directly from the grid. Over and above single-cell editing, Ext JS 4 introduces a new row-editing plugin, which renders a row's fields as editable and displays an **Update** and **Cancel** button for when the user is finished.

The **RowEditor** turns each cell into an editable field (`Ext.form.field`), which the user can interact with when editing data. The fields are not limited to `textfields` either as it's possible to add any type of field, such as `datefields`, `numberfields`, or `comboboxes`.

This recipe will demonstrate how to turn a basic grid panel into an editable grid using the `RowEditor` plugin. We will demonstrate how to render different field types and configurations, depending on the type of data in the column. By the end of the recipe, the edited data will be sent to the server for processing through the grid's `store` and `proxy`:

Row Editing Example			
Client ▲	Date	Amount	Status
Ace Outsourcing Resources	08/10/2011	500.50	Sent
Acme Corporation	08/10/2011	1000	Viewed
Acme Corporation	Update Cancel	380.00	Paid
Global Interactive Technologies		200.00	Paid

Getting ready

We are going to use the Invoice example that we have used throughout this chapter. We will start by including the Model and Store files to our HTML page:

```
<script type="text/javascript" src="invoices-model.js">
</script>
<script type="text/javascript" src="invoices-store.js">
</script>
```

How to do it...

1. We need to ensure that the store is ready for submitting saved data to the server. In this case we are going to define a `JsonWriter` on the store. Set the writer to only submit changed fields to the server:

    ```
    var invoiceStore = Ext.create('Ext.data.Store', {
        ...
        proxy: {
            ...
            writer: {
                type: 'json',
                writeAllFields: false
            }
        }
    });
    ```

     As we only want to submit the rows we have edited, we will need to ensure that the Model has the correct `idProperty` defined. Set `idProperty: 'InvoiceID'` in the model. Failing to do this will result in all records being sent to the server.

2. The next step is to create the `RowEditing` plugin. It's possible to add custom configuration to the plugin. For example, set `clicksToEdit: 1` so that the `RowEditor` will appear after a click to a cell:

    ```
    var rowEditing = Ext.create('Ext.grid.plugin.RowEditing', {
        clicksToEdit: 1
    });
    ```

3. Create a grid panel that is bound to the `invoiceStore`.

4. Add the `rowEditing` plugin and set the Grid's selection model to `rowmodel`.

```
Ext.create('Ext.grid.Panel', {
    title: 'Row Editing Example',
    height: 300,
    width: 600,
    store: invoiceStore,
    plugins: [rowEditing],
    selType: 'rowmodel',
    columns: [],
    style: 'margin: 50px',
    renderTo: Ext.getBody()
});
```

5. Finally, define the columns for the grid. We also add an `editor` configuration to each of the columns that require editing capabilities. These editors are the fields rendered when in edit mode:

```
Ext.create('Ext.grid.Panel', {
    ...
    columns: [{
        header: 'Client',
        dataIndex: 'Client',
        flex: 1,
        editor: {
            allowBlank: false
        }
    }, {
        header: 'Date',
        dataIndex: 'Date',
        format: 'd/m/Y',
        xtype: 'datecolumn',
        editor: {
            xtype: 'datefield',
            format: 'd/m/Y',
            allowBlank: false
        }
    }, {
        header: 'Amount',
        dataIndex: 'Amount',
        xtype: 'numbercolumn',
        editor: {
            xtype: 'numberfield',
            allowBlank: false,
            hideTrigger: true,
            minValue: 1,
            maxValue: 150000
```

```
                }
        }, {
            header: 'Status',
            dataIndex: 'Status'
        }],
        ...
    });


    Ext.create('Ext.grid.Panel', {
        ...
        plugins: [cellEditing],
        selType: 'cellmodel',
        columns: [{
            header: 'Client',
            dataIndex: 'Client',
            flex: 1,
            editor: {
                allowBlank: false
            }
        }, {
            header: 'Date',
            dataIndex: 'Date',
            format: 'd/m/Y',
            xtype: 'datecolumn',
            editor: {
                xtype: 'datefield',
                format: 'd/m/Y',
                allowBlank: false
            }
        }, {
            header: 'Amount',
            dataIndex: 'Amount',
            xtype: 'numbercolumn',
            editor: {
                xtype: 'numberfield',
                allowBlank: false,
                hideTrigger: true,
                minValue: 1,
                maxValue: 150000
            }
        }, {
```

```
        header: 'Status',
        dataIndex: 'Status'
    }],
    ...
});
```

 If no `xtype` is defined the editor will default to being a `TextField`.

How it works...

There are three key points to note about using a RowEditor to update grid data:

1. **Ensure that the proxy and store are ready**: To enable the grid to write the data back to our server we need to check that:

   - The proxy has a writer. You may also wish to consider setting `writeAllFields: false` if you only want to send the updated data back to the server (as opposed to the entire record).

   - If your identity field is not named `id`, make sure you have set the `idProperty`. Failure to do so will result in all records being sent to the server.

   - Unless you intend to manually send the data to the server it can be helpful to define `autoSync: true` on the store. On every update the store will synchronize the data with the server.

   Having set the proxy and store we can now save the data. When we change the `Client` field for the third invoice, the following data is submitted:

After processing your submitted data, your server must respond with the complete record so that the store can complete the save process. By doing this the records will be marked as clean again and any IDs generated for new records will be assigned to the record.

2. **Configure the Row Editing plugin on the grid**: Adding the `RowEditing` plugin and `RowEditor` to a grid requires little configuration. Achieving this is done by creating an instance of `Ext.grid.plugin.RowEditing` in the grid's `plugins` collection.

   We've configured this `RowEditing` plugin to activate on a click of the mouse (on a cell) by setting `clicksToEdit: 1`.

    It's important to ensure that the selection model for the grid is `rowmodel` when using a `RowEditor`.

   The `RowEditing` plugin will now handle the rest for us by rendering a floating dialog to present the editable fields with an **Update** and **Cancel** button.

3. **Define editors for the editable columns**: The editors are the configuration for `Form` fields that will be rendered when the `RowEditing` plugin is active. The editor defaults to `textfield`, however it's possible to replace this with any field and configuration specific to the field type. This has been demonstrated with the date field and number field, which were applied to the **Date** and **Amount** columns.

There's more...

The `RowEditor` provides an excellent way to update the data across all columns of a row. However, there are some instances where we may wish to edit a grid's data on a cell-by-cell basis.

Editing grid data with a celleditor

In this example, when the user clicks on a cell, the cell's editor will be activated:

Cell Editing Example			
Client ▲	Date	Amount	Status
Ace Outsourcing Resources	08/10/2011	500.50	Sent
Acme Corporation|	08/10/2011	1,000.00	Viewed
Acme Corporation	08/10/2011	380.00	Paid
Global Interactive Technologies	08/10/2011	200.00	Paid

To achieve this, all that we are required to do is swap out the `RowEditing` plugin for a `CellEditing` plugin and change the row-selection model to a cell-selection model:

```
var cellEditing = Ext.create('Ext.grid.plugin.CellEditing', {
    clicksToEdit: 1
});

Ext.create('Ext.grid.Panel', {
```

```
...
    plugins: [cellEditing],
    selType: 'cellmodel',
    columns: [{
        header: 'Client',
        dataIndex: 'Client',
        flex: 1,
        editor: {
            allowBlank: false
        }
    }, {
        header: 'Date',
        dataIndex: 'Date',
        format: 'd/m/Y',
        xtype: 'datecolumn',
        editor: {
            xtype: 'datefield',
            format: 'd/m/Y',
            allowBlank: false
        }
    }, {
        header: 'Amount',
        dataIndex: 'Amount',
        xtype: 'numbercolumn',
        editor: {
            xtype: 'numberfield',
            allowBlank: false,
            hideTrigger: true,
            minValue: 1,
            maxValue: 150000
        }
    }, {
        header: 'Status',
        dataIndex: 'Status'
    }],
    ...
});
```

See also

▸ For a reminder on using the `Form` fields in this example take a look at *Chapter 6, Using and Configuring Form Fields*.

▸ A more detailed explanation of models and stores can be found in the previous chapter.

Adding a paging toolbar for large datasets

When you need to load a large dataset there are a number of options available to enhance the experience for the user and reduce load on the server. A paging toolbar (`Ext.toolbar.Paging`) enables you to request that a limited number of records returned from the server. The toolbar will then display a series of buttons to allow the user to move from page to page.

Global Interactive Technologies (6)	Sun Apr 03 201...	282.66	Paid
Global Interactive Technologies (7)	Tue May 17 201...	74.13	Draft
Global Interactive Technologies (8)	Wed Jun 08 201...	207.93	Draft
Global Interactive Technologies (9)	Mon Jun 14 201...	9.39	Viewed
Global Interactive Technologies (10)	Sun Oct 25 200...	138.29	Draft

|◀ ◀ Page 1 of 120 ▶ ▶| ⟳   Displaying Invoices 1 - 50 of 6000

In this recipe, we will render a grid with a paging toolbar that loads a maximum of 50 records at a time.

Getting ready

We are going to use the Invoice example that we have used throughout this chapter. So we will start by including the Model file to our HTML page:

```
<script type="text/javascript" src="invoices-model.js">
</script>
```

Additionally, the Store will request data from `invoices.php`, which is provided, to return 6,000 dynamically generated records and handle the requests from the client. For more information on creating the large dataset see *Dealing with large datasets with an infinite scrolling grid*.

How to do it...

1. Define a Store with an `AjaxProxy` for binding to the grid. Set the store's `pageSize` configuration option to `50`. Assign the store to the variable `invoiceStore`:

```
var invoiceStore = Ext.create('Ext.data.Store', {
    autoLoad: true,
    model: 'Invoice',
    pageSize: 50,
    proxy: {
        type: 'ajax',
        url: 'invoices.php',
        reader: {
```

```
            type: 'json',
            root: 'rows'
        }
    }
});
```

2. Create a grid that is bound to the `invoiceStore` (created in step 1) with the following column configuration:

```
Ext.create('Ext.grid.Panel', {
    title: 'Paging Toolbar',
    height: 300,
    width: 600,
    store: invoiceStore,
    columns: [{
        header: 'Client',
        dataIndex: 'Client',
        flex: 1
    }, {
        header: 'Date',
        dataIndex: 'Date'
    }, {
        header: 'Amount',
        dataIndex: 'Amount'
    }, {
        header: 'Status',
        dataIndex: 'Status'
    }],
    renderTo: Ext.getBody()
});
```

3. In the grid's configuration add an `Ext.PagingToolbar` docked to the bottom of the grid through the `bbar` config option. The paging toolbar should also be bound to the same Store as the grid (`invoiceStore`):

```
Ext.create('Ext.grid.Panel', {
    ...
    bbar: Ext.create('Ext.PagingToolbar', {
        store: invoiceStore,
        displayInfo: true,
        displayMsg: 'Displaying Invoices {0} - {1} of {2}',
        emptyMsg: "No invoices to display"
    })
    ...
});
```

How it works...

As the example shows, it's very straightforward adding a paging toolbar to a grid. The requests made to the server have three additional parameters when a paging toolbar is defined:

- page
- start
- limit

On the `invoiceStore` (an instance of `Ext.data.Store`) we are only required to define the `pageSize`. The `pageSize` is used for the `limit` parameter that is sent to the server, which is in this case 50. Therefore, the user interface is requesting up to 50 records at a time.

When the data is returned from the server you must ensure that the `total` property contains the total number of possible records in the dataset.

```
{
    "success": true,
    "total": 6000,
    "rows": [{}]
}
```

The paging toolbar uses the value of `total` to calculate the page we are on, the records we are viewing, and the total number of pages available. In this case, it calculates `total/pageSize` = 120.

The `start` parameter is used to inform the server where we want to start the dataset from. It could, for example, start from record 300 with a limit of 50 therefore return rows 300 to 350.

See also

- The next recipe for an alternative to paging.
- The *Creating a DataView bound to a Data Store* recipe in *Chapter 4, UI Building Blocks—Trees, Panels, and Data Views*, which includes details about adding filtering controls to a toolbar.

Dealing with large datasets with an infinite scrolling grid

Coping with large amounts of data has always been a problem in web applications. We are often faced with extensive datasets that the browser simply can't cope with rendering all at once.

We have already explored a traditional solution for combating this by paging the data and offering the user previous/next buttons that navigate them to the next subset of data. This approach has proven its success across the web, with the majority of the big players using it across their sites. We will demonstrate a slightly different approach to solving this problem that removes the paging interaction of the user.

The infinite scrolling grid is designed to trick the user into thinking that they are dealing with one large data grid containing all of their data. However, what is actually happening is that they are seeing many smaller datasets, stitched together and dynamically loaded as the scroll position changes.

This recipe is going to show how this technique can be achieved to create a data grid that will progressively load thousands of records.

Getting ready

There are a couple of tasks we must do before we start creating our grid, namely creating a data source and importing our Invoice Model:

Creating a large data source: In order to demonstrate the infinite scrolling in action, we are going to need a large dataset. We are going to stick with our Invoice Management grid example; but we will cheat a little bit and create a PHP file, which will generate the set of data that we are looking for with some indexes in the **Client** field so we can see it is changing. We will be sending up a `limit` and `start` parameter to let the server know what slice of the result set the grid requires, and so we will use these to loop on and create an array of data. The following code snippet demonstrates this loop:

```
$total = 6000;
$limit = $_GET['limit'];
$start = $_GET['start'];
$invoices = array();
$statuses = array('Paid', 'Viewed', 'Draft', 'Partial');

for($i = $start; $i< $start + $limit; $i++){
    $invoice = array('InvoiceID' => ($i),
    'Client' => 'Global Interactive Technologies (' . ($i) . ')',
    'Description' => 'Creating an Invoice management system',
    'Date' => date("c", rand(time()-63113851,time())),
    'Amount' =>number_format((rand()+1)/100, 2),
    'Currency' => 'GBP',
    'Status' => $statuses[rand(0,3)]);
    $invoices[] = $invoice;
}

echo json_encode(array('success' => true, 'total' => $total,
'rows' => $invoices));
```

Importing our Invoice Model: We are going to reuse the Invoice Model we created in this chapter's first recipe and so we must include the `invoice-model.js` file into our HTML page.

How to do it...

Now that we have a large data source and our Invoice Model set up we can start to create our infinite scrolling grid.

1. We start by creating an `Ext.data.Store` with an AJAX proxy pointing to our `invoices.php` file discussed in the Getting Started section. The store includes two new options that we haven't seen before. The `buffered` and `pageSize` options are required for the store to load a page at a time. We also give the store the `autoLoad: true` configuration so it will load our data immediately.

```
var invoiceStore = Ext.create('Ext.data.Store', {
    model: 'Invoice',
    pageSize: 50,
    buffered: true,
    autoLoad: true,
    proxy: {
        type: 'ajax',
        url: 'invoices.php',
        reader: {
            type: 'json',
            root: 'rows'
        }
    }
});
```

2. All we need to do now is to create a very simple `Ext.grid.Panel`, bound to the `invoiceStore`, with a simple column configuration. If we load up our example and start scrolling we will see the data load as we scroll down.

```
Ext.create('Ext.grid.Panel', {
    title: 'Chapter 8 - Grids',
    height: 300,
    width: 600,
    store: invoiceStore,
    columns: [{
        header: 'Client',
        dataIndex: 'Client'
    }, {
        header: 'Date',
        dataIndex: 'Date'
    }, {
        header: 'Amount',
        dataIndex: 'Amount'
```

```
    }, {
        header: 'Status',
        dataIndex: 'Status'
    }],
    renderTo: Ext.getBody()
});
```

How it works...

As already mentioned, the infinite scrolling grid works by tricking the user into thinking that they are scrolling through the complete data set when actually they are only actually scrolling through a small subset with the next portion being loaded as it is needed.

If you dig into the HTML that is generated for this grid you will notice that the scrollbar and the actual grid rows are completely separate. The visible scrollbar is actually scrolling a very tall, narrow div, which represents the height the grid would be, if the entire dataset were to be loaded and rendered at once.

The highlighted element in the following screenshot shows this div, with a height of 120,000 pixels:

```
▼<div id="gridpanel-1009-body" class="x-panel-body x-grid-body x-panel-body-default x-panel-body-
default x-layout-fit" style="width: 600px; left: 0px; height: 253px; top: 47px; ">
    ▼<div id="gridview-1015" class="x-grid-view x-fit-item x-grid-view-default x-unselectable" style=
    "overflow: auto; position: relative; -webkit-user-select: none; margin: 0px; width: 598px; height:
    251px; " tabindex="-1">
        <div style="position: absolute; width: 1px; top: 0px; left: 0px; height: 120000px; " id="ext-
        gen1042"></div>
        ▶<table class="x-grid-table x-grid-table-resizer" border="0" cellspacing="0" cellpadding="0" style=
        "width: 585px; position: absolute; top: 0px; ">…</table>
    </div>
</div>
```

As the user moves the scrollbar and starts to near the end of the rendered rows the store is notified and it sends a call to the server requesting the next page of data adjusting the start parameter as needed.

If a user was to scroll down the grid very quickly, the scroller is clever enough to realize that it doesn't need any of the rows in between the old scroll position and the new, so misses out these pages and only loads the one that equates to its new position.

The Ext.grid.PagingScroller class is responsible for applying this functionality to the grid and is created internally when a buffered store is used. We can configure this class by supplying an object literal to the verticalScroller configuration of the grid panel.

The Ext.data.Store requires very few configuration changes to get this functionality working. The Store has a pageSize defined, which is used as the limit parameter that is sent to the server. By tweaking this option you can optimize the performance of the grid loading to suit the height of your grid. If your grid is taller than our example, you will want to increase this value so more records are fetched with each store load so a new set isn't fetched as often.

The `buffered` option tells the Store that it will be used in conjunction with a view that will be progressively loading records as they are needed.

There's More...

It is possible to further tune the behavior of the paging scroller through a few of its configuration options. These can be applied by including the `verticalScroller` option in the grid's configuration:

- ▶ `leadingBufferZone`: This represents the number of rows to render ahead of the leading side of the scrolling view's visible area.
- ▶ `trailingBufferZone`: This represents the number of rows to render behind the scrolling view's visible area.
- ▶ `scrollToLoadBuffer`: This determines the number of milliseconds to buffer the next page load. We can use this to avoid wasted AJAX calls when scrolling very fast through a list.

In addition to tweaking the paging scroller's configuration we can also tune our grid's performance by adding some config options to our data store:

- ▶ `leadingBufferZone`: This determines how many records are cached ahead of the grid view's visible area. By increasing this number you will require fewer server requests as the user scrolls.
- ▶ `trailingBufferZone`: Similarly, this will determine how many records are retained behind the view's visible area.

Try playing with the values of these properties to see how the number of AJAX requests and the number of table rows in the DOM changes.

See also

- ▶ The first recipe in this chapter that focuses on the basics of grid panels.
- ▶ The previous recipe provides an example of paging a grid and contains further background information that you might find useful.

Dragging-and-dropping records between grids

Allowing users to drag-and-drop items from one container to another is a very visual and user-friendly way of manipulating data. Ext JS provides us with very easy-to-use drag-and-drop classes that make including this functionality in grids simple.

Once again we will base our example on the Invoice Management scenario and we will create two grids. The first will contain unpaid invoices and the second paid invoices. We are going to set up drag-and-drop to allow the user to move an invoice from the unpaid invoices grid to the paid invoices grid and vice versa.

Getting ready

We are going to use the Invoice example that we have used throughout this chapter, so we will start by including the Model and Store files to our HTML page:

```
<script type="text/javascript" src="invoices-model.js">
</script>
<script type="text/javascript" src="invoices-store.js">
</script>
```

How to do it...

1. Having included our basic Invoice Store and Model, our first step is to create our two grids. The first, containing unpaid invoices, will be bound to our `invoicesStore`, and the second bound to a new empty store:

```
var unpaidInvoicesGrid = Ext.create('Ext.grid.Panel', {
    title: 'Unpaid Invoices',
    height: 300,
    width: 600,
    store: invoiceStore,
    columns: [{
        header: 'Client',
        dataIndex: 'Client'
    }, {
        header: 'Date',
        dataIndex: 'Date'
    }, {
        header: 'Amount',
        dataIndex: 'Amount'
    }, {
        header: 'Status',
        dataIndex: 'Status'
    }],
    renderTo: Ext.getBody()
});

var paidInvoicesGrid = Ext.create('Ext.grid.Panel', {
    title: 'Unpaid Invoices',
    height: 300,
```

```
        width: 600,
        store: new Ext.data.Store({
            model: 'Invoice'
        }),
        columns: [{
            header: 'Client',
            dataIndex: 'Client'
        }, {
            header: 'Date',
            dataIndex: 'Date'
        }, {
            header: 'Amount',
            dataIndex: 'Amount'
        }, {
            header: 'Status',
            dataIndex: 'Status'
        }],
        renderTo: Ext.getBody()
});
```

2. Next, we configure the `Ext.grid.plugin.DragDrop` plugin as part of each grid's view configuration. It takes two options, in addition to its `ptype` value, namely `dragGroup` and `dropGroup`:

```
// Unpaid Invoices Grid
...
viewConfig: {
    plugins: [{
      ptype: 'gridviewdragdrop',
      dragGroup: 'unpaid-group',
      dropGroup: 'paid-group'
    }]
}
...


// Paid Invoices Grid
...
viewConfig: {
    plugins: [{
      ptype: 'gridviewdragdrop',
      dragGroup: 'paid-group',
      dropGroup: 'unpaid-group'
    }]
}
...
```

3. With the `Ext.grid.plugin.DragDrop` plugin configured on both grids, the drag-and-drop functionality is complete and rows can be dragged from one grid to another as shown as follows:

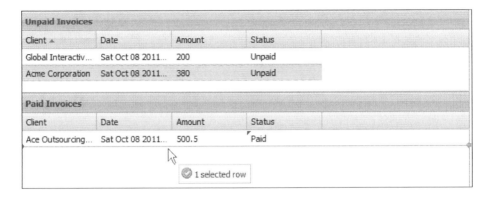

How it works...

The `Ext.grid.plugin.DragDrop` plugin encapsulates the drag-and-drop functionality and gives us a simple interface to create draggable grid rows.

The `dragGroup` and `dropGroups` work together across all the created `DragDrop` plugin instances to link grids together in terms of where rows can be dragged to and from.

In our unpaid grid we gave it a `dragGroup` of `unpaid-group`; we then specify a `dropGroup` of `unpaid-group` in our paid grid. By giving these properties equivalent values, it tells the plugin that any rows of `dragGroup` unpaid-group can be dropped in any grid that has a `dropGroup` of unpaid-group too.

Similarly the unpaid grid has a `dropGroup` matching the paid grid's `dragGroup` to allow rows to be dragged back again.

When a row is dragged from one grid to another, the Model that the row represents is removed from its original grid's data store and added to the destination grid's store. If we have `autoSync` set to true on these stores, and a proxy defined, you will see an AJAX call being made to save the newly added record in the target store and a delete call being made for the source store's removed record.

There's more...

We will now explore how to perform some actions after a row has been successfully dropped and also how to enable rows to be dropped within the same grid allowing rows to be reordered.

Updating a row's data after dropping

The `Ext.grid.plugin.DragDrop` plugin adds two events to the grid's view class—`beforedrop` and `drop`. We will use the `drop` event to update our dropped model instance with its new status:

1. We start by adding a listener for the `drop` event to the `viewConfig` of the unpaid invoices grid:

```
. . .
viewConfig: {
    plugins: [{
      ptype: 'gridviewdragdrop',
      dragGroup: 'unpaid-group',
      dropGroup: 'paid-group'
    }],
    listeners: {
        drop: function(node, data, overModel, dropPosition){
        }
    }
}
. . .
```

2. We can now access an array of the models that are being dragged from the `data` parameter's `records` property. We will then iterate through this array and update each model's `Status` field to `Unpaid`:

```
. . .
drop: function(node, data, overModel, dropPosition){
    var records = data.records;
    Ext.each(records, function(record){
        record.set('Status', 'Unpaid');
    });
}
. . .
```

3. We can add the same code to the paid invoices grid; but replacing the `Unpaid` string with `Paid`:

```
. . .
    drop: function(node, data, overModel, dropPosition){
        var records = data.records;
        Ext.each(records, function(record){
            record.set('Status', 'Unpaid');
        });
    }
. . .
```

Allowing rows to be reordered with drag-and-drop

In our first example, we defined our DragDrop plugins to allow dragging between the two grids by matching the dragGroup and dropGroup values. We can define as many Ext.grid.plugin.DragDrop instances as we like to allow dragging between any number of grids within your application.

By simply defining another Ext.grid.plugin.DragDrop instance with the dragGroup and dropGroup set to the same value, we are able to drag-and-drop within the same grid. The following code shows this second plugin instance configured to allow rows to be reordered:

```
viewConfig: {
    plugins: [{
      ptype: 'gridviewdragdrop',
      dragGroup: 'unpaid-group',
      dropGroup: 'paid-group',
    }, {
      ptype: 'gridviewdragdrop',
      dragGroup: 'unpaid-group',
      dropGroup: 'unpaid-group',
    }],
    listeners: {
        drop: function(node, data, overModel, dropPosition){
            var records = data.records;

            Ext.each(records, function(record){
                record.set('Status', 'Unpaid');
              });
          }
        }
      }
    }
```

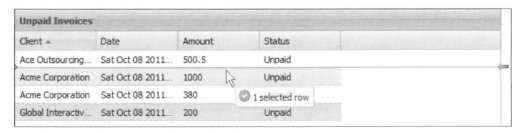

See also

▸ The previous chapter for more information on models and stores.

▸ The final chapter of the book, which discusses how to create your own plugins.

Creating a grouped grid

Grouping data together helps present the information clearly to users. Ext JS 4 provides a grouping feature (`Ext.grid.feature.Grouping`) that groups records using the Store's `groupers` and displays a title for each group:

Grouping Example			
Client ▲	Date	Amount	Status
▣ Client: Ace Outsourcing Resources (1 Invoice)			
Ace Outsourcing Resources	08/10/2011	500.50	Sent
▣ Client: Acme Corporation (2 Invoices)			
Acme Corporation	08/10/2011	1,000.00	Viewed
Acme Corporation	08/10/2011	380.00	Paid
▣ Client: Global Interactive Technologies (1 Invoice)			
Global Interactive Technologies	08/10/2011	200.00	Paid

To demonstrate the grouping feature we will group all invoices by **Client**.

Getting ready

We are going to use the Invoice example that we have used throughout this chapter so we will start by including the Model and Store files to our HTML page:

```
<script type="text/javascript" src="invoices-model.js">
</script>
<script type="text/javascript" src="invoices-store.js">
</script>
```

How to do it...

Now that you have included the necessary Model and Store we need to make a few changes:

1. Add a `groupField` to the `invoiceStore`. We will group this grid by the `Client` field. It is also possible to define more elaborate groupers using the `Ext.util.Grouper` class.

```
var invoiceStore = Ext.create('Ext.data.Store', {
    ...
    groupField: 'Client',
    proxy: {
        ...
    }
});
```

2. Assign a grouping feature to the variable `grouping`. The configuration of this grouping feature will give the group a customized header to display the client name and number of invoices in that group:

```
var grouping = Ext.create('Ext.grid.feature.Grouping', {
    groupHeaderTpl: 'Client: {name} ({rows.length}
Invoice{[values.rows.length> 1 ? "s" : ""]})'
});
```

3. Create a basic grid bound to the `invoiceStore`. Include the grouping feature created above by adding the `grouping` variable to the `features` collection:

```
Ext.create('Ext.grid.Panel', {
    title: 'Grouping Example',
    height: 300,
    width: 600,
    store: invoiceStore,
    features: [grouping],
    columns: [{
        header: 'Client',
        dataIndex: 'Client',
        flex: 1
    }, {
        header: 'Date',
        dataIndex: 'Date',
        xtype: 'datecolumn',
        format: 'd/m/Y'
    }, {
        header: 'Amount',
        dataIndex: 'Amount',
        xtype: 'numbercolumn'
    }, {
        header: 'Status',
        dataIndex: 'Status'
    }],

    style: 'margin: 50px',
    renderTo: Ext.getBody()
});
```

How it works...

The grouping feature makes use of grouped data that is aggregated by the `groupers` we set on the Store. To achieve this grouping we have defined the `groupField` property as `Client`.

With the grouped data ready (in the store) the grid panel's grouping feature takes care of the rest. It's simply a case of adding the feature to the grid's `features` collection. It is also possible to do this inline in the grid in the following way:

```
features: [{
    ftype: 'grouping',
    groupHeaderTpl: '...'
}]
```

 An `ftype` is a shorthand way of instantiating a feature in the same way as an `xtype` is used for widgets and a `ptype` is used for plugins.

The `Ext.grid.feature.Grouping` that we created has a customized group header, which was created by defining the `groupHeaderTpl` property. The underlying processing for `groupHeaderTpl` is done with an `Ext.Template`. Therefore, we are able to customize the output of this with the passed `values`.

 For more information about templates please refer to *Chapter 4*, where they are discussed in greater depth.

There's more...

The grouping feature adds a number of extra events that are fired when the user interacts with the group. For instance, when the group is clicked or expanded we can add additional custom processing to create the desired experience. A number of methods are also inherited in the grouping feature.

Making use of the grouping feature events and methods

When grid grouping is enabled five additional events are available to the grid. These can be accessed by adding a listener to the grid's configuration like so:

```
Ext.create('Ext.grid.Panel', {
    ...
    listeners: {
        groupclick: function(grid, node, group){
            alert(group);
        }
    },
    ...
});
```

The `groupclick` listener is fired every time the user clicks on the group header. In this example the group name appears in a JavaScript alert.

We can also add additional configurations to the grouping feature. The `startCollapsed` config option here collapses all the groups when first rendered:

```
var moreGrouping = Ext.create('Ext.grid.feature.Grouping', {
    groupHeaderTpl: 'Client: {name}',
    startCollapsed: true
});
```

The buttons in this top toolbar call the `enable` and `disable` methods available to the instantiated grouping feature:

```
Ext.create('Ext.grid.Panel', {
    ...
    features: [moreGrouping],
    tbar: [{
        text: 'Enable Groups',
        handler: function(){
            moreGrouping.enable();
        }
    }, {
        text: 'Disable Groups',
        handler: function(){
            moreGrouping.disable();
        }
    }],
    ...
});
```

See also

▶ You may find the recipes in *Chapter 4* useful when working with XTemplates.

Custom rendering of grid cells with TemplateColumns

The `Ext.grid.column.Template` class is a new column type that has been introduced in Ext JS 4. It allows a very easy mechanism for formatting a grid's columns with an `Ext.XTemplate` so you can have full control over your grid's displayed data.

We will continue with our Invoice Management example, and in this recipe we are going to explore how to use this new class to add extra information and formatting to the **Client** and **Amount** grid columns.

Getting ready

As with all the recipes in this chapter so far, we are going to use the generic Invoices `Ext.data.Model` and `Ext.data.Store`, which can be found in the `invoices-store.js` and `invoices-model.js`. These have been bundled with the resources for this chapter and both files will need to be included in your HTML like so:

```
<script type="text/javascript" src="invoices-model.js">
</script>
<script type="text/javascript" src="invoices-store.js">
</script>
```

How to do it...

1. Now we have the Model and Store in place. We can create a basic grid panel that is bound to our `invoiceStore`. This grid has columns defined for four of the Model's fields: `Client`, `Date`, `Amount`, and `Status`:

```
Ext.create('Ext.grid.Panel', {
    title: 'Chapter 8 - Grids',
    height: 300,
    width: 600,
    store: invoiceStore,
    columns: [{
        header: 'Client',
        dataIndex: 'Client'
    }, {
        header: 'Date',
        dataIndex: 'Date'
    }, {
        header: 'Amount',
        dataIndex: 'Amount'
    }, {
        header: 'Status',
        dataIndex: 'Status'
    }]
});
```

2. Now we have our basic structure in place we can define the Client column as an `Ext.grid.column.Template` column. We do this by adding an `xtype` to its column definition and giving it the value `templatecolumn`:

```
...
xtype: 'templatecolumn',
...
```

3. We can add the `tpl` configuration option and assign it a string containing our template. We will simply display the client's value and then the invoice's description in a span under it. We are also going to add a QuickTip to it in case it is too long for the cell to contain:

```
{
    xtype: 'templatecolumn',
    header: 'Client',
    dataIndex: 'Client',
    tpl: '{Client}<br/><span class="description" data-qtip="{Descr
iption}">{Description}</span>'
}
```

4. Finally, we'll add a quick CSS style to make it look a bit better:

```
.description {
    color: #666;
    font-size: 0.9em;
    margin-top: 4px;
}
```

5. We can now see the output in the following screenshot:

How it works...

Although it gives us a lot of control over our grid cells, the `Ext.grid.column.Template` class must be one of the smallest in the framework. It extends the base `Ext.grid.column.Column` class and naturally can be configured with all of its options.

The `Ext.grid.column.Template` class makes use of the base column's `renderer` option and creates a new `renderer` function that applies the current grid row's Model instance (and all of its loaded associated data) to the column's `tpl` property. If this property is a string it is used to create a new `Ext.XTemplate` instance, otherwise the instance is used directly. The output of applying the Model's data to this template is then displayed in the cell.

> The `renderer` option of a column allows the cell's data and appearance to be manipulated before it is rendered to the screen. For example, it can be used to apply conditional styles to a cell or to calculate a new value based on other data in the Model instance.

There's more...

As well as accepting a string the `tpl` option can accept an actual `Ext.XTemplate` instance. We will show this in action by converting the `Amount` column into a `template` column, and using an explicit `Ext.XTemplate` instance to format the currency and add the `Currency` field:

1. As before, we start by adding the `Ext.grid.column.Template` column's xtype (`templatecolumn`) to the column.

2. Our next step is to assign the `tpl` option an `Ext.XTemplate` object and define the template string itself:

```
. . .
tpl: new Ext.XTemplate(
   '{Amount}',
   '<span class="currency">{Currency}</span>'
)
. . .
```

3. If you view this you will see the `Currency` field showing but our `Amount` field is not showing two decimal places. We can fix this by adding a formatting function as part of our `Ext.XTemplate` (as we have done in previous chapters) and use this to format our float:

```
tpl: new Ext.XTemplate(
      '{Amount:this.formatAmount}',
      '<span class="currency">{Currency}</span>', {
      formatAmount: function(val){
            return val.toFixed(2);
      }
)
```

4. As in the first example, we will add some CSS styling to format our currency type and the outcome can be seen in the following screenshot:

See also

▸ For a more detailed explanation of XTemplates, it's worth looking back to *Chapter 4* where we've provided a number of useful examples.

Creating summary rows aggregating the grid's data

It is often useful to summarize data that is displayed in a grid. For example, you may wish to display the number of rows, sum the values in a column, or calculate the average (mean) for a column.

Ext JS 4 provides a useful feature for grids to allow us to display a summary row in the last row or, if it is a grouped grid, in the last row of each group. The `Ext.grid.feature.Summary` and `Ext.grid.feature.GroupingSummary` classes provide the tools required to do so:

This recipe will demonstrate how to add a summary row to your grid and perform custom rendering on the value.

Getting ready

We are going to use the Invoice example that we have used throughout this chapter so we will start by including the Model and Store files to our HTML page:

```
<script type="text/javascript" src="invoices-model.js">
</script>
<script type="text/javascript" src="invoices-store.js">
</script>
```

How to do it...

1. Create a grid panel with the following configuration and column configuration:

```
Ext.create('Ext.grid.Panel', {
    title: 'Summary Example',
    height: 300,
    width: 600,
    store: invoiceStore,
    columns: [{
        header: 'Client',
        dataIndex: 'Client',
        flex: 1
    }, {
        header: 'Date',
        dataIndex: 'Date',
        xtype: 'datecolumn',
        format: 'd/m/Y'
    }, {
        header: 'Amount',
        dataIndex: 'Amount',
        xtype: 'numbercolumn'
    }, {
        header: 'Status',
        dataIndex: 'Status'
    }],
    style: 'margin: 50px',
    renderTo: Ext.getBody()
});
```

2. In the grid's `features` collection add `summary` as `ftype`. Then add a `summaryType` and custom `summaryRenderer` to the `Amount` column to sum the total value of all invoices:

```
Ext.create('Ext.grid.Panel', {
    ...
```

```
        features: [{
          ftype: 'summary'
        }],
        columns: [{
            header: 'Client',
            dataIndex: 'Client',
            flex: 1
        }, {
            header: 'Date',
            dataIndex: 'Date',
            xtype: 'datecolumn',
            format: 'd/m/Y'
        }, {
            header: 'Amount',
            dataIndex: 'Amount',
            xtype: 'numbercolumn',
            summaryType: 'sum',
            summaryRenderer: function(value, summaryData, field){
                return '&pound;' + Ext.Number.toFixed(value, 2);
            }
        }, {
            header: 'Status',
            dataIndex: 'Status'
        }],
        ...
    });
```

3. Finally, add a `count` summary to the `Client` column and apply a custom `summaryRenderer` to display the total number of invoices in this grid:

```
    Ext.create('Ext.grid.Panel', {
        ...
        columns: [{
            header: 'Client',
            dataIndex: 'Client',
            flex: 1,
            summaryType: 'count',
            summaryRenderer: function(value, summaryData, field){
                return Ext.String.format('{0} Invoice{1}', value,
    value !== 1 ? 's' : '');
            }
        },
        ...
        ]
        ...
    });
```

4. To customize the style of the summary row, add the following CSS in the HEAD element of your HTML page:

```
<style type="text/css">
    .x-grid-row-summary .x-grid-cell-inner {
        font-weight: bold;
    }
</style>
```

How it works...

The summary-row feature is added to the grid by adding `ftype: 'summary'` to the grid's `features` collection. Having done this, it's now simply a case of adding the `summaryType` option to the desired column's configuration.

Ext JS 4 provides five built-in summary types that are listed as follows:

- count
- sum
- min
- max
- average

These perform the calculation on the specified record's fields. Of course, it is possible to write a custom `summaryType` by supplying a function definition, for example:

```
summaryType: function(value) { // Calculation code here }
```

We use the `summaryRenderer` to customize the output value of the summary.

The `Amount` column's `summaryRenderer` ensures that the summed value is displayed to two decimal places with a pound sterling symbol.

In the `Client` column, we define our parameterized string (`{0} Invoice{1}`) and pass the desired arguments to replace the parameters. The first parameter is replaced with `value` (the count of all rows) and the second is replaced with the outcome of the following condition:

```
value !== 1 ? 's' : ''
```

This enables us to display the word *Invoices* when the number of rows is greater than one.

There's more...

In addition to adding a summary to the last row of a grid, it's also possible to summarize the data in a grouping grid.

Summary data in a grouping grid

Swap out the grouping `ftype` from the features collection for a `groupingsummary` `ftype`.
We can define other grouping configuration options (such as the `groupHeaderTpl`)
here as well. The `summaryType` and `summaryRenderer` are the same as the standard
summary feature:

```
Ext.create('Ext.grid.Panel', {
    ...
    features: [{
      groupHeaderTpl: 'Client: {name}',
      ftype: 'groupingsummary'
    }],
    columns: [{
        header: 'Client',
        dataIndex: 'Client',
        flex: 1,
        summaryType: 'count',
        summaryRenderer: function(value, summaryData, field){
            return Ext.String.format('{0} Invoice{1}', value,
            value !== 1 ? 's' : '');
        }
    }, {
        header: 'Date',
        dataIndex: 'Date',
        xtype: 'datecolumn',
        format: 'd/m/Y'
    }, {
        header: 'Amount',
        dataIndex: 'Amount',
        xtype: 'numbercolumn',
        summaryType: 'sum',
        summaryRenderer: function(value, summaryData, field){
                return '&pound;' + Ext.Number.toFixed(value, 2);
        }
    }, {
        header: 'Status',
        dataIndex: 'Status'
    }],
    ...
});
```

Displaying full-width row data with the RowBody feature

Although grids are generally about rows and columns of individual values, we often have a need to display some extra information that describes the entire row rather than a single column. In a traditional HTML table we could display this as a second TR containing a cell spanning all of the table's columns. This would then allow extra information, which might be too large for a single cell to display, alongside the separate cell values.

Ext JS contains a similar feature that allows us to create a full-width row below the column-separated row to display additional information relating to that row.

This recipe will show how we can achieve this to display one of our Model's fields, and then how to expand it to contain HTML generated from an `Ext.XTemplate`. The following screenshot shows our final goal:

Chapter 8 - Grids			
Client ▲	Date	Amount	Status
Ace Outsourcing Resources	Sat Oct 08 2011 00:00:00 GMT+010...	500.5	Sent
Description: Design and build a Sencha Touch mobile application.			
Acme Corporation	Sat Oct 08 2011 00:00:00 GMT+010...	1000	Viewed
Description: Develop an Ext JS 4 CMS			
Acme Corporation	Sat Oct 08 2011 00:00:00 GMT+010...	380	Paid
Description: Train our staff how to use Ext JS 4			
Global Interactive Technologies	Sat Oct 08 2011 00:00:00 GMT+010...	200	Paid
Description: Creating an Invoice management system			

Getting ready

We will include the standard Invoices Model and Store we have used throughout this chapter into our HTML page with the following code.

```
<script type="text/javascript" src="invoices-model.js">
</script>
<script type="text/javascript" src="invoices-store.js">
</script>
```

How to do it...

1. As before we start with a basic grid, containing four columns, which is bound to our Invoice's Store:

```
Ext.create('Ext.grid.Panel', {
    title: 'Chapter 8 - Grids',
    height: 300,
    width: 600,
    store: invoiceStore,
    columns: [{
        header: 'Client',
        dataIndex: 'Client',
        flex: 1
    }, {
        header: 'Date',
        dataIndex: 'Date',
        width: 200
    }, {
        header: 'Amount',
        dataIndex: 'Amount'
    }, {
        header: 'Status',
        dataIndex: 'Status'
    }],
    renderTo: Ext.getBody()
}];
```

2. Our next step is to create a new `Ext.grid.feature.RowBody` instance and add it to our grid's `features` configuration option:

```
...
features: [Ext.create('Ext.grid.feature.RowBody', {})],
...
```

3. If we view the result so far, we can see the RowBody being added but it is empty.

4. We must now configure it to display the data we want. We do this by overriding the `getAdditionalData` method of the `Ext.grid.feature.RowBody` class, which returns an object literal that is applied to the RowBody's markup template. We set the `rowBody` property of the returned object to the description contained in our Model's data.

```
features: [Ext.create('Ext.grid.feature.RowBody', {
    getAdditionalData: function(data){
        var headerCt = this.view.headerCt,
            colspan = headerCt.getColumnCount();
```

```
        return {
            rowBody: data.Description,
            rowBodyCls: this.rowBodyCls,
            rowBodyColspan: colspan
        };
    }
```

5. Our result now looks much better with each Invoice's description being displayed under its main row. However, the two rows look very disconnected and the grid's selection model does not include the RowBody in its selection styling:

Chapter 8 - Grids			
Client ▲	Date	Amount	Status
Ace Outsourcing Resources	Sat Oct 08 2011 00:00:00 GMT+010...	500.5	Sent
Design and build a Sencha Touch mobile application.			
Acme Corporation	Sat Oct 08 2011 00:00:00 GMT+010...	1000	Viewed
Develop an Ext JS 4 CMS			
Acme Corporation	Sat Oct 08 2011 00:00:00 GMT+010...	380	Paid
Train our staff how to use Ext JS 4			
Global Interactive Technologies	Sat Oct 08 2011 00:00:00 GMT+010...	200	Paid
Creating an Invoice management system			

6. We solve this problem by adding another grid feature called the `Ext.grid.feature.RowWrap` to the grid's `features` array. We do this by using its `ftype` (which, as mentioned earlier, is similar to an `xtype` but is specific for features):

```
. . .
{
    ftype: 'rowwrap'
}
. . .
```

How it works...

The `Ext.grid.features.RowBody` class works by injecting extra HTML into the grid's view based on the returned template from the class's `getRowBody` method. This template is used in conjunction with the data object that is created within the `getAdditionalData` method that we created in step 4. The important output of this method is the `rowBody` property of the returned object. This value is used to replace the RowBody's main template placeholder and forms the content of the new row.

The other two properties of the returned object, `rowBodyCls` and `rowBodyColspan`, are used to define the CSS class applied to the RowBody's TR element and the number that is given to the table cell's `colspan` property respectively.

The final step adds the `Ext.grid.feature.RowWrap` class that wraps the grid's row content with a child table element containing the grid's normal row, and the extra row added by the `RowBody` feature. By using this feature it makes the `RowBody` part of the selectable area and combines the two rows in a much more visually appealing way.

There's more...

The value of the `rowBody` property discussed in step 4 above is simply injected into the row's only cell and so can contain any text or markup that we want. We will demonstrate this by creating a simple `Ext.XTemplate`, which will allow us to format the content of the RowBody:

1. We start by creating an `Ext.XTemplate` as a property of the `Ext.grid.feature.RowBody` instance applied to the grid:

```
Ext.create('Ext.grid.feature.RowBody', {
    rowBodyTpl: new Ext.XTemplate('<span style="font-weight:
bold;">Description: </span>{Description}'),

    getAdditionalData: function(data){
        var headerCt = this.view.headerCt,
            colspan = headerCt.getColumnCount();

        return {
            rowBody: data.Description,
            rowBodyCls: this.rowBodyCls,
            rowBodyColspan: colspan
        };
    }
});
```

2. We can then access this template, apply the data parameter to it, and assign the
   output to the `rowBody` property:

```
Ext.create('Ext.grid.feature.RowBody', {
    rowBodyTpl: new Ext.XTemplate('<span style="font-weight:
bold;">Description: </span>{Description}'),

    getAdditionalData: function(data){
        var headerCt = this.view.headerCt,
            colspan = headerCt.getColumnCount();

        return {
            rowBody: this.rowBodyTpl.apply(data),
            rowBodyCls: this.rowBodyCls,
            rowBodyColspan: colspan
        };
    }
});
```

3. The output of this shows a bold **Description** label beside each row's description value
   as seen in the screenshot at the beginning of the recipe.

> The `getAdditionalData` method runs in the scope of the
> `Ext.grid.feature.RowBody`'s instance and so allows us
> to access the `Ext.XTemplate` stored in the `rowBodyTpl`
> property using the `this` keyword.

See also

▶ For further information on XTemplate's please refer back to *Chapter 4*.

Adding a context menu to grid rows

Context menus are a huge part of desktop computing: often, when we right-click on an object,
we expect to see a list of actions that can be performed.

This recipe is going to explain how we can create a context menu that will be shown when the
user right-clicks on a row, and that will allow them to instigate an action upon it.

We are going to use the Invoice example that we have used throughout this chapter, so we will start by including the Model and Store files to our HTML page:

```
<script type="text/javascript" src="invoices-model.js">
</script>
<script type="text/javascript" src="invoices-store.js">
</script>
```

How to do it...

1. Our first step is to create a basic grid, such as the one we created in the first recipe of this chapter:

```
var invoicesGrid = Ext.create('Ext.grid.Panel', {
    title: 'Chapter 8 - Grids',
    height: 300,
    width: 600,
    store: invoiceStore,
    columns: [{
        header: 'Client',
        dataIndex: 'Client'
    }, {
        header: 'Date',
        dataIndex: 'Date'
    }, {
        header: 'Amount',
        dataIndex: 'Amount'
    }, {
        header: 'Status',
        dataIndex: 'Status'
    }],
    renderTo: Ext.getBody()
});
```

2. We now instantiate an `Ext.menu.Menu` object and configure it with a height, width, and a collection of `Ext.menu.Items` that will be our action buttons:

```
var contextMenu = Ext.create('Ext.menu.Menu', {
    height: 100,
    width: 125,
    items: [{
        text: 'View Invoice',
        icon: 'icons/document-text.png'
```

```
        }, {
            text: 'Edit Invoice',
            icon: 'icons/pencil.png'
        }, {
            text: 'Re-Send Invoice',
            icon: 'icons/envelope-label.png'
        }, {
            text: 'Delete Invoice',
            icon: 'icons/minus-circle.png'
        }]
    });
```

3. We can now hook the right-click event of the grid to a function that will show our menu. This event is named `itemcontextmenu` and will fire when a grid row is right-clicked.

4. We add a handler by using the grid's `on` method and make two method calls inside it. The first, `stopEvent`, prevents the right-click event from showing the browser's native context menu; and the second displays our menu at the position the right-click occurred:

```
invoicesGrid.on({
    itemcontextmenu: function(view, record, item, index, e){
        e.stopEvent();

        contextMenu.showAt(e.getXY());
    }
});
```

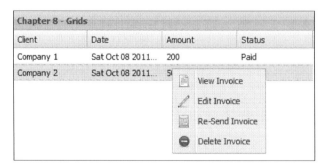

5. Our final step is to handle each of our menu items' click event, so that we can perform an action. We will do this by using the `defaults` option of the `Ext.menu.Menu` class and define a click handler that will log the text of the button that was clicked:

```
defaults: {
    listeners: {
        click: function(item){
```

```
            console.log(item.text + ' Clicked!');
        }
    }
},
```

How it works...

The important part of this recipe is the `itemcontextmenu` event of the `Ext.grid.Panel` class. This allows us to react to a user's right-click and displays a menu when it occurs.

The call to the `Ext.EventObject`'s `stopEvent` method stops the event from cascading to other components and also stops the browser handling the event itself, thus preventing the browser's native context menu from appearing.

In step 4 we have made use of the `defaults` configuration option, which every subclass of `Ext.container.AbstractContainer` has. This option allows a set of properties to be defined in one place, and they will be applied to each of the container's child items. In our case, this meant we only had to define the menu items' click handler once, reducing the amount of code we have to write and maintain.

There's more...

Obviously when a user right-clicks on a specific row and chooses an option, we want to pass information about the targeted row to the action's code. We will now demonstrate a quick way of getting the selected record, which can then be passed through and used in our action code:

1. We start by adding an `itemId` to each of our menu items. This will allow us to figure out which button was clicked while maintaining a single-click handling function:

```
[{
    text: 'View Invoice',
    icon: 'icons/document-text.png',
    itemId: 'viewButton'
}, {
    text: 'Edit Invoice',
    icon: 'icons/pencil.png',
    itemId: 'editButton'
}, {
    text: 'Re-Send Invoice',
    icon: 'icons/envelope-label.png',
    itemId: 'resendButton'
}, {
    text: 'Delete Invoice',
```

```
        icon: 'icons/minus-circle.png',
        itemId: 'deleteButton'
}]
```

2. Next, we use the `getSelection` method of the grid's selection model class to return an array of the selected rows. In our example, only one row is selectable at a time and this selection changes on each right-click:

```
var selectedRecords = invoicesGrid.getSelectionModel().
getSelection();
```

3. Finally, we check to ensure that there is a row selected and use the first one in a switch statement to execute the correct code for the clicked menu item:

```
if (selectedRecords.length > 0) {
  var record = selectedRecords[0];
    switch (item.itemId) {
        case 'viewButton':
            // Do View logic
            break;
        case 'editButton':
            // Do Edit logic
            break;
        case 'resendButton':
            // Do Re-Send logic
            break;
        case 'deleteButton':
            // Do Delete logic
            break;
    }
    console.log(Ext.String.format('{0} - {1} for {2} {3}', item.
text, record.get('Client'), record.get('Amount'), record.
get('Currency')));
}
```

See also

▶ We explore buttons and menus in more detail in *Chapter 9, Constructing Toolbars with Buttons and Menus.*

Populating a form from a selected grid row

Binding grid data to other components provides a useful way to display data differently or enable users to edit the data away from the grid. This recipe will demonstrate how to bind a grid to a form, update the record, and have the grid reflect the changes.

Getting ready

We are going to use the Invoice example that we have used throughout this chapter. So we will start by including the Model and Store files to our HTML page:

```
<script type="text/javascript" src="invoices-model.js">
</script>
<script type="text/javascript" src="invoices-store.js">
</script>
```

How to do it...

1. Create a grid bound to the `invoiceStore` with the following column configuration:

```
var grid = Ext.create('Ext.grid.Panel', {
    title: 'Chapter 8 - Grids',
    height: 300,
    width: 600,
    store: invoiceStore,
    columns: [{
        header: 'Client',
        dataIndex: 'Client',
        flex: 1
    }, {
        header: 'Date',
        dataIndex: 'Date'
    }, {
        header: 'Amount',
        dataIndex: 'Amount'
    }, {
        header: 'Status',
        dataIndex: 'Status'
    }],
    style: 'margin: 50px',
    renderTo: Ext.getBody()
});
```

2. Create a form panel with the following field configuration. Ensure the field names map directly between the Model and the Form. Additionally, the date field's `submitFormat` must be the same as the Model's date format:

```
var formPanel = Ext.create('Ext.form.Panel', {
    title: 'Invoice Form',
    bodyPadding: 5,
    width: 350,
    layout: 'anchor',
```

```
        defaults: {
            anchor: '100%'
        },
        defaultType: 'textfield',
        items: [{
            fieldLabel: 'Client',
            name: 'Client'
        }, {
            fieldLabel: 'Date',
            name: 'Date',
            xtype: 'datefield',
            submitFormat: 'c'
        }, {
            fieldLabel: 'Amount',
            name: 'Amount',
            xtype: 'numberfield',
            hideTrigger: true,
            keyNavEnabled: false,
            mouseWheelEnabled: false
        }, {
            fieldLabel: 'Status',
            name: 'Status',
            xtype: 'displayfield'
        }],

        style: 'margin: 50px',
        renderTo: Ext.getBody()
    });
```

3. Ensure the grid has a row selection model and add a `listener` to listen to the `select` event of `Ext.selection.RowModel`. When a row is selected we load the record into the form panel:

```
var grid = Ext.create('Ext.grid.Panel', {
    ...
    selType: 'rowmodel',
    listeners: {
        select: function(RowModel, record, index, eOpts){
            formPanel.loadRecord(record);
        }
    },
    ...
});
```

4. Add a button to the form panel to submit the data back to the Model. This will update the grid and submit the data to the server.

```
var formPanel = Ext.create('Ext.form.Panel', {
    ...
    buttons: [{
        text: 'Update Data',
        handler: function(){
            var form = this.up('form').getForm();
            var recordIndex = form.getRecord().index;
            var formValues = form.getValues();
            var record = grid.getStore().getAt(recordIndex);

            record.beginEdit();
            record.set(formValues);
            record.endEdit();
        }
    }],
    ...
});
```

The up method used in the previous function allows us to move up the tree of components; looking for the first component that matches the specified Ext.ComponentQuery selector. In our example we are looking for a component with an xtype of form, which will return the button's parent form panel. Similarly, components have a down method that works the same way but looks for a child component that matches the selector.

How it works...

When populating a form with data from a grid we use the select event that is fired when the user clicks a row. This select event is provided by the Ext.selection.RowModel (rowmodel) class which is applied to the grid using the selType configuration option.

By calling the loadRecord method of the Form panel, we are able to load the record directly into the form. Populating the fields is taken care of by the framework where it loops through the form, mapping the model field to the form field by name.

We then let the user edit data with the form and update the Model. When the Model is updated we can send the newly edited data to the server through the AJAX proxy. We have done this by defining autoSync: true on the Store, however, if required this can be done manually.

We can split the update handler down into three tasks:

1. Get the form values:

```
var form = this.up('form').getForm();
var formValues = form.getValues();
```

2. Get the correct record from the grid's store using the store's `getAt` method:

```
var recordIndex = form.getRecord().index;
var record = grid.getStore().getAt(recordIndex);
```

3. Set the newly updated values to the Model and, if desired, write the data to the server through the proxy:

```
record.beginEdit();
record.set(formValues);
record.endEdit();
```

We have called the `beginEdit` and `endEdit` methods to ensure that the data is sent to the server in one batch. By calling these methods no events are raised to the parent store until the `endEdit` method is called, at which point the events will fire.

See also

▸ To learn more about forms and populating forms it's worth having a look at *Chapter 5*.

▸ We've described form fields in greater detail in *Chapter 6*.

▸ A similar example can be found in *Chapter 4* in the recipe titled *Displaying a detailed window after clicking a DataView node*.

Adding buttons to grid rows with action columns

The action column enables you to define a column with a series of clickable icons that allow users to interact with the grid on a row-by-row basis.

This example will demonstrate how to create an action column for a grid with multiple icons that can be clicked:

Action Column Example: with multiple icons/actions				
Client ▲	Date	Amount	Status	
Ace Outsourcing Resources	Sat Oct 08 2011...	500.5	Sent	🖉 ⊖ 🖼
Acme Corporation	Sat Oct 08 2011...	1000	Viewed	🖉 ⊖ 🖼
Acme Corporation	Sat Oct 08 2011...	380	Paid	🖉 ⊖ 🖼
Global Interactive Technologies	Sat Oct 08 2011...	200	Paid	🖉 ⊖ 🖼

Getting ready

We are going to use the Invoice example that we have used throughout this chapter so we will start by including the Model and Store files to our HTML page:

```
<script type="text/javascript" src="invoices-model.js">
</script>
<script type="text/javascript" src="invoices-store.js">
</script>
```

How to do it...

1. Initialize the `QuickTipManager` to ensure that tooltips are displayed:

```
Ext.tip.QuickTipManager.init();
```

2. Create a basic grid that is bound to the `invoiceStore` with the following columns configuration:

```
Ext.create('Ext.grid.Panel', {
    title: 'Action Column Example',
    height: 150,
    width: 600,
    store: invoiceStore,
    columns: [{
        header: 'Client',
        dataIndex: 'Client',
        flex: 1
    }, {
        header: 'Date',
        dataIndex: 'Date'
    }, {
        header: 'Amount',
        dataIndex: 'Amount'
    }, {
        header: 'Status',
        dataIndex: 'Status'
    }],

    style: 'margin: 50px',
    renderTo: Ext.getBody()
});
```

3. Add a fifth column to the column configuration. This will be an `actioncolumn` with a pencil icon. The action's click handler will display a JavaScript alert:

```
Ext.create('Ext.grid.Panel', {
    ...
    columns: [
    ...
    {
        xtype: 'actioncolumn',
        icon: 'icons/pencil.png',
        tooltip: 'Edit',
        handler: function(grid, rowIndex, colIndex){
            alert('Show "Edit Invoice" component');
        }
    }]
    ...
});
```

4. We can add multiple icons to an `actioncolumn` by defining the actions in the `Ext.grid.column.Action`'s `items` collection. Each action will have its own click handler:

```
Ext.create('Ext.grid.Panel', {
    ...
    columns: [
    ...
    {
        xtype: 'actioncolumn',
        items: [{
            icon: 'icons/pencil.png',
            tooltip: 'Edit',
            handler: function(grid, rowIndex, colIndex){
                alert('Show "Edit Invoice" component');
            }
        }, {
            icon: 'icons/minus-circle.png',
            tooltip: 'Delete',
            handler: function(grid, rowIndex, colIndex){
                Ext.Msg.show({
                    title: 'Delete Invoice',
                    msg: 'Confirm deleting this invoice',
                    buttons: Ext.Msg.YESNO,
                    icon: Ext.Msg.QUESTION
                });
            }
        }, {
            icon: 'icons/money.png',
            tooltip: 'Enter Payment',
            handler: function(grid, rowIndex, colIndex){
```

```
                              Ext.Msg.prompt('Enter Payment', 'Payment
      Amount:');
                      }
               }]
         }]
         ...
      });
```

The action column is defined in the grid's column collection. We're using lazy instantiation by creating a column with `xtype: 'actioncolumn'`, which will have the configuration and click handler(s) required.

Firstly, we need to ensure that the action displays an icon to the user. This is done by defining the `icon` config option. For example, `icon: 'icons/pencil.png'` will display the `pencil.png` image located in the `icons` directory.

Secondly, if the user were to click on the icon, we may wish to carry out a task (for example, display a message). The `handler` function is used for this purpose. It will be called every time the icon is clicked.

> ▸ **Multiple actions in one column**: We are able to add multiple icons to one column with individual click handlers. This is done by defining each individual `icon/ handler` inside the `items` collection of the `actioncolumn`.

> ▸ **Icon tooltips**: The `tooltip` config option of an `actioncolumn` adds a tooltip message to the icon when the user hovers over the icon. In order for this to display you must initialize the `Ext.tip.QuickTipManager`.

It's possible to take this one step further and configure the `actioncolumn` to switch between icons dynamically.

Change the icon dynamically

Here we can see that a green tick appears when the data in the `Status` column is `Paid` and a red cross for all other `Status` types:

1. We need to create a CSS class for each of our dynamic icons/actions:

```
<style type="text/css">
    .paid {
        background-image: url(icons/tick.png);
        width: 16px;
    }

    .not-paid {
        background-image: url(icons/cross.png);
        width: 16px;
    }
</style>
```

2. The action column uses a `getClass` function to return the desired CSS class depending on the value in the `Status` field. It is also possible to set a different tooltip for each case. The click `handler` applies to all icons for this action, however, it would be straightforward to add a similar switch statement to customize the outcome of the click.

LC: please replace the entire block with :

```
Ext.create('Ext.grid.Panel', {
    ...
    columns: [{
        xtype: 'actioncolumn',
        hideable: false,
        items: [{
            getClass: function(v, meta, rec){
                switch (rec.get('Status')) {
                    case 'Paid':
                        this.items[3].tooltip = 'This invoice has
been paid.';
                        return 'paid';
                    default:
                        this.items[3].tooltip = 'This invoice has
not yet been paid.';
                        return 'not-paid';
                }
            },
            handler: function(grid, rowIndex, colIndex){
                var rec = grid.getStore().getAt(rowIndex);
                alert('Status: ' + rec.get('Status'));
            }
        }]
    }],
    ...
});
```

Prevent the column appearing in the hide/show column menu

By default, the action column will appear in the above list. Furthermore, because we have not assigned a column header the column name will be empty. To hide the column from this menu set `hideable: false` in the `actioncolumn` configuration:

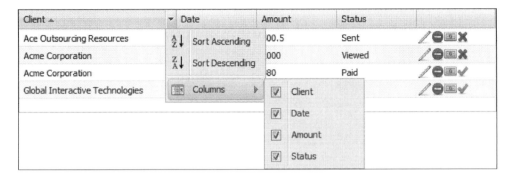

See Also

▶ For another way of displaying actions relating to a grid row see the recipe *Adding a context menu to grid rows*.

9
Constructing Toolbars with Buttons and Menus

In this chapter, we will cover:

- ▶ Creating a split button
- ▶ Working with context menus
- ▶ Adding a combobox to a toolbar to filter a grid
- ▶ Using the color picker in a menu

Introduction

Toolbars, buttons, and menus are the foundation for giving users the means to interact with our applications. They are a navigation and action-launching paradigm that almost all computer users are familiar with and so making use of them in your applications will give users a head start in finding their way around.

This chapter will explore these crucial components and demonstrate how to add them to your application to provide an interactive and dynamic user experience.

Creating a split button

Split buttons are a great way of offering the user multiple actions while keeping the most common default action at the top level, and minimizing the number of buttons cluttering up the viewport.

This recipe will explain how to create a simple split button offering the user a choice of which format they would like to save their document.

How to do it...

1. We start with a blank HTML document with the Ext JS framework included and an `onReady` function ready to have our code added.

2. Now we have our structure, we create a new `Ext.button.Split` instance with some simple configuration. We start by giving it a `text` value, a `tooltip`, and a `handler` function:

```
var splitButton = Ext.create('Ext.button.Split', {
    text: 'Save...',
    tooltip: 'Click the arrow to choose what format to save
in...',
    handler: function(){
        console.log('Save as Default');
    }
});
```

3. Now we have our button we will create a simple `Ext.panel.Panel` with a toolbar to contain our button:

```
var panel = Ext.create('Ext.panel.Panel', {
    renderTo: Ext.getBody(),
    height: 300,
    width: 400,
    html: 'Panel Contents',
    dockedItems: [{
        xtype: 'toolbar',
        dock: 'top',
        items: [splitButton]
    }]
});
```

4. We can now see the button in place and the console log when the button is clicked:

5. We continue by configuring our split button to have an `Ext.menu.Menu` instance attached to its `menu` property. This menu will be shown when the split button's arrow is clicked:

```
var splitButton = Ext.create('Ext.button.Split', {
    text: 'Save...',
    tooltip: 'Click the arrow to choose what format to save
in...',
    handler: function(){
        console.log('Save as Default');
    },
    menu: Ext.create('Ext.menu.Menu', {
        items: [{
            text: 'Save as Image',
            handler: function(){
                console.log('Save as Image');
            }
        }, {
            text: 'Save as PDF',
            handler: function(){
                console.log('Save as PDF');
            }
        }, {
            text: 'Save as Word Document',
            handler: function(){
                console.log('Save as Word Document');
            }
        }]
    })
});
```

6. Now that we have added our menu we can see it appear when we click the split button's arrow:

How it works...

The split buttons work by having an `Ext.menu.Menu` instance attached to them, which is displayed under the main button, when its arrow is clicked. This menu can be configured in exactly the same way as if were it being placed anywhere in your application (for example, as a context menu or directly on a toolbar).

The `handler` option that we gave to the button in step 2 is the function that will be executed when the button's main body (that is, not the arrow) is clicked. This allows us to assign the default behavior of the button. Each of the menu's items contains their own `handler` functions, which will be executed when each of them is clicked.

> Just like a regular `Ext.button.Button` we can configure a split button to display an icon by adding the `icon` or `iconCls` configuration options.

There's more...

We will now look into how to remove the split button's default behavior and instead always have the menu display on a click. We will also explore the `Ext.button.Cycle` component, a subclass of the `Ext.button.Split` component, and demonstrate an example using it.

Removing the default action and always showing the menu

1. We will start with the simple split button that we created in step 3, but we will remove the handler configuration:

```
var splitButton = Ext.create('Ext.button.Split', {
    text: 'Save...',
    tooltip: 'Click the arrow to choose what format to save
in...',
    menu: Ext.create('Ext.menu.Menu', {
        items: [{
            text: 'Save as Image',
            handler: function(){
                console.log('Save as Image');
            }
        }, {
            text: 'Save as PDF',
            handler: function(){
                console.log('Save as PDF');
            }
        }, {
```

```
                    text: 'Save as Word Document',
                    handler: function(){
                        console.log('Save as Word Document');
                    }
                }]
            })
        });
```

2. We will now bind a function to the button's click event:

```
splitButton.on({
    click: function(){

    },
    scope: this
});
```

3. We can now complete the task by adding a call to the `showMenu` method of the `Ext.button.Split` class,which will display the configured menu below the button when the button, as well as the arrow, is clicked:

```
splitButton.on({
    click: function(){
        splitButton.showMenu();
    },
    scope: this
});
```

Using the Ext.button.Cycle component

The `Ext.button.Cycle` class is a subclass of the `Ext.button.Split` class. It alters the behavior so that when we press the button, the next item in the menu becomes active. We create a similar **Save** button using this component with the following code:

```
var cycleButton = Ext.create('Ext.button.Cycle', {
    showText: true,
    prependText: 'Save as ',
    menu: {
        items: [{
            text: 'Image'
        }, {
            text: 'PDF'
        }, {
            text: 'Word Document'
        }]
    }
});
```

The `showText` option determines whether the active item's text is displayed as the main button's text. The `prependText` value is used to prefix the active item's text value. By default the first item is considered the active item but this can be determined by adding `checked: true` to one of the menu items.

> The menu is defined as a simple object literal rather than a concrete `Ext.menu.Menu` instance. This is required for the cycle button to work.

There are several useful methods and events that can be used to hook into the button's cycling functionality:

- `changeHandler`: A function set to this option gets attached to the button's `change` event and is executed whenever the button's active item is changed. Alternatively the `change` event can be listened for explicitly.

- `getActiveItem`/`setActiveItem`: These two methods allow the active item to be retrieved or set.

- `toggleSelected`: This method lets us programmatically toggle the active item to the next one in the menu.

Working with context menus

A **context menu** is a menu that contains actions that are specific to the item the cursor is pointing at. These menus are normally accessed through the right mouse button.

This recipe builds upon the example *Adding a context menu to grid rows* from *Chapter 8, Displaying and Editing Tabular Data* by showing a context menu when the user right-clicks on a row. Depending on the values in the selected row we will enable/disable certain options from the menu. The final result can be seen in the following screenshot:

Chapter 9				
Client ▲		Date	Amount	Status
Ace Outsourcing Resources		10/08/2011	500.5	Sent
Acme Corpor...	View Invoice	10/08/2011	1000	Viewed
Acme Corpo	Edit Invoice	10/08/2011	380	Paid
Global Intera	Re-Send Invoice	10/08/2011	200	Paid
	Archive Invoice			
	Delete Invoice			

Getting ready

To get us up and running quickly we will reuse the Invoices Model and Store that we used in the previous chapter. If you aren't familiar with them please revisit that chapter and remind yourself of their code.

How to do it...

1. We start by including the Invoices Model and Store files into our HTML file. The code for these files can be seen in *Chapter 8*.

   ```
   <script type="text/javascript" src="invoices-model.js"></script>
   <script type="text/javascript" src="invoices-store.js"></script>
   ```

2. The next step is to create a basic grid and render it to the document's body:

   ```
   var invoicesGrid = Ext.create('Ext.grid.Panel', {
       title: 'Chapter 9',
       height: 300,
       width: 600,
       store: invoiceStore,
       columns: [{
           header: 'Client',
           dataIndex: 'Client',
           flex: 1
       }, {
           header: 'Date',
           dataIndex: 'Date',
           xtype: 'datecolumn',
           dateFormat: 'd/m/Y'
       }, {
           header: 'Amount',
           dataIndex: 'Amount'
       }, {
           header: 'Status',
           dataIndex: 'Status'
       }],

       renderTo: Ext.getBody()
   });
   ```

3. We now instantiate an `Ext.menu.Menu` object and configure it with a height, width, and a collection of `Ext.menu.Items` that will be our action buttons:

   ```
   var contextMenu = Ext.create('Ext.menu.Menu', {
       height: 100,
       width: 125,
   ```

```
        items: [{
            text: 'View Invoice'
        }, {
            text: 'Edit Invoice'
        }, {
            text: 'Re-Send Invoice'
        }, {
            text: 'Archive Invoice'
        }, {
            text: 'Delete Invoice'
        }]
    });
```

4. We can now hook the right-click event (`itemcontextmenu`) of the grid to a function that will show our menu. This function contains the logic to enable/disable the buttons depending on the values in the row:

```
invoicesGrid.on({
    itemcontextmenu: function(grid, record, item, index, e, eOpts)
    {
        e.stopEvent();

        var viewBtn = contextMenu.items.get(0);
        var editBtn = contextMenu.items.get(1);
        var resendBtn = contextMenu.items.get(2);
        var archiveBtn = contextMenu.items.get(3);
        var deleteBtn = contextMenu.items.get(4);

        var status = record.get('Status');

        switch (status) {
            case 'Paid':
                viewBtn.enable();
                editBtn.disable();
                resendBtn.disable();
                archiveBtn.enable();
                deleteBtn.disable();
                break;
            case 'Sent':
                viewBtn.enable();
                editBtn.enable();
                resendBtn.enable();
                archiveBtn.disable();
                deleteBtn.enable();
                break;
```

```
            case 'Viewed':
                viewBtn.enable();
                editBtn.enable();
                resendBtn.enable();
                archiveBtn.disable();
                deleteBtn.enable();
                break;
            default:
        }

        contextMenu.showAt(e.getXY());
    }
});
```

How it works...

To invoke the context menu we listen for the `itemcontextmenu` event of the `Ext.grid.Panel` class. This allows us to react to a user's right-click and display a menu when it occurs.

The call to the `stopEvent` method of the `Ext.EventObject` class stops the event from bubbling to other components and also stops the browser handling the event itself, thus preventing the browser's native context menu from appearing.

We use the `get` method on the items collection of `contextMenu` to create a reference to the individual menu items. This is done for convenience.

To determine the value of the `Status` column we call `record.get('Status')`. The record is passed as a parameter on the `itemcontextmenu` event. We then use a `switch` statement calling the `enable` or `disable` method on each button depending on the value of `Status`.

The call to `contextMenu.showAt(e.getXY())` displays our menu at a position where the right-click happened.

See also

► For a detailed look at grids we recommend you refer back to the previous chapter.

► The recipe *Adding a context menu to grid rows* in *Chapter 8, Displaying and Editing Tabular Data* introduces the context menu on a grid.

Adding a combobox to a toolbar to filter a grid

As well as buttons and text, form fields can be easily added to toolbars. We will use this recipe to show you how to place a combobox on a panel's docked toolbar that will then be used to filter the contents of a grid.

We will then expand on this by adding a free-text filter to the grid by positioning a text field on the toolbar.

Getting ready

To get us up and running quickly we will reuse the Invoices Model and Store we used in the previous chapter. If you aren't familiar with them please revisit that chapter and remind yourself of the code.

How to do it...

1. We start by including the Invoices Model and Store files into our HTML file:

```
<script type="text/javascript" src="invoices-model.js"></script>
<script type="text/javascript" src="invoices-store.js"></script>
```

2. As we are creating a combobox we will need a data store for it to bind to. We will create a simple store with some static data representing the possible status values of our Invoices:

```
var statusStore = Ext.create('Ext.data.Store', {
    fields: ['Status'],
    data: [{
        Status: 'All'
    }, {
        Status: 'Paid'
    }, {
        Status: 'Viewed'
    }, {
        Status: 'Sent'
    }, {
        Status: 'Draft'
    }]
});
```

3. Next we create an `Ext.form.field.ComboBox` bound to our new store, with its `displayField` and `valueField` properties set to our store's only field:

```
var filterCombo = Ext.create('Ext.form.field.ComboBox', {
    fieldLabel: 'Status Filter',
    labelWidth: 70,
    queryMode: 'local',
    displayField: 'Status',
    valueField: 'Status',
    store: statusStore
});
```

4. Now we create a simple grid panel, bound to the Invoices Store that we included in step 1. We also create a toolbar as part of the `dockedItems` collection, which has one child item—`filterCombo`:

```
var invoicesGrid = Ext.create('Ext.grid.Panel', {
    title: 'Chapter 9',
    height: 300,
    width: 600,
    store: invoiceStore,
    dockedItems: [{
      xtype: 'toolbar',
      dock: 'top',
      items: [filterCombo]
    }],
    columns: [{
        header: 'Client',
        dataIndex: 'Client'
    }, {
        header: 'Date',
        dataIndex: 'Date'
    }, {
        header: 'Amount',
        dataIndex: 'Amount'
    }, {
        header: 'Status',
        dataIndex: 'Status'
    }],

    renderTo: Ext.getBody()
});
```

We can see the outcome of this in the following screenshot:

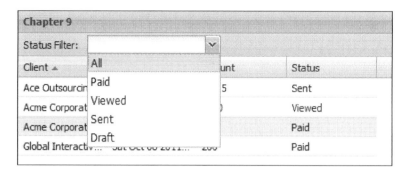

5. Our next step is to listen for the combobox's `select` event and then filter the Invoices Store based on the chosen value. We start by using the `on` method to attach a handler function to the event:

```
filterCombo.on('select', function(combo, records, opts){

});
```

6. Finally, we perform the filter by first clearing any existing filters. Following this we use the grid's store's `filter` method to exclude any records with Statuses that don't match our chosen item:

```
filterCombo.on('select', function(combo, records, opts) {
    invoicesGrid.getStore().clearFilter();
    // if there are selected records and the first isn't
    // 'All' then apply the filter
    if(records.length > 0 && records[0].get('Status') !== 'All') {
        var filterStatus = records[0].get('Status');
        invoicesGrid.getStore().filter('Status', filterStatus);
    }
});
```

How it works...

Comboboxes extend the `Ext.Component` class, along with the entire framework's other widgets. This common base class means that any `Ext.Component` can be nested inside any `Ext.Container` class and be successfully laid out using the framework's layout classes.

This hierarchy means that the combobox can be added to containers, such as toolbars, as easily as they can be to forms.

The combobox's `select` event is fired when an option is chosen from its drop-down list. It passes three parameters to any handler functions—the combobox itself, an array of the selected records, and an options object.

In our handler function, we clear the filters currently applied to the store of `invoiceGrid`. This is necessary to prevent the next added filter being applied in addition to the previous ones.

Next we check that at least one record is present in the `records` array and that the selected status does not equal `'All'`. By doing this we leave the store unfiltered if the user chooses the `All` option.

Finally, the filter is applied by passing the field name to be filtered on and the selected status's value to the store's `filter` method.

There's more...

We will now demonstrate how to add a text field to our grid's toolbar and use it to allow users to filter the grid by typing the start of a client's name and having the grid filter in real-time.

1. We start by creating a text field:

    ```
    var searchTextField = Ext.create('Ext.form.field.Text', {
        fieldLabel: 'Client Search'
    });
    ```

2. Next we enable the field's key events (for example, `keydown`, `keypress`, and `keyup`) so we can use them to perform our filtering:

    ```
    var searchTextField = Ext.create('Ext.form.field.Text', {
        fieldLabel: 'Client Search',
        enableKeyEvents: true
    });
    ```

3. Now we attach a listener to the field's `keyup` event. This will fire after the user presses a key and then lets us filter the grid based on the value entered:

    ```
    var searchTextField = Ext.create('Ext.form.field.Text', {
        fieldLabel: 'Client Search',
        enableKeyEvents: true,
        listeners: {
            keyup: {
                fn: function(field, e){

                }
            }
        }
    });
    ```

4. We use the grid store's `filterBy` method that allows us to define our own function, which is executed for every record in the store and, if true is returned from it, we will include that record in its filtered collection:

```
fn: function(field, e){
    var val = field.getValue();

    invoicesGrid.getStore().filterBy(function(record){
        return record.get('Client').substring(0, val.length) ===
val;
    }, this);
}
```

5. We want to prevent this handler from being run if lots of characters are being typed in quick succession. We can do this by providing a `buffer` option that tells the handler to only run after this number of milliseconds has elapsed. If the event is fired again, before this time has passed, then the timer will start again and the previous event does not execute:

```
...
keyup: {
        fn: function(field, e){
            ...
        },
        buffer: 250
}
...
```

6. Lastly, we add the text field to the grid's toolbar:

```
invoicesGrid.getDockedItems()[1].add(searchTextField);
```

The following screenshot shows the text field in place and a filter applied:

 ▶ For more information on grids take another look at *Chapter 8*. The recipe *Displaying simple tabular data* is a particularly good starting point.

 ▶ Models and Stores are covered in greater depth in *Chapter 7, Working with the Ext JS Data Package*.

Using the color picker in a menu

The **Color Picker** component provides a straightforward way for the user to select a color from a defined array of color hex codes:

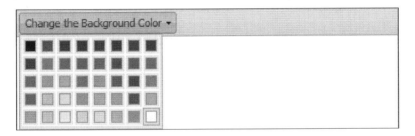

This recipe will demonstrate how to use the color picker in a menu to change the body background color. We will use the default 40-color palette that is provided by the framework.

How to do it...

1. Start by creating a button and add a new instance of a `ColorPicker` to the button's menu property:

```
var button = Ext.create('Ext.button.Button', {
    text: 'Change the Background Color',
    menu: new Ext.menu.ColorPicker({
        ...
    })
});
```

2. Create a Panel with the button in a toolbar that's docked to the top.

```
var panel = Ext.create('Ext.Panel', {
    height: 300,
    width: 400,
    dockedItems: [{
        xtype: 'toolbar',
        dock: 'top',
        items: [button]
```

```
    }],
    renderTo: Ext.getBody(),
    style: 'margin: 50px'
});
```

3. Add a handler to the `ColorPicker` to change the body background color to the selected color:

```
...
menu: new Ext.menu.ColorPicker({
    handler: function(picker, color){
        Ext.getBody().setStyle('background-color', '#' + color);
    }
})
...
```

How it works...

The color picker is defined in the menu property of the button. The resulting output of this is a button that, when clicked, displays an `Ext.picker.Color` component.

However, as this particular example demonstrates the color picker as a menu, we create a new instance of `Ext.menu.ColorPicker`, which is a menu (`Ext.menu.Menu`) containing our `Ext.picker.Color` component.

When a color is selected the `select` event is fired. We see this behavior in the handler we specified. The `color` parameter in the `select` event contains the selected hex code, which we use to set the body's background color.

 The hex code does not contain the hash (#) symbol.

In the body's element (retrieved through `Ext.getBody()`) we call the `setStyle` method, specifying the CSS attribute that we wish to set:

```
Ext.getBody().setStyle('background-color', '#' + color);
```

The value is a concatenation of a # symbol and the selected color (from the `color` parameter).

There's more...

It's possible to customize the colors available to pick from by defining an array of hex codes in the colors property:

```
var redHuePicker = new Ext.menu.ColorPicker({
    componentCls: 'x-color-picker custom',
    colors: ['E78A61', 'F9966B', 'EE9A4D', 'F660AB', 'F665AB',
'E45E9D', 'C25283', '7D2252', 'E77471', 'F75D59', 'E55451', 'C24641',
'FF0000', 'F62217', 'E41B17', 'F62817', 'E42217', 'C11B17', 'FAAFBE',
'FBBBB9', 'E8ADAA', 'E7A1B0', 'FAAFBA', 'F9A7B0', 'E799A3', 'C48793',
'C5908E', 'B38481', 'C48189', '7F5A58', '7F4E52', '7F525D'],
    handler: function(picker, color){
        Ext.getBody().setStyle('background-color', '#' + color);
    }
});
```

As there are less than 40 colors in the palette, we will also assign a custom CSS class to resize the height and width of the component:

```
x-color-picker.custom {
    width: 150px;
    height: 70px;
    cursor: pointer;
}
```

10
Drawing and Charting

In this chapter, we will cover:

- ▶ Drawing basic shapes
- ▶ Applying gradients to shapes
- ▶ Drawing paths
- ▶ Transforming and interacting with shapes
- ▶ Creating a bar chart with external data
- ▶ Creating a pie chart with local data
- ▶ Creating a line chart with updating data
- ▶ Customizing labels, colors, and axes
- ▶ Attaching events to chart components
- ▶ Creating a live updating chart bound to an editable grid

Introduction

This chapter will demonstrate the new charting and drawing features introduced to Ext JS 4. In particular, you will discover how to chart data for presentation in numerous ways.

We will take you through the `Ext.draw` package which, as you will learn, is used as the basis of the charting package that we explore later. The first recipes introduce the tools available for drawing shapes and text before moving onto the fully featured `Ext.chart` classes that enable you to quickly create and integrate attractive, interactive charts into your apps.

Drawing basic shapes

Ext JS 4 introduces a brand new drawing package that gives us the opportunity to create complex graphics directly in the browser. The framework itself leverages this package to render all of the new charts.

This recipe will explore how we go about using this new package to draw some simple shapes. Before this, we will explain what classes the package consists of and how they work and fit together:

- ▶ `Ext.draw.Surface`: The surface class provides us with an abstracted interface into the underlying drawing technology, which changes across different browsers depending on what technologies they support. The concrete implementations of the surface class use SVG (`Ext.draw.engine.Svg`) in all capable browsers with VML (`Ext.draw.engine.Vml`) being used in the remaining incapable ones (namely, Internet Explorer 6, 7, and 8). This abstraction lets us only worry about what we want to draw and leave the responsibility of how to actually draw it to the framework.

- ▶ `Ext.draw.Sprite`: A sprite is an entity that is drawn onto the drawing surface. In terms of the drawing package, this could be a circle, a rectangle, a square, some text, or an arbitrary path. Sprites expose various methods and events for manipulating and interacting with them, which we will explore later in this chapter.

- ▶ `Ext.draw.Component`: The draw package's component class references an instance of `Ext.draw.Surface` (available from the component's `surface` property) and allows sprites to be added to it in the same way we would add other components to containers.

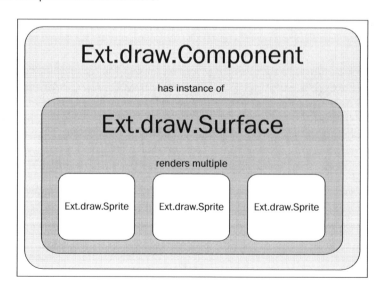

How to do it...

We will demonstrate how to create a couple of basic shapes (or sprites) by creating a very simple map-pin icon consisting of a circle and a rectangle:

1. We start by creating an instance of the Ext.draw.Component class that we render to the document's body:

```
var mapPin = Ext.create('Ext.draw.Component', {
    renderTo: Ext.getBody(),
    width: 500,
    height: 500,
    viewBox: false
});
```

The viewBox configuration option tells the component whether to scale its sprites to fill the component's size or not (while maintaining the aspect ratio). For example, with viewBox set to false our shapes will be sized by our configuration. However, if we set it to true our shape will scale to fill its parent component.

2. Next we create our map pin's head. We define a sprite, with a type of 'circle' and some basic sizing and styling configuration, and add it to the component's items collection:

```
var mapPin = Ext.create('Ext.draw.Component', {
    renderTo: Ext.getBody(),
    width: 500,
    height: 500,
    viewBox: false,

    items: [{
        type: 'circle',
        x: 50,
        y: 50,
        radius: 10,
        fill: '#2D00B3'
    }]
});
```

3. We now add the pin. This will be made up of a single rectangular sprite, positioned under the circle. Note that we add it *before* the circle so it appears behind it:

```
var mapPin = Ext.create('Ext.draw.Component', {
    renderTo: Ext.getBody(),
    width: 500,
    height: 500,
    viewBox: false,
    items: [{
        type: 'rect',
        x: 49,
        y: 58,
        width: 3,
        height: 30,
        fill: '#999'
    }, {
        type: 'circle',
        x: 50,
        y: 50,
        radius: 10,
        fill: '#2D00B3'
    }]
});
```

4. Finally, we add a small rotation to the pin so that it looks more realistic. We do this by adding the `rotate` configuration option and giving it a value of -7 degrees:

```
var mapPin = Ext.create('Ext.draw.Component', {
    renderTo: Ext.getBody(),
    width: 500,
    height: 500,
    viewBox: false,
    items: [{
        type: 'rect',
        x: 52,
        y: 58,
        width: 3,
        height: 30,
        fill: '#999',
        rotate: {
            degrees: -7
        }
    }, {
        type: 'circle',
        x: 50,
```

```
            y: 50,
            radius: 10,
            fill: '#2D00B3'
        }]
    });
```

How it works...

The `mapPin` variable holds a reference to our `Ext.draw.Component` instance, which can have any number of `Ext.draw.Sprite` instances added to it and have them drawn to the browser.

The `type` option of the sprite configuration tells the class what kind of shape to draw. Each of the types (`rect`, `circle`, `square`, `text`, and `path`) offer slightly different options.

All types accept positioning coordinates through the x and y options. These determine the sprite's position within the `Ext.draw.Component`. They also may have a `fill` value, which should be a string containing a color.

The rectangle type accepts a `width` and `height` option that will determine the dimensions of the shape.

A circle sprite accepts a `radius` configuration, which establishes the size of the circle from its center that corresponds to the provided x and y values.

> Sprites can be added to `Ext.draw.Component` instances at runtime by using the `Ext.draw.Surface`'s add method:
>
> ```
> var sprite = drawingComponent.surface.add({...});
> sprite.show();
> ```

In step 4 we configured the pin to be rotated by 7 degrees. This was achieved by using the `rotate` option which accepts a configuration object containing a `degrees` property, defining the number of degrees to rotate the shape by, and, optionally, an x and y property that allows us to move the center of rotation.

> Two additional transformation options exist to allow us to `scale` and `translate` sprites. They both accept an object containing x and y properties defining the scale factor or translation distance in the horizontal and vertical planes.

In modern browsers the drawing is created using SVG markup. The output of this drawing can be seen in the following screenshot. We will see in the *Drawing paths* recipe how closely related the Ext JS syntax for creating drawings is to the commands used when creating regular SVG drawings:

```
▼<div id="draw-1014" class="x-surface x-surface-default" style="width: 250px; height: 250px; " role=
"presentation">
  ▼<svg xmlns="http://www.w3.org/2000/svg" version="1.1" width="250" height="250" id="ext-gen1015" style=
  "width: 250px; height: 250px; ">
    <defs></defs>
    <rect width="100%" height="100%" fill="#000" stroke="none" opacity="0" id="ext-gen1016"></rect>
    <rect id="ext-sprite-1013" style="-webkit-tap-highlight-color: rgba(0, 0, 0, 0); " zIndex="0" x="52"
    y="58" width="3" height="30" fill="#999" ry="0" rx="0" transform=
    "matrix(0.9925,-0.1219,0.1219,0.9925,-8.4977,7.0641)"></rect>
    <circle id="ext-sprite-1014" style="-webkit-tap-highlight-color: rgba(0, 0, 0, 0); " zIndex="0" x="50"
    y="50" r="10" fill="#2D00B3" cx="50" cy="50" transform="matrix(1,0,0,1,0,0)"></circle>
  </svg>
</div>
```

There's more...

As well as basic shapes, Ext JS draw package allows us to draw text and configure and manipulate it in the same way as other sprites. We will now demonstrate how to define a text sprite and how it can be configured:

1. We start by creating our usual `Ext.draw.Component` instance, which will give us our drawing surface:

```
var textComponent = Ext.create('Ext.draw.Component', {
    renderTo: Ext.getBody(),
    width: 500,
    height: 250,
    viewBox: false,
    items: []
});
```

2. We then use the 'text' `type` to define our new sprite and position it within our component with a `fill` color of black:

```
var textComponent = Ext.create('Ext.draw.Component', {
    renderTo: Ext.getBody(),
    width: 500,
    height: 250,
    viewBox: false,
    items: [{
        type: 'text',
        x: 100,
        y: 100,
        fill: '#000'
    }]
});
```

3. So far we won't see any output from our code, so we must add the `text` configuration. This defines what text will be drawn onto the drawing surface. We also add the `font` option to draw our text in the lovely *Times New Roman* font:

```
var textComponent = Ext.create('Ext.draw.Component', {
    renderTo: Ext.getBody(),
    width: 500,
    height: 250,
    viewBox: false,
     items: [{
        type: 'text',
        x: 100,
        y: 100,
        font: '32px "Times New Roman"',
        text: 'Ext JS 4 Cookbook',
        fill: '#000'
    }]
});
```

See also

▶   The next recipe, which enhances this example by adding a gradient to the map pin.

Applying gradients to shapes

Gradients can help add realism to drawings or provide the final polish for a design. They can be easily added to any sprite created with the `Ext.draw` package.

We will continue to work on our map-pin example from the previous recipe and add gradients to its sprites to make them appear a little more realistic.

How to do it...

1. We will start with our finished map pin from the first recipe:

```
var mapPin = Ext.create('Ext.draw.Component', {
    renderTo: Ext.getBody(),
    width: 500,
    height: 500,
    viewBox: false,

    items: [{
        type: 'rect',
        x: 52,
        y: 58,
```

```
            width: 3,
            height: 30,
            fill: '#999',
            rotate: {
                degrees: -7
            }
        }, {
            type: 'circle',
            x: 50,
            y: 50,
            radius: 10,
            fill: '#2D00B3'
        }]
    });
```

2. We now define a gradient for the map pin's pin. We want a linear gradient going across the pin to give the effect of it being metal. We add this to the `gradients` collection of `Ext.draw.Component`:

```
...
gradients: [{
    id: 'pin-gradient',
    type: 'linear',
    angle: -7,
    stops: {
        0: {
            color: '#eee'
        },
        100: {
            color: '#999'
        }
    }
}]
...
```

3. This gradient can now be attached to the pin sprite by referencing its `id` in the sprite's `fill` config:

```
...
fill: 'url(#pin-gradient)'
...
```

4. The map pin's head requires a radial gradient to give it the effect of being a sphere, rather than a flat circle. We add this as a second item in the `gradients` array:

```
...
{
    id: 'head-gradient',
    type: 'radial',
    centerX: '25%',
    centerY: '25%',
    focalX: '60%',
    focalY: '60%',
    radius: 4,
    stops: {
        0: {
            color: '#9F80FF'
        },
        25: {
            color: '#2D00B3'
        },
        100: {
            color: '#2D00B3'
        }
    }
}
...
```

5. This gradient is added to the pin's head sprite in the same way as we did for the pin.

```
...
fill: 'url(#head-gradient)'
...
```

6. The final result can be seen below.

How it works...

Gradients are defined in the `gradients` configuration option of the `Ext.draw.Component` class. Any gradients you want to apply to a sprite must be declared here.

There are two gradient types, linear and radial, which both accept an `id`, a `type`, and a `stops` object literal.

The `stops` object defines the colors that the gradient will have at specific points across it. These are defined by providing the gradient's properties at individual percentage points. In our linear gradient we define that the gradient's color will be #EEE 0% of the way across the shapes length (i.e. at the start) and that it will end with a color of #999 (at 100%). We can add as many of these stops as we like to achieve any gradient style.

Finally our gradient can be applied to a sprite by referencing its ID using the special syntax `fill: 'url(#gradient-id-here)'`.

Linear gradients also accept an optional option of angle, which we have used in our map pin's gradient. This will define the angle (in degrees) that the gradient will run in.

See also

 ▶ The previous recipe, *Drawing basic shapes*, for a more detailed explanation on how to draw the map pin used in this example.

Drawing paths

As well as simple geometric shapes the `Ext.draw` package allows us to create any shape we can think of using the 'path' sprite `type`. This type of sprite lets us use an SVG-like syntax to define the points that the path will pass through.

We will first explore how to create simple straight-line shapes and then move on to create more complex curved paths.

How to do it...

In our example we will draw a simple house with a sky and some grass that a 3-year-old would be embarrassed to call his own:

1. We start by creating an `Ext.draw.Component` to contain our sprites:

```
var house = Ext.create('Ext.draw.Component', {
    renderTo: Ext.getBody(),
    width: 800,
    height: 550,
    viewBox: false,
    items: []
});
```

2. Next we add two rectangles, one blue and one green, to represent the sky and grass respectively:

```
var house = Ext.create('Ext.draw.Component', {
    renderTo: Ext.getBody(),
```

```
            width: 800,
            height: 550,
            viewBox: false,
            items: [{
                type: 'rect',
                x: 200,
                y: 0,
                width: 500,
                height: 250,
                fill: '#3BB9FF'
            }, {
                type: 'rect',
                x: 200,
                y: 250,
                width: 500,
                height: 100,
                fill: '#7CFC00'
            }]
        });
```

3. We now add a sprite of type 'path' to the `items` collection. We give it a `fill`, `stroke` color, and a `stroke width`:

```
...
{       type: 'path',
        fill: '#98AFC7',
        stroke: '#000',
        'stroke-width': 2
}
...
```

4. Finally, we define the `path` configuration that accepts a string containing the instructions on how to draw the shape we want, in our case a house. We define this as an array of strings with a call to its `join` method that will concatenate them all together. By doing this it makes it easier to follow what each instruction is doing and to edit them later.

```
{
  type: 'path',
  fill: '#9B4645',
  stroke: '#000',
  "stroke-width": 2,
  path: [
    'M 300 290',    // Point 1
    'l 0 -60',      // Point 2
    'l -10 0',      // Point 3
```

```
        '1 60 -40',    // Point 4
        '1 60 40',     // Point 5
        '1 -10 0',     // Point 6
        '1 0 60',      // Point 7
        '1 -100 0',    // Point 8
        'm 43 0',      // Point 9
        '1 0 -25',     // Point 10
        '1 15 0',      // Point 11
        '1 0 25'       // Point 12
    ].join(' ')
}
```

This path should give us the following output:

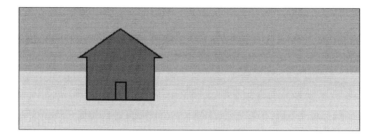

How it works...

Paths are defined in exactly the same way as all of the other sprites we have seen except for one important detail—the `path` configuration. This configuration accepts a string containing a series of commands, which effectively guides the pen across the drawing surface and tells it how and where to draw the lines.

The first command is M 300 290. The M command tells the pen to lift off the page and move to a specific coordinate location within the drawing surface in the format 'x y'. So this command moves the pen to position 1 in the following diagram. The other numbers on the diagram relate to the instructions (within step 4's code listing) that got the path to that point:

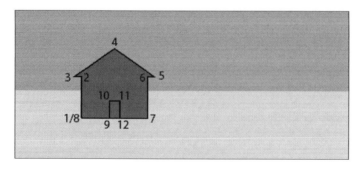

The drawing surface's 0,0 position is located in the top left.

It is important to note that a lowercase m would move the pen by the amount specified relative to its current position. So, if our example was 'm 300 290', we would move 300 pixels to the right and 290 pixels down, rather than to the coordinate 300, 290. This rule can be applied to all of the command letters.

The next series of items use the l command. This command draws a line from the pen's current position to a new position decided by the numbers that follow it.

We have used a lowercase l so the first command tells us to move 0 pixels on the x-axis and -60 pixels on the y-axis. In other words, stay in the same horizontal position but move 60 pixels up. This command takes us to position 2.

You can follow the next six commands clockwise around the outside of the house shape and back to our starting position.

 Your path will automatically be closed by the most direct route if you don't complete it yourself.

The next command moves the pen into the center of the house to draw the door. It does this by moving 43 pixels horizontally, relative to its last position.

There's more...

It is also possible to draw curved lines using the path sprite. We will draw a simple moon using two Bezier curves to achieve the following drawing:

1. We once again start by creating an Ext.draw.Component with a simple rectangle sprite to give us a blue background:

```
var moon = Ext.create('Ext.draw.Component', {
    renderTo: Ext.getBody(),
    width: 500,
```

```
      height: 500,
      viewBox: false,

      items: [{
        type: 'rect',
        x: 0,
        y: 0,
        width: 500,
        height: 500,
        fill: '#060429'
      }]
    });
```

2. We then add our path sprite and define a starting point of (300, 180) using the command M 300 180:

```
var moon = Ext.create('Ext.draw.Component', {
    renderTo: Ext.getBody(),
    width: 500,
    height: 500,
    viewBox: false,
    items: [{
        type: 'rect',
        x: 0,
        y: 0,
        width: 500,
        height: 500,
        fill: '#060429'
    }, {
        type: 'path',
        fill: '#FEF6B1',
        path: [
            'M 300 180'
        ].join(' ')
    }]
});
```

3. Now we add our first Bezier curve to create the inner arc of the moon (highlighted in light grey):

Simple Bezier curves work by adding an invisible control point to the end points of a line. These control points influence the magnitude and direction of the curve. The following diagram shows the approximate position of the curves' control points:

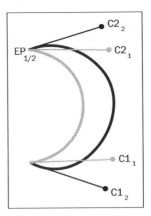

4. To create this we use the c command, which accepts three sets of x y pairs. The first pair defines the coordinates (or relative coordinates if you use a lowercase 'c') of the starting point's control point (shown as **C1** in the diagram). The second pair defines the end point's control point (**C2**), and the third identifies the position the line will finish (**EP**). Using this structure, the command we use to create the first line can be seen as follows:

```
C 350 110, 350 170, 300 180
```

5. Similarly our outer line is defined using the same format and can be seen as follows:

```
C 380 200, 380 80, 300 180
```

The complete code for the drawing is as follows:

```
var moon = Ext.create('Ext.draw.Component', {
    renderTo: Ext.getBody(),
    width: 500,
    height: 500,
    viewBox: false,
    items: [{
        type: 'rect',
        x: 0,
        y: 0,
        width: 500,
        height: 500,
        fill: '#060429'
    }, {
```

```
        type: 'path',
        fill: '#FEF6B1',
        path: [
            'M 300 180',
            'C 350 110, 350 170, 300 180',
            'C 380 200, 380 80, 300 180'
        ].join(' ')
    }]
});
```

See also

▶ The next recipe, to learn how to animate your drawings.

▶ The first recipe, *Drawing basic shapes*, for a quick reminder on the basics of the
   Ext.draw package.

Transforming and interacting with shapes

Once we have created a drawing we will sometimes want to update it to reflect a change in
the data it is representing or a change in the situation the shape finds itself in. Whatever
the reason, the drawing package allows us to easily reconfigure a sprite's characteristics
programmatically, both instantly and through a progressive animation.

We will demonstrate how to achieve this by changing the properties of a simple rectangle
sprite. The first method we will use is the setAttributes method of the Ext.draw.
Sprite class and then we will move on to using the animate method.

How to do it...

1. Our first step is to create a sprite to work with. We will create a very simple dark blue
    rectangle and add it to an Ext.draw.Component instance:

```
var rectangle = Ext.create('Ext.draw.Sprite', {
    type: 'rect',
    x: 150,
    y: 150,
    width: 100,
    height: 30,
    fill: '#060429'
});
```

```
var shape = Ext.create('Ext.draw.Component', {
    renderTo: Ext.getBody(),
    width: 1000,
    height: 500,
    viewBox: false,

    items: [rectangle]
});
```

2. We will start by scaling the rectangle to three times its original dimensions. We can use the reference to the rectangle sprite (`rectangle`) to call its `setAttributes` method passing in a configuration object telling it to scale its height (y) and width (x) by a factor of 3:

```
rectangle.setAttributes({
    translate: {
        x: 200,
        y: 50
    }
}, true);
```

3. Other attributes that can be updated are the rotation and fill of the sprite. The following code demonstrates how to update these two attributes with a single call rotating the shape by 30 degrees and turning it green:

```
rectangle.setAttributes({
    rotate: {
        degrees: 30
    },
    fill: '#3B5323'
}, true);
```

4. The final attribute we can transform is the sprite's position. We use the `translate` property to instruct the sprite to be moved by x pixels horizontally and y pixels vertically:

```
rectangle.setAttributes({
    translate: {
        x: 200,
        y: 50
    }
}, true);
```

5. These transformations can be combined with the `Ext.util.Animate` class's included functionality (as it is a mixin. See *Chapter 1, Classes, Object-Oriented Principles, and Structuring your Application* for more details on mixins) to make them animated. We simply call the sprite's `animate` method passing in a configuration object:

```
rectangle.animate({
    to: {
        fill: '#FF0000'
    },
    duration: 2000,
    callback: function(){
        rectangle.setAttributes({
            rotate: {
                degrees: 60
            }
        }, true);
    }
}, true);
```

This code will fade our rectangle's fill color from green to red, after which it will rotate 60 degrees.

How it works...

The `setAttribute` method allows us to redefine any of the characteristics we set on a sprite when it was first created, namely the rotation, scale, translation, and fill color. Any number of these attributes can be set in a single call to the method.

> You can retrieve references to individual sprites that have been added to `Ext.draw.Component` by querying the `items` collection of its `Ext.draw.Surface` class, accessible through the `surface` property. For example, `drawComponent.surface.items.get(0)`.

The second parameter of the `setAttribute` method is a Boolean value that tells the sprite whether it should redraw itself immediately. By setting this to true you will instantly see the results of the transformation. However, if you are applying many updates you may see a performance improvement by delaying a redraw until the last transformation has been applied.

Our final animation example shows the `animate` method being passed a configuration object specifying the state the rectangle will be in after the animation is complete (found in the `to` property), allowing it to calculate the intermediate stages.

The `callback` option is also used to perform further transformations after the animation (which will last for two seconds) has completed.

There's more...

Sprites expose various events allowing us to capture and react to user interaction with each shape we create. This opens up huge possibilities for how we can utilize the drawing package in our applications and plays a large role in the charting package, which we will discuss later in this chapter.

We are going to work through an example where we change the color of a shape when the user hovers over it and, when clicked, animates the shape scaling to twice its original size:

1. First of all we create a simple, blue rectangular sprite with dimensions of 100 pixels by 30 pixels:

```
var rectangle2 = Ext.create('Ext.draw.Sprite', {
    type: 'rect',
    x: 150,
    y: 150,
    width: 100,
    height: 30,
    fill: '#060429'
});
```

2. Next we add a `listeners` configuration, like we have done with many of the other widgets of Ext JS, and add handlers for the `mouseover` and `mouseout` events. In these events we add a function to change the shape's `fill` color to green and then back to blue on `mouseout`:

```
var rectangle2 = Ext.create('Ext.draw.Sprite', {
  type: 'rect',
  x: 150,
  y: 150,
  width: 100,
  height: 30,
  fill: '#060429',
  listeners: {
    mouseover: function(){
      rectangle2.setAttributes({
        fill: '#3B5323'
      }, true);
    },
    mouseout: function(){
```

```
        rectangle2.setAttributes({
          fill: '#060429'
        }, true);
      }
   });
```

3. We also add a listener for the `mouseup` event (fired when the left mouse button is clicked and released) and call the sprite's `animate` method with the new width and height values:

```
...
mouseup: function(){
  rectangle2.animate({
    to: {
      width: 200,
      height: 60
    },
    duration: 2000
  }, true);
}
...
```

4. Lastly, we can add the rectangle to an `Ext.draw.Component` instance and see our code in action!

```
var shape2 = Ext.create('Ext.draw.Component', {
    renderTo: Ext.getBody(),
    width: 1000,
    height: 500,
    viewBox: false,

    items: [rectangle2]
});
```

Creating a bar chart with external data

A bar chart is an incredibly useful way of presenting quantitative data to users. This recipe will demonstrate how to create a bar chart and have it load data asynchronously from your server.

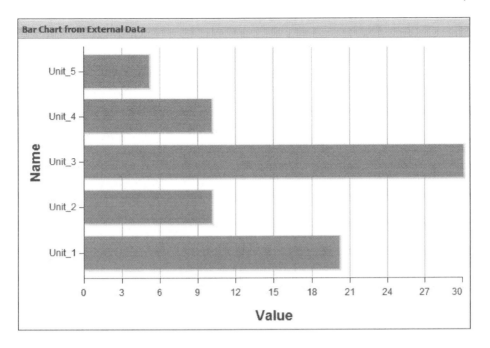

This recipe requires the use of a web server for serving the chart's data. A JSON file is provided with example data.

How to do it...

1. Start by defining a model to define the data we are loading:

```
Ext.define('Chart', {
    extend: 'Ext.data.Model',
    fields: [{
        name: 'name',
        type: 'string'
    }, {
        name: 'value',
        type: 'int'
    }]
});
```

2. Create a store with an AJAX proxy:

```
var store = Ext.create('Ext.data.Store', {
    model: 'Chart',
    proxy: {
        type: 'ajax',
        url: 'BarChart.json',
        reader: {
            type: 'json',
            root: 'data'
        }
    },
    autoLoad: true
});
```

3. Create a panel with a `fit` layout and render it to the document's body:

```
var panel = Ext.create('Ext.Panel', {
    width: 600,
    height: 400,
    title: 'Bar Chart from External Data',
    layout: 'fit',
    items: [
        ...
    ],
    style: 'margin: 50px',
    renderTo: Ext.getBody()
});
```

4. In the panel's `items` collection add a basic chart bound to the store created in step 2. The chart requires `numeric` and `category` axes and a `bar` series:

```
var panel = Ext.create('Ext.Panel', {
    ...
    items: {
        xtype: 'chart',
        animate: true,
        store: store,
        axes: [{
            type: 'Numeric',
            position: 'bottom',
            fields: ['value'],
            title: 'Value'
        }, {
            type: 'Category',
            position: 'left',
```

```
            fields: ['name'],
            title: 'Name'
        }],
        series: [{
            type: 'bar',
            axis: 'bottom',
            xField: 'name',
            yField: 'value'
        }]
    },
    ...
});
```

How it works...

We have started by defining a Model to represent an individual record being retrieved by the store. As the data that we return from the server has a `name` and `value` field we have defined these here.

The next piece of the puzzle is an `Ext.data.Store` that we use as the client-side cache for our data. We associate the chart model to the `Ext.data.Store` to ensure that it understands how the data is represented. The AJAX proxy (`Ext.data.proxy.Ajax`) is used for loading data into the store.

Now that the store is ready we just need a component to bind it to. We have created our component from the `Ext.chart.Chart` class using `xtype: 'chart'`. This gives us basic charting functionality, which we add our store, axes, and series to.

The axes are used to define the boundaries of the chart and, in this instance, create the horizontal and vertical axes. There are four types of axis available to us: numeric, category, time, and gauge. We have used the numeric and category types in our example and they allow us to plot numeric data and data representing names and other non-quantitive values.

The series handles the rendering of the data points across the chart. Here we've used the `Ext.chart.series.Bar` class to create a simple bar chart.

See also

▶ It may be worth reminding yourself of the data package for more information on working with Stores and Models. The first few recipes in *Chapter 7, Working with the Ext JS Data Package*, will be particularly useful.

Creating a pie chart with local data

The pie chart is a very common chart type and is very good at representing proportional data where each slice of the pie equates to the percentage that particular slice holds against the sum of the entire dataset.

This recipe is going to demonstrate how to create a pie chart representing the distribution of GitHub repositories across programming languages.

How to do it...

1. As with all of our data-bound examples, we start by creating an `Ext.data.Model`. We give it two fields—`Language` and `Percentage`:

```
Ext.define('LanguageShare', {
    extend: 'Ext.data.Model',
    fields: [{
        name: 'Language',
        type: 'string'
    }, {
        name: 'Percentage',
        type: 'int'
    }]
});
```

2. Now we define a data set to display in our chart. I have omitted some of the data for brevity:

```
var languageShareData = [{
  Language: 'C',
  Percentage: 7
},
...
{
  Language: 'Others',
  Percentage: 22
}];
```

3. Next we create an `Ext.data.Store` and load in our dataset. This will be used to bind to our chart:

```
var languageShareStore = Ext.create('Ext.data.Store', {
    model: 'LanguageShare',
    data: languageShareData
});
```

4. Define an `Ext.Panel` containing an `Ext.chart.Chart` configuration object, using its `xtype`, as its only item:

```
var panel = Ext.create('Ext.Panel', {
    width: 600,
    height: 400,
    title: 'Pie Chart - Language\'s Share of GitHub Repositories',
    layout: 'fit',
    items: [{
        xtype: 'chart'
    }],
    style: 'margin: 50px',
    renderTo: Ext.getBody()
});
```

5. We can now bind our chart to the Store we created in Step 3:

```
...
{
    xtype: 'chart',
    store: languageShareStore
}
...
```

6. Our next step is to create our `Ext.chart.series.Pie` instance that will tell the chart that we want the data to be represented as a pie chart. We tell it that the `Percentage` field is the one to use to calculate the size of each slice:

```
{
    xtype: 'chart',
    store: languageShareStore,
    series: [{
        type: 'pie',
        angleField: 'Percentage'
    }]
}
```

7. At this stage our pie chart will render our data but, by default, won't have any labels attached so we don't know which slice refers to which data! We can add a label to each slice by using the `label` property and configuring it with the field to grab the label value from and some other display properties:

```
{
    type: 'pie',
    angleField: 'Percentage',
    label: {
        display: 'rotate',
```

```
        contrast: true,
        field: 'Language'
    }
}
```

Our final pie chart can be seen in the following screenshot:

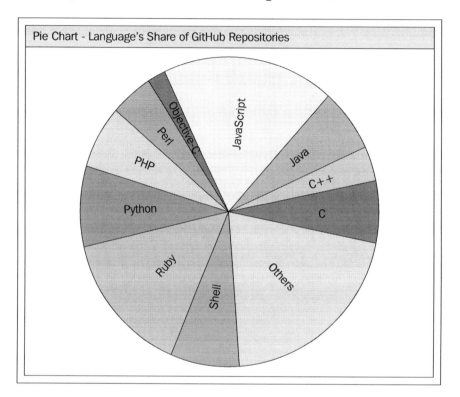

How it works...

As with all of the other chart types the `Ext.chart.Chart` class provides the infrastructure and canvas for our specific chart type to be rendered to.

We use the pie series `type` to have the `Ext.chart.series.Pie` class process the records contained in the bound store and turn it into a series of sprites to form a chart. This series will convert each of the records in the Store into a slice of the pie. All of the work to create the sprites is taken care of by the framework and so we don't need to work with the drawing package directly.

The most important configuration of this series type is the `angleField`. This tells the series which of our model fields holds the value that will be used when calculating the size of each record's slice.

We add labels to the chart by using the labels configuration that is used to configure the `Ext.chart.Label` mixin, which is applied to the `Ext.chart.series.Pie` class. These options allow us to configure how the labels are positioned and styled.

By choosing the `rotate` value for the `display` property the labels are positioned along the length of the slice. We also choose to set the `contrast` property to true so that the labels' colors are tailored to suit the underlying slice's color and therefore they can be easily read.

There's more...

The pie series offers us numerous other options to customize and tart up our charts. We will now explore two of these options to add that extra bit of flair to our pie chart.

Highlight each slice as users hover

We can easily apply styles to a pie's slice when the user hovers over it by using the `highlight` configuration option of the series. We pass this a `segment` object literal containing the styles we would like to apply to the segment when it is hovered over:

```
highlight: {
  segment: {

  }
}
```

We are going to apply a `margin` of `40` pixels to our slices so they slide outwards, exposing the slice individually, allowing a better look at its size:

```
highlight: {
  segment: {
    margin: 40
  }
}
```

We can see the outcome in the following diagram:

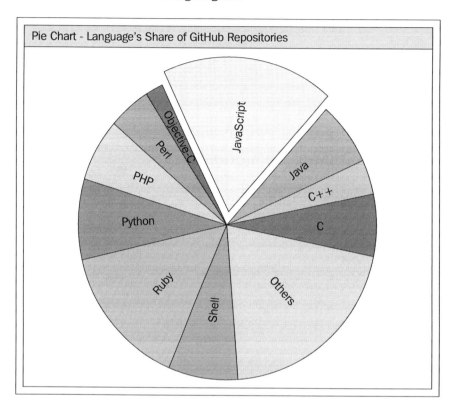

Scaling the slices in line with their magnitude

The pie series offers another piece of functionality that allows us to vary the size of the slice depending on the value contained in one of the model's fields. We will apply this feature simply based on the `Percentage` field, but it could equally be a different field.

We utilize the `lengthField` configuration of the pie series and pass it the name of the desired field as a string value. The following code demonstrates this:

```
...
lengthField: 'Percentage',
...
```

As we can see from the screenshot, this effect serves to exaggerate and emphasize each slice's size, or it can allow us to incorporate a second value in the same graph if we use a different `lengthField`.

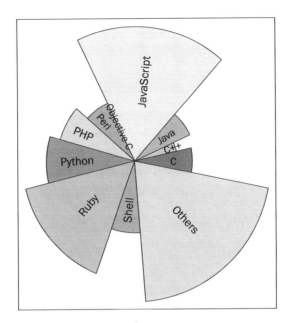

Creating a line chart with updating data

Line charts are one of the most commonly used types of graphs and are most suited to represent trending data, which is often regularly updated and required to be analyzed in real time.

In this recipe, we will look into creating a line chart that polls the server every second to retrieve a new record and plots that new point on the graph.

We will use the scenario of a heart-rate monitor, displaying someone's current heart rate at a specific time after loading the chart.

Getting ready...

We will be using a small PHP script to generate our data and will supply our Ext JS code with a single record on each load. The script accepts a single parameter called `currentCount` to ensure the `SecondsElapsed` field is correctly populated with the next value, but this would not be necessary if we were querying a real data source.

```php
$currentCount = $_GET['currentCount'];
$min = 150;
$max = 180;

$data = array();

$data[] = array(
    'SecondsElapsed' => $currentCount,
    'BeatsPerMinute' => rand($min, $max)
);

$output = array(
    'success'=> true,
    'data' => $data,
    'results' => count($data)
);

print json_encode($output);
```

How to do it...

1. We start by creating a simple `Ext.data.Model` to represent our `HeartRate` data object:

```javascript
Ext.define('HeartRate', {
    extend: 'Ext.data.Model',
    fields: [{
        name: 'SecondsElapsed',
        type: 'int'
    }, {
        name: 'BeatsPerMinute',
        type: 'int'
    }]
});
```

2. Next we create an `Ext.data.Store` that we will bind to our chart. We set this up to point to our `HeartRate.php` file discussed earlier. We also attach a handler function to our store's `beforeload` event where we increment the `currentCount` variable and attach it as a parameter to our AJAX calls:

```
var currentCount = 0;
var maxDisplayCount = 20;
var heartRateStore = Ext.create('Ext.data.Store', {
    model: 'HeartRate',
    proxy: {
      type: 'ajax',
      url: 'HeartRate.php',
      reader: {
        type: 'json',
        root: 'data'
      }
    },
    autoLoad: true,
    listeners: {
      beforeload: function(store, operation, opts){
        currentCount++;
        operation.params = {
          currentCount: currentCount
        };
      }
    }
});
```

3. Now we add a listener to the store's `load` event. This listener will be tasked with updating the chart's x-axis' `minimum` and `maximum` values so that they stay in sync with the data and only show 20 values at a time (defined by our `maxDisplayCount` variable). We then redraw the chart:

```
load: function(store, records){
  var chart = panel.items.get(0),
    secondsElapsedAxis = chart.axes.get(1),
    secondsElapsed = records[0].get('SecondsElapsed');

  secondsElapsedAxis.maximum = store.getCount() < maxDisplayCount
? maxDisplayCount : secondsElapsed;
  secondsElapsedAxis.minimum = store.getCount() < maxDisplayCount
? 0 : secondsElapsed - maxDisplayCount;

  chart.redraw();
}
```

4. The next step is to create an `Ext.Panel` with an `Ext.chart.Chart` instance within it. The chart should then be bound to `heartRateStore`:

```
var panel = Ext.create('Ext.Panel', {
    width: 600,
    height: 400,
    title: 'Line Chart - Heart Rate Monitor',
    layout: 'fit',
    items: [{
        xtype: 'chart',
        animate: true,
        store: heartRateStore
    }],
    style: 'margin: 50px',
    renderTo: Ext.getBody()
});
```

5. We are now able to define the chart's `series` as the 'line' type and set its `xField` and `yField` to be the `SecondsElapsed` and `BeatsPerMinute` fields respectively:

```
...
series: [{
    type: 'line',
    smooth: false,
    axis: 'left',
    xField: 'SecondsElapsed',
    yField: 'BeatsPerMinute'
}]
...
```

6. The chart's numeric axes are now declared. The y-axis is bound to the `BeatsPerMinute` field and given a position of left. The x-axis is bound to the `SecondsElapsed` field and positioned at the bottom:

```
...
axes: [{
        type: 'Numeric',
        grid: true,
        position: 'left',
        field: ['BeatsPerMinute'],
        title: 'Beats per Minute',
        minimum: 0,
        maximum: 200,
        majorTickSteps: 5
}, {
        type: 'Numeric',
        position: 'bottom',
        fields: 'SecondsElapsed',
        title: 'Seconds Elapsed',
        minimum: 0,
        maximum: 20,
```

```
        decimals: 0,
        constrain: true,
        majorTickSteps: 20
    }],
    ...
```

7. Finally, we make the magic happen by creating a repeating function using the `setInterval` function. We pass this a simple function that calls the `heartRateStore`'s `load` method, which is configured to append the newly loaded records to the existing ones, instead of replacing them:

```
setInterval(function(){
    heartRateStore.load({
        addRecords: true
    });
}, 1000);
```

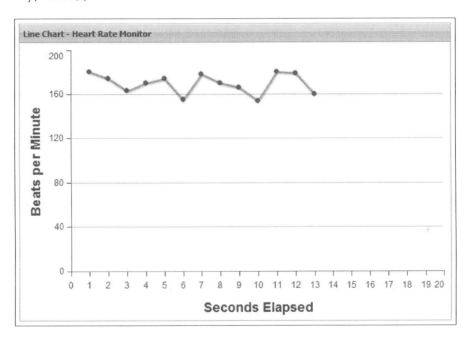

How it works...

The line chart we have created is setup in a fairly standard way. The two numeric axes bind to the integer fields within the `HeartRate` model and are displayed by the `Ext.chart.series.Line` class.

The hard work is done by our store's `load` event handler. This method effectively moves the chart's visible x-axis numbers to the left by one on each store load, where a new record is added. This gives the effect of the chart scrolling sideways.

We achieve this by retrieving a reference to the x-axis instance through the `Ext.chart.Chart` class' axes property. We then update its `minimum` and `maximum` values (these provide the range of numbers that are shown at the bottom), which will be updated when the chart is redrawn.

The other key area is the `addRecords` configuration passed into the heartRateStore's `load` method. By setting this property to true any new records retrieved by the load operation are appended to the existing dataset rather than replacing what is already there, which is the default behavior.

See also

> ▸ For more information on Stores and Models we recommend you revisit *Chapter 7, Working with the Ext JS Data Package*. The first few recipes in the chapter are particularly useful.

Customizing labels, colors, and axes

With little configuration it is possible to customize the look and feel of your chart. This recipe will demonstrate how easy it is to apply different themes, tweak colors, add grid lines, and ensure that your axes are presented neatly for a bar chart.

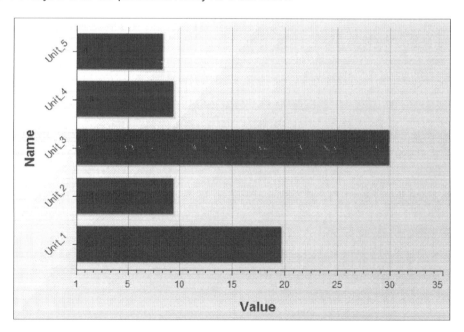

Getting ready

A web server is required for this recipe so the sample JSON data can be loaded. This is supplied in separate JSON file.

How to do it...

1. Start by defining a model to define the data we are loading:

```
Ext.define('Chart', {
    extend: 'Ext.data.Model',
    fields: [{
        name: 'name',
        type: 'string'
    }, {
        name: 'value',
        type: 'int'
    }]
});
```

2. Create a store with an AJAX proxy:

```
var store = Ext.create('Ext.data.Store', {
    model: 'Chart',
    proxy: {
        type: 'ajax',
        url: 'BarChart.json',
        reader: {
            type: 'json',
            root: 'data'
        }
    },
    autoLoad: true
});
```

3. Create a chart bound to the store and render it to the document's body:

```
var chart = Ext.create('Ext.chart.Chart', {
    width: 600,
    height: 400,
    animate: true,
    store: store,
    style: 'margin: 50px',
    renderTo: Ext.getBody()
});
```

4. Add the `theme` config to the chart and set it to red, then apply a gradient to the `background`:

```
var chart = Ext.create('Ext.chart.Chart', {
    ...
    theme: 'Red',
    background: {
        gradient: {
            angle: 30,
            stops: {
                0: {
                    color: '#FFFFFF'
                },
                100: {
                    color: '#FFDBDB'
                }
            }
        }
    }
});
```

5. We need `axes` for the bar chart. Add a `Numeric` and `Category` axis as follows:

```
var chart = Ext.create('Ext.chart.Chart', {
    ...
    axes: [{
        type: 'Numeric',
        position: 'bottom',
        fields: ['value'],
        title: 'Value',
        minimum: 1,
        maximum: 35,
        decimals: 0,
        majorTickSteps: 10,
        minorTickSteps: 5,
        grid: {
            'stroke-width': 2
        }
    }, {
        type: 'Category',
        position: 'left',
        fields: ['name'],
        title: 'Name',
        label: {
            rotate: {
```

```
                    degrees: 315
                }
            }
        }]
    });
```

6. Finally, add a bar series. The label, in this case, adds the values for each bar:

```
var chart = Ext.create('Ext.chart.Chart', {
        ...
    series: [{
        type: 'bar',
        axis: 'bottom',
        xField: 'name',
        yField: 'value',
        label: {
            field: 'value',
            display: 'insideStart',
            orientation: 'horizontal',
            color: '#333'
        }
    }]
});
```

How it works...

We've started by defining an Ext.data.Model and Ext.data.Store that we are using to remotely load data for our bar chart. We can split the results of this recipe into three sections:

► **Changing the colors and theme**: Step 4 above demonstrates how straightforward it is to change the theme of the charts. The theme configuration option of Ext.chart. Chart takes a string, which is the name of the theme you desire. The framework is supplied with a variety of themes such as Base, Green, Sky, Red, and Purple. A full list of supplied themes is available in the Ext.chart.Chart documentation. By default the theme is Base. It's also possible to create your own theme if required. This is explained in more detail in the following *There's More* section.

The background gradient is applied through the background config option. The gradient is created with the Ext.draw.Component. The angle property is used to ensure that the gradient starts in the top left and goes to the bottom right. The value is set in degrees. The stops object takes keys (in our case 0 and 100) that contain the desired style variations. In this example our gradient starts at white (#FFFFFF) and ends pink (#FFDBDB).

▶ **Configuring the Axes**: We have configured the numeric axis and defined a `maximum` (35) and `minimum` (1) for the axis. The `majorTickSteps` and `minorTickSteps` properties allow us to present the axis to the user in a fixed manner. In this case for each major tick there will be five minor ticks. Further configuration is available from the `Ext.chart.axis.Axis` class.

▶ **Adding Labels**: The label property in the `Ext.chart.series.Series` class allows us to add a label to the chart's item showing the value of a field. In this example we have added a label to display the columns value by setting the `Ext.chart.Label` class's `field` property to `value`.

There's more...

As mentioned above we're going to see what's required to create our own custom theme for a chart using the `Ext.chart.theme.Theme` class.

Creating a bespoke theme

Creating a bespoke theme is done by extending the `Ext.chart.theme.Base` class and adding your own custom styles/colors to its various properties.

The following theme is by no means complete. However, it illustrates how to go about creating one:

```
Ext.define('Ext.chart.theme.MyTheme', {
    extend: 'Ext.chart.theme.Base',

    constructor: function(config){

        this.callParent([Ext.apply({
            axis: {
                fill: '#ccc',
                stroke: '#ccc'
            },
            colors: ['#111', '#333', '#555', '#777', '#000']
        }, config)]);
    }
});
```

Now that we have defined the class `Ext.chart.theme.MyTheme`, we can use it in our charts by specifying `theme: 'MyTheme'`. For a complete listing of the configurable properties we recommend you to look at the source code in the `Ext.chart.theme.Base` class.

- ▸ The comprehensive guide in the Ext JS documentation, which goes into great detail on the options available.

- ▸ The *Creating a bar chart with external data* recipe for an introduction into creating charts.

- ▸ For further details about Models and Stores look back at *Chapter 7, Working with the Ext JS Data Package*.

- ▸ To learn about theming a full application see *Chapter 12, Advanced Ext JS for the Perfect App*.

Attaching events to chart components

It's possible to listen out for events on charts allowing users to interact with the data being presented. This includes interactions, such as clicking on charts' series (bars, lines, and so on) and hovering over specific areas of a graph.

By adding support for these types of interactions to your charts you will enhance the user experience and allow more in-depth data to be revealed when it's needed.

This example will demonstrate how to listen for various mouse events, such as clicking and hovering.

Getting ready

This recipe requires the use of a web server for serving the charts data. A JSON file is provided with example data.

How to do it...

1. Start by defining a model for the data we are loading into the chart:

```
Ext.define('Chart', {
    extend: 'Ext.data.Model',
    fields: [{
        name: 'name',
        type: 'string'
    }, {
        name: 'value',
        type: 'int'
    }]
});
```

2. Create a store with an AJAX proxy. Set `autoLoad: true` to load the data automatically:

```
var store = Ext.create('Ext.data.Store', {
    model: 'Chart',
    proxy: {
        type: 'ajax',
        url: 'BarChart.json',
        reader: {
            type: 'json',
            root: 'data'
        }
    },
    autoLoad: true
});
```

3. Create a basic chart rendered to the document's body. Give it a `Numeric` and `Category` axis and set a `bar` series:

```
var chart = Ext.create('Ext.chart.Chart', {
    width: 600,
    height: 400,
    animate: true,
    store: store,
    axes: [{
        type: 'Numeric',
        position: 'bottom',
        fields: ['value'],
        title: 'Value'
    }, {
        type: 'Category',
        position: 'left',
        fields: ['name'],
        title: 'Name'
    }],
    series: [{
        type: 'bar',
        axis: 'bottom',
        xField: 'name',
        yField: 'value'
    }],
    style: 'margin: 50px',
    renderTo: Ext.getBody()
});
```

4. In the bar series add a `listener` and listen for the `itemmouseup` event. When the mouse click is released the function will be called passing the `item` argument:

```
var chart = Ext.create('Ext.chart.Chart', {
    ...
    series: [{
        type: 'bar',
        axis: 'bottom',
        xField: 'name',
        yField: 'value',
        listeners: {
            itemmouseup: function(item){
                console.log('Column Value: ' + item.value[1] + ',
Column Name: ' + item.value[0]);
            }
        }
    }],
    ...
});
```

5. Run the code in a browser and watch the console as you click on the bars. The output will be like this:

```
Column Value: 30, Column Name: Unit_3
```

6. To demonstrate this working in a line chart change the series to the following:

```
var chart = Ext.create('Ext.chart.Chart', {
    ...
    series: [{
        type: 'line',
        axis: 'left',
        xField: 'name',
        yField: 'value',
        listeners: {
            itemmousedown: function(item){
                console.log('Mouse Pressed');
            },
            itemmouseup: function(item){
                console.log('Mouse Up');
            },
```

```
            itemmouseout: function(item){
                console.log('Mouse Out');
            },
            itemmouseover: function(item){
                console.log('Mouse Over');
            }
        }
    }],
    ...
});
```

7. When looking at the console in the browser the output will be determined by how you move the mouse and where you click:

How it works...

This works by listening to the events available in the `Ext.chart.series.Series` class. When the event is triggered, for example, by mouse interaction, the `getItemForPoint` method is called, which finds the corresponding item in the series.

The item returned from this method is passed into our function, which is then fired. From here we can do additional processing or display feedback/messages to the user.

Inside our event handler we can use the object passed in to determine more information about the item that was retrieved. The item object contains the `series` object, a `value` object with the item's value(s), the x/y coordinates or point, and the item's rendering sprite.

See also

► The recipes on event handling in *Chapter 2, Manipulating the DOM, Handling Events, and Making AJAX Requests*, which explores the finer details of listening for, and binding handlers to, events.

► The *Creating bar charts with external data* recipe for an introduction into creating charts.

► To find out more about data storage see *Chapter 7*.

Creating a live updating chart bound to an editable grid

While the animations in Ext JS 4's charts might be pleasant to watch it's often useful to have charts updating on the fly as your users manipulate data. Here we'll explore how to bind a chart to an editable grid. The user will make changes to the data in the grid and the pie chart will immediately reflect the change.

While you may wish to save the changes made in the grid to your database, you'll notice that the store doesn't need to be reloaded for the pie chart to change.

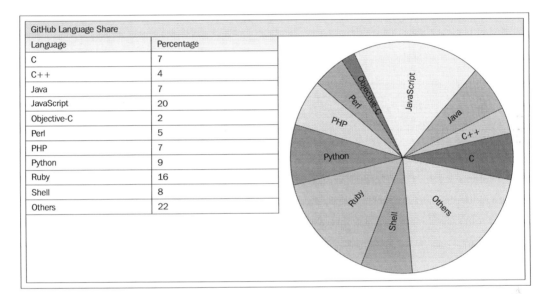

GitHub Language Share

Language	Percentage
C	7
C++	4
Java	7
JavaScript	20
Objective-C	2
Perl	5
PHP	7
Python	9
Ruby	16
Shell	8
Others	22

How to do it...

1. Start by defining a model for the data we are loading into the chart and grid:

```
Ext.define('LanguageShare', {
    extend: 'Ext.data.Model',
    fields: [{
        name: 'Language',
        type: 'string'
```

```
    }, {
        name: 'Percentage',
        type: 'int'
    }]
});
```

2. Now define a dataset for the chart and grid:

```
var languageShareData = [{
    Language: 'C',
    Percentage: 7
}, {
    Language: 'C++',
    Percentage: 4
}, {
    Language: 'Java',
    Percentage: 7
}, {
    Language: 'JavaScript',
    Percentage: 20
}, ...];
```

3. Create an `Ext.data.Store` and load in our dataset. This will be used to bind the data to the grid and chart:

```
var languageShareStore = Ext.create('Ext.data.Store', {
    model: 'LanguageShare',
    data: languageShareData
});
```

4. Create a basic chart with a `pie` series. Assign it to the variable `chart`:

```
var chart = Ext.create('Ext.chart.Chart', {
    height: 400,
    width: 400,
    store: languageShareStore,
    animate: true,
    series: [{
        type: 'pie',
        angleField: 'Percentage',
        label: {
            display: 'rotate',
            contrast: true,
            field: 'Language'
        }
    }]
});
```

5. Create a grid panel with a `CellSelectionModel` and `CellEditing` plugin. Ensure that the `Percentage` column is editable by adding a `numberfield`. Assign the editor grid to the variable `grid`:

```
var grid = Ext.create('Ext.grid.Panel', {
    store: languageShareStore,
    height: 400,
    width: 400,
    border: 0,
    columns: [{
        header: 'Language',
        dataIndex: 'Language',
        flex: 1
    }, {
        header: 'Percentage',
        dataIndex: 'Percentage',
        flex: 1,
        field: {
            xtype: 'numberfield',
            allowBlank: false
        }
    }],
    selType: 'cellmodel',
    plugins: [Ext.create('Ext.grid.plugin.CellEditing', {
        clicksToEdit: 1
    })]

});
```

6. Finally, create a panel with an `hbox` layout and render it to the document's body. Add the `grid` and `chart` to the panel's `items` collection:

```
var panel = Ext.create('Ext.Panel', {
    width: 800,
    height: 427,
    title: 'GitHub Language Share',
    layout: {
        type: 'hbox',
        align: 'stretch'
    },
    items: [grid, chart],
    style: 'margin: 50px',
    renderTo: Ext.getBody()
});
```

How it works...

As you can see it's surprisingly straightforward to produce a dynamic chart that changes as the stores data changes. In this example, both `grid` and `chart` are bound to the same store—`languageShareStore`. When the values in the grid are changed the `languageShareStore` is updated to reflect the new value, which consequently results in the pie chart being redrawn with the updated data.

See also

▸ To see further examples of each of the chart types see the earlier recipes in this chapter.

▸ *Chapter 8, Displaying and Editing Tabular Data*, explains how to use and configure grids and editor grids.

▸ For more details about data modeling and storage revisit *Chapter 7*.

11
Theming your Application

In this chapter, we will cover:

- ▶ Compiling SASS with Compass
- ▶ Introduction to SASS
- ▶ Using Ext JS' SASS variables
- ▶ Using the UI config option
- ▶ Creating your own theme mixins
- ▶ Restyling a panel
- ▶ Creating images for legacy browsers

Introduction

Changing the look and feel of an Ext JS application has always been a big task involving getting your hands dirty, trawling through CSS styles, and creating custom image sprites to support those pesky legacy browsers. Ext JS 4 has addressed this problem in a spectacular fashion and it is now very easy to move away from the default theme.

This chapter describes the tasks involved in customizing the look and feel of your Ext JS application. You will learn the basics of SASS and Compass, and move on to compiling the framework's SASS. We will then explore how to customize your theme with SASS options and custom mixins. Finally, we will demonstrate how to take care of legacy browsers using the Sencha SDK tools' slicer tool.

Compiling SASS with Compass

Ext JS 4's entire style set is built upon SASS and Compass and makes changes to the framework's style a walk in the park. By utilizing these technologies the look and feel of your Ext JS application can be altered with extreme flexibility. It will also help in increasing the maintainability of your code because of the reduction in code needed and the greater organization.

This recipe will start by explaining what SASS and Compass are and how they fit into the web-development workflow. We will then move on to learn how to set up your development environment to take advantage of these two tools. Finally, we will move onto compiling our complete framework's CSS stylesheet, ready for customization following the subsequent recipes in this chapter.

Getting ready

It is important to understand how these two tools fit together and how they can play such a big role in making our application's style so flexible.

What is SASS?

SASS (Syntactically Awesome Stylesheets) is an enhancement of the CSS language that extends it by adding additional functionality and capabilities. SASS introduces the idea of variables, mixins, and maths to our CSS while also bringing in a nested syntax and selector inheritance allowing us to remove large amounts of duplication.

This extended CSS syntax is then compiled into regular CSS, which can then be included in your website.

A simple SASS snippet with its compiled CSS equivalent can be found as follows:

```
// Sass
table
{
  width: 100%;
  color: #3F4E5E;
  background-color: #EEE;

  tbody
  {
    td
    {
      border-bottom: 1px solid #999;
      border-left: 1px solid #000;
    }
```

```
  }
}

// Generated CSS
table {
  width: 100%;
  color: #3F4E5E;
  background-color: #EEE;
}

table tbody td {
  border-bottom: 1px solid #999;
  border-left: 1px solid #000;
}
```

What is Compass?

Compass is a CSS authoring framework that uses SASS as its foundation and provides us with a whole host of helper functions, mixins, cross-browser compatibility tools, and a lot more. All these features make creating CSS even simpler.

How to do it...

First we will look at setting up our development environment so we can use SASS and Compass. If you are on a Windows machine you will first have to install Ruby; for Mac OS X users this comes preinstalled so you can skip to step 4:

1. Compass is written in Ruby, so we must first install Ruby on our machines. To do this, simply navigate to `http://rubyforge.org/frs/?group_id=167` and download the latest version.

2. Once downloaded run the executable and follow the wizard to install, accepting all of the default settings.

3. Now Ruby is installed, we must open the command prompt with Ruby by using the **Start Command Prompt with Ruby** shortcut created within Ruby's start menu folder:

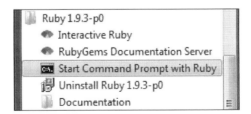

4. SASS and Compass are both installed through RubyGems so we can install them by typing the following into the command prompt (or Terminal, if you are on OS X) window:

   Windows: `gem install compass`

   OS X: `sudo gem install compass`

5. With Ruby and Compass installed we can now start using it to compile Ext JS stylesheets. We will demonstrate this by simply recreating the standard theme from our own `.scss` file.

6. Ext JS provides sample `config.rb` and `my-ext-theme.scss` files, which are needed to configure Compass and define how our SASS will be compiled. We will start by copying these files from the `resources\themes\templates\resources\sass` folder within the Ext JS SDK (left-hand side of the following image) into another folder that we will name `cookbook` in the main `resources` folder, shown on the right. We have then renamed the `.scss` file to `cookbook-theme.scss`.

 `.scss` is the file extension given to SASS stylesheets. This file type can be compiled into regular CSS.

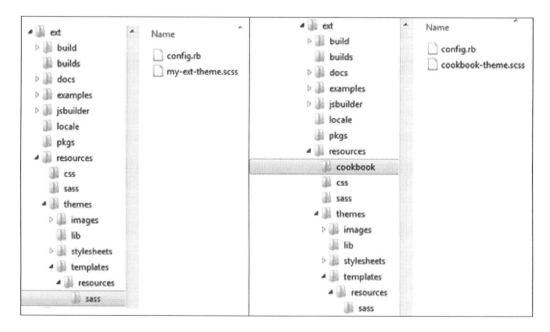

7. Next we open the `config.rb` file and edit the `$ext_path` variable, which defines how Compass can get from this file's location to the root of the Ext JS SDK. In our case we change this to move up two folder levels:

   `$ext_path = "../.."`

8. The `cookbook-theme.scss` file contains the style definitions that Compass will compile. This file contains definitions to import all of Ext JS SASS components.

9. Our last step is to compile our SASS and have it generate our `cookbook-theme.css` file containing the framework's complete styles. First, within our Ruby command prompt, we navigate to our new `cookbook` folder. Next, we use the command `compass compile`, which will start to compile the SASS. We can then look in the `resources/css` folder and find our newly created `cookbook-theme.css` file:

How it works...

The `config.rb` file contains all the configuration options that will be used when Compass is executed and our SASS is compiled. There are a variety of options that can be set, which will affect how the CSS is built.

The `.scss` file contains the entire SASS markup that will be compiled into a plain CSS file. This sample file basically imports all of the required SASS mixins provided by the framework from other `.scss` files, resulting in a full CSS file.

See also

▶ The Compass homepage (`http://compass-style.org`), which has lots of resources available from getting started guides to advanced usage examples.

▶ The next recipe, *Introduction to SASS*, which will explain the syntax and main features of SASS.

Introduction to SASS

As we have mentioned, SASS is an enhancement to the CSS language that, when compiled, produces CSS style rules ready for inclusion in our websites. By using it we gain access to a huge range of powerful features to make creating CSS styles much quicker, easier, and which will increase the maintainability of your app's styles greatly.

This recipe will be a short introduction to the main syntax and concepts of SASS, which are used within Ext JS' styles. By mastering these basics it will make theming our Ext JS applications a breeze and allow us to customize them with the same levels of flexibility.

Getting ready

This recipe will require SASS and Compass to be set up so we can compile our SASS stylesheets. If you haven't already done so, please revisit the first recipe in this chapter and follow the instructions to get you started.

In addition to setting up SASS and Compass, we are going to need to create a `config.rb` file within the directory that we are running this example from. The contents of this file simply need to contain the location of the SASS files, the output location, and the output mode:

```
sass_path = File.dirname(__FILE__)

css_path = sass_path

output_style = :expanded
```

How to do it...

To demonstrate how to style an HTML page with SASS we are going to create a very simple page with some details about this chapter of the book:

1. We start by defining an HTML page that contains a couple of heading elements, a div element, and a list of the chapter's recipes:

```
<div class="cookbook">

  <h1>Ext JS 4 Cookbook</h1>
```

```
<div class="chapter">

  <h2>Theming your Application</h2>

  <div class="description">
    This chapter describes the tasks involved for customizing
the look and feel of an Ext JS application.
  </div>

  <ul class="recipes">
    <li>Compiling SASS with Compass</li>
    <li class="current-recipe">Introduction to SASS</li>
    <li>Using SASS Variables in Ext JS</li>
    <li>Using the UI Config Option</li>
    <li>Creating your own Theme Mixins</li>
    <li>Restyling a Panel</li>
    <li>Creating images for Legacy Browsers</li>
  </ul>

</div>

</div>
```

2. Next we create a `.scss` file which will contain our SASS code. We create this in the same folder as our HTML file to keep things simple.

3. We can now start writing our SASS styles. We start by importing the Compass library so we can take advantage of all its built-in mixins and functions. Then we define a variable containing a base color that our page will use:

```
@import "compass";
$base-color: #545454;
```

4. We define our first style to attach to elements with the `cookbook` class. This is done using a familiar CSS syntax. We then give it a `color` using our `$base-color` variable and define its `font` style using SASS's nested syntax:

```
.cookbook
{
  color: $base-color;
  font: {
    family: Helvetica;
    size: 0.9em;
  }
}
```

5. Now we define the style of the H1 tags within the cookbook DIV. We do this by nesting the H1 tag within the curly braces of the cookbook's style. We give this style a font-size of 2.5em and a color value 20 percent darker than our predefined base color using Compass's darken function:

```
.cookbook
{
  color: $base-color;
  font: {
    family: Helvetica;
    size: 0.9em;
  }
  h1
  {
    font-size: 2.5em;
    color: darken($base-color, 20%);
  }
}
```

6. Once again nested within the .cookbook's curly braces we define the styles for our chapter class. We set this to have a width of 50% and a box shadow using the box-shadow mixin, which produces full cross-browser box-shadow CSS:

```
.chapter
{
  @include box-shadow(0 0 3px darken($base-color, 40%));
  width: 50%;
}
```

7. We now define the style for a chapter's H2, UL, and DIV tags. We do this by simply nesting the selectors within the chapter's definition. We use another function of Compass—the complement function. This takes our base color and returns a complementing color:

```
h2
{
  font-size: 1.5em;
  color: complement($base-color);
}

ul, div
{
  margin: 0 30px;
}
```

8. Our next element is our recipe list. We style this by nesting the LI selector inside UL and give it some padding:

```
ul
{
  li
  {
    padding: 5px 0;
  }
}
```

9. Finally, in our HTML, you will see we have added a current-recipe class to the second recipe LI. We can define this element's style by using the & selector, which adds a reference to the current selector's parent selector and combines them:

```
ul
{
    li
    {
        padding: 5px 0;
        &.current-recipe
        {
            background-color: yellow;
        }
    }
}
```

10. If we now compile our SASS (using the compass compile command), it will produce a raw CSS file with the following styles:

```
.cookbook {
  color: #545454;
  font-family: Helvetica;
  font-size: 0.9em;
}
.cookbook h1 {
  font-size: 2.5em;
  color: #212121;
}
.cookbook .chapter {
  -moz-box-shadow: 0 0 3px black;
  -webkit-box-shadow: 0 0 3px black;
  -o-box-shadow: 0 0 3px black;
  box-shadow: 0 0 3px black;
  width: 50%;
}
```

```
.cookbook .chapter h2 {
  font-size: 1.5em;
  color: #545454;
}
.cookbook .chapter ul, .cookbook .chapter div {
  margin: 0 30px;
}
.cookbook .chapter ul li {
  padding: 5px 0;
}
.cookbook .chapter ul li.current-recipe {
  background-color: yellow;
}
```

The result of all these steps can be seen in the following screenshot:

ExtJS 4 Cookbook

Theming your Application

This chapter describes the tasks involved for customising the look and feel of an ExtJS application.

- Compiling SASS with Compass
- Introduction to SASS
- Using ExtJS' SASS Variables
- Using the UI Config Option
- Creating your own Theme Mixins
- Restyling a Panel
- Creating images for Legacy Browsers

How it works...

Now, that was a lot to take in one go, so we will take each main concept individually and explain how it works:

▶ **Variables**: Our very first step was to define a variable that would control the base color of our page. SASS variables work as they do in any other language, in that they can be referenced instead of a hard value and assigned to at any point.

They must be prefixed with a $ symbol and are assigned to using a colon instead of an equals (=) symbol as you will probably be used to.

▶ **Nesting**: As you have seen we have used a lot of nesting in our SASS stylesheet. By nesting selectors SASS combines the preceding parent selectors with the current one, to produce a fully qualified CSS selector.

In our simple example's output, you can see that the `.cookbook .chapter ul` selector is written three times and we are only applying three styles! By nesting our styles we remove this repetition, which previously had to be entered by hand, and let SASS take care of it for us. In addition to the nesting of selectors you will also have noticed the way we defined the `font` property using a JS-style object literal. By using this syntax SASS will combine the parent property-name (that is, `font`) with each of the object's properties to produce individual CSS properties:

```
font: {
  family: Helvetica;
  size: 0.9em;
}
```

becomes

```
font-family: Helvetica;
font-size: 0.9em;
```

▶ **Functions**: We have made use of two of SASS's built-in functions, namely `darken` and `complement`. These work in the same way as any other language's functions. They accept parameters within parenthesis and return a value. The `darken` function takes a color and a percentage value and returns a color that is darker than the original by the percentage value. Similarly the `complement` function accepts a color and returns its complementary color.

▶ **Mixins**: Mixins are a very important feature of SASS and are used heavily within Ext JS, as you will find out in the later recipes. Mixins are similar to functions but can return a series of CSS statements rather than just a single value. In our example we use the built-in `box-shadow` mixin. This allows us to specify our box shadow's characteristics once and have SASS extrapolate that into all of the separate rules required for cross-browser compatibility. We can see below our single mixin call and then the output once it has been compiled:

```
@include box-shadow(0 0 3px darken($base-color, 40%));


// output
-moz-box-shadow: 0 0 3px black;
-webkit-box-shadow: 0 0 3px black;
-o-box-shadow: 0 0 3px black;
box-shadow: 0 0 3px black;
```

This quickly saves us a lot of hassle in both maintenance and the headache of having to remember all of the different prefixes and rule syntaxes. SASS offers a mixin for almost all of the usual CSS3 properties, making writing it much quicker!

▶ **& Selector**: The & selector is used to reference the parent of our current selector. By adding the & character before a selector its parent's selector will be added to its definition allowing us deeper control over our selectors. In our example, we wanted to give a specific style to the LI element that had the class `current-recipe`. If we had omitted the & keyword we would have had a simple nested statement of `.cookbook .chapter ul li .current-recipe`, which would not have worked. By including the & keyword we combine the parent selector (`li`) with our `.current-recipe` class producing `.cookbook .chapter ul li.current-recipe`.

There's more...

Another feature of SASS that we did not use in our previous example is its maths support. SASS enables us to perform simple calculations that allow us to have our style's sizing and layout properties adjust dynamically based upon a master value.

We will demonstrate this with a slightly contrived example using the HTML we created at the beginning of this recipe. Imagine we always want to keep the top and bottom padding of our LI elements exactly 1/6th of our UL's left margin.

Traditionally we would have to remember to update our LI's padding value if our margin changed. In this example, this isn't a huge problem but in large applications this can quickly become a maintenance nightmare. We use SASS's maths support to have this ratio maintained automatically:

▶ First we define a variable to hold our UL's left and right margin values:

```
$element-side-margin: 30px;
```

▶ Next we set our LI's top and bottom padding to this variable's value, divided by six. The syntax for this is identical to most other languages, using the traditional maths operators:

```
padding: $element-side-margin / 6;
```

If we now compile this, we will see the padding value has compiled to 5 px. Try updating the variable's value and recompiling, and you will see the padding value adjusting accordingly.

See also

▶ The SASS homepage (`http://sass-lang.com`) to get more information of SASS and its features.

▶ The previous recipe that will walk you through setting up Compass so that you can compile your SASS stylesheets.

▶ The next recipe in this chapter looks at utilizing variables in SASS with a focus on using the SASS variables that control Ext JS styles.

Using Ext JS' SASS variables

One of the main reasons that Ext JS theming is so flexible is that it extracts almost every detail of each component's style into its own SASS variable. This means that we can configure the entire framework by simply setting some variables to our desired value and have them propagate throughout the stylesheet when it is compiled.

This recipe will highlight some of the most important global variables that can be used to customize the default Ext JS theme.

Getting ready

We start by making a copy of the template `config.rb` and `my-ext-theme.scss` files, which will be used as our base. These can be found in the `resources\themes\ templates\resources\sass` folder of your Ext JS SDK.

We copy them into a new folder and rename the `.scss` file to `cookbook-theme.scss`.

Next we must compile this SASS file using the `compass compile` command to produce a `cookbook-theme.css file`.

To demonstrate our examples we have copied the "themes" example from the "examples" folder and referenced our new CSS file from it. We are now able to see all of the framework's widgets on one page with the default theme. We can now start to customize it using variables.

How to do it...

We will take a few of the main SASS variables in turn and show how to set them and what effect they will have on our app.

$base-color

This is the most influential SASS variable and affects almost every component in the framework. By updating this color value all the components will be updated relative to it and provides us a quick and easy way to customize our entire application's look.

We can see this by assigning a new color to it at the start of our `.scss` file to a light purple color:

```
$base-color: #B89FED;
```

After recompiling our SASS and reloading our themes example, we can see our application's look has changed completely:

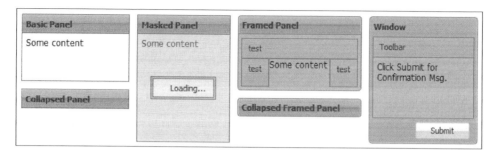

 You must include any variable definitions before importing `ext/default/all` into our `custom.scss` file.

$font-size and $font-family

We can also globally control the size and style of the application's font by setting the `$font-size` and `$font-family` variables at the start of our SASS file. We can demonstrate this by increasing the font size from its default `12` to `16` pixels and changing the font to `Times New Roman`:

```
$font-size: 16px;
$font-family: Times New Roman;
```

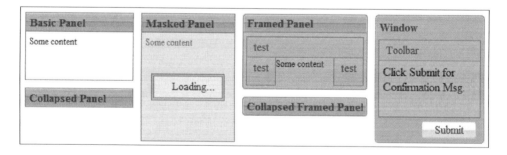

Widgets

Each widget in the framework has its own set of variables that define how it looks. All of these can be customized within our SASS file and the CSS will be altered accordingly. For example, a simple button has almost 100 variables that can be used to change its appearance. The following list contains some of the variables that are available to change a small button:

- `$button-small-border-radius`
- `$button-small-border-width`

- ▶ `$button-small-padding`
- ▶ `$button-small-text-padding`
- ▶ `$button-small-font-size`
- ▶ `$button-small-font-size-over`
- ▶ `$button-small-font-size-focus`
- ▶ `$button-small-font-size-pressed`
- ▶ `$button-small-font-size-disabled`
- ▶ `$button-small-font-weight`
- ▶ `$button-small-font-weight-over`
- ▶ `$button-small-font-weight-focus`
- ▶ `$button-small-font-weight-pressed`
- ▶ `$button-small-font-weight-disabled`
- ▶ `$button-small-font-family`
- ▶ `$button-small-font-family-over`
- ▶ `$button-small-font-family-focus`
- ▶ `$button-small-font-family-pressed`
- ▶ `$button-small-font-family-disabled`
- ▶ `$button-small-icon-size`

We can assign a new value to these in the same way we have done in our previous examples and recompile our CSS to see the changes. We will change the border radius of our buttons to 15 pixels as a demonstration:

```
$button-small-border-radius: 15px;
```

How it works...

Ext JS defines all of its variables and their default values in separate files, which are included at the beginning of the project when the `_all.scss` file is imported with the call `@import 'ext4/default/all';`. Any custom definitions must therefore come before this so they can be used within all of the subsequently imported SASS files.

▸ The first two recipes of this chapter that explain how to set up Compass, and give an introduction into SASS and how to use it.

Using the UI config option

Sencha provide a series of mixins with Ext JS 4 that allow you to quickly and easily create custom styles for a wide range of components. These mixins can be used to create custom UI styles, which you can apply to panels, buttons, and so on.

For example, the default styling for a button is available for a variety of sizes of button. However, in each case the color is the same. By creating a button `ui` with the `extjs-button-ui` mixin you can create a button with a different color for use with a different action. This recipe will demonstrate the principles and steps required to use the `ui` mixins and apply them to your components.

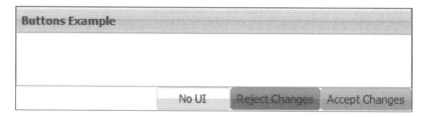

Getting ready

This recipe will require SASS and Compass to be set up so we can compile our SASS stylesheets. If you haven't already done so, please revisit the first recipe in this chapter and follow the instructions to get you started.

You'll need to prepare a `config.rb` file for compiling your SASS like so:

```
$ext_path = "../extjs"
sass_path = File.dirname(__FILE__)
css_path = sass_path
output_style = :expanded
load File.join(File.dirname(__FILE__), $ext_path, 'resources',
'themes')
```

How to do it...

1. Start by creating a `.scss` file called `CustomTheme.scss` and adding some basic configuration to it:

```
$include-default: false;

@import 'ext4/default/all';

@include extjs-panel;
@include extjs-button;
```

2. Compile the SASS with the `compass compile` command so that the file `CustomTheme.css` is generated.

3. Include the stylesheet in your HTML file:

```
<link rel="stylesheet" type="text/css" href="CustomTheme.css">
```

4. Render a panel to the document's body with buttons in the panel's `buttons` collection:

```
Ext.onReady(function(){
    Ext.create('Ext.panel.Panel', {
        title: 'Buttons Example',
        width: 400,
        height: 100,
        buttons: [{
            text: 'No UI'
        }, {
            text: 'Reject Changes'
        }, {
            text: 'Accept Changes'
        }],
        renderTo: Ext.getBody(),
        style: 'margin: 50px'
    });
});
```

5. Using the `extjs-button-ui` mixin, create a UI to apply custom styles to the button. Place this inside your SASS file and pass it the desired configuration. This will create the necessary styles for a green button:

```
@include extjs-button-ui(
    'accept-small',

    $border-radius: $button-small-border-radius,
    $border-width: $button-small-border-width,
```

```
$border-color: #90EE90,
$border-color-over: #90EE90,
$border-color-focus: #90EE90,
$border-color-pressed: #90EE90,
$border-color-disabled: #90EE90,

$padding: $button-small-padding,
$text-padding: $button-small-text-padding,

$background-color: #90EE90,
$background-color-over: #90EE90,
$background-color-focus: #90EE90,
$background-color-pressed: #90EE90,
$background-color-disabled: #90EE90,

$background-gradient: $button-default-background-gradient,
$background-gradient-over: $button-default-background-
gradient-over,
$background-gradient-focus: $button-default-background-
gradient-focus,
$background-gradient-pressed: $button-default-background-
gradient-pressed,
$background-gradient-disabled: $button-default-background-
gradient-disabled,

$color: #333,
$color-over: #333,
$color-focus: #333,
$color-pressed: #333,
$color-disabled: #333,

$font-size: $button-small-font-size,
$font-size-over: $button-small-font-size-over,
$font-size-focus: $button-small-font-size-focus,
$font-size-pressed: $button-small-font-size-pressed,
$font-size-disabled: $button-small-font-size-disabled,

$font-weight: $button-small-font-weight,
$font-weight-over: $button-small-font-weight-over,
$font-weight-focus: $button-small-font-weight-focus,
$font-weight-pressed: $button-small-font-weight-pressed,
$font-weight-disabled: $button-small-font-weight-disabled,

$font-family: $button-small-font-family,
$font-family-over: $button-small-font-family-over,
$font-family-focus: $button-small-font-family-focus,
$font-family-pressed: $button-small-font-family-pressed,
```

```
        $font-family-disabled: $button-small-font-family-disabled,

        $icon-size: $button-small-icon-size
    );
```

6. Do the same again to create the styles for a red button (some configuration options have been omitted for brevity).

```
@include extjs-button-ui(
    'reject-small',

    ...

    $border-color: #F08080,
    $border-color-over: #F08080,
    $border-color-focus: #F08080,
    $border-color-pressed: #F08080,
    $border-color-disabled: #F08080,

    ...

    $background-color: #F08080,
    $background-color-over: #F08080,
    $background-color-focus: #F08080,
    $background-color-pressed: #F08080,
    $background-color-disabled: #F08080,

    ...

    $color: #333,
    $color-over: #333,
    $color-focus: #333,
    $color-pressed: #333,
    $color-disabled: #333,

    ...
);
```

7. Re-compile the SASS using the command `compass compile`.

8. We're now ready to apply the UIs to the buttons. This is achieved via the `ui` config option. Update the buttons on the panel with their respective UIs.

```
Ext.create('Ext.panel.Panel', {
    ...
    buttons: [{
        text: 'No UI'
    }, {
        text: 'Reject Changes',
        ui: 'reject'
```

```
    }, {
        text: 'Accept Changes',
        ui: 'accept'
    }],
    ...
});
```

How it works...

The `ui` config option allows you to set the style for a component. By default the buttons element will have the CSS class `x-btn-default-small`; however, by changing the ui value, the framework will replace that class with `x-btn-accept-small` or `x-btn-reject-small` and apply the styles associated with those classes.

We create the custom classes using the `extjs-button-ui` mixin provided in the framework's SASS definition and pass various arguments into it. The first argument taken is the UI's name, which is what will be used in the `ui` config option.

 We have named our UIs "accept-small" and "reject-small" because it is possible to have small, medium, and large buttons. This provides flexibility to stylize each size separately.

We can see what other arguments the `extjs-button-ui` accepts by looking in the `_button.scss` file provided with the framework files. It's located in `resources\themes\stylesheets\ext4\default\widgets\_button.scss`.

 We can find all the `ui` mixins for other components by looking through the SASS files in this directory.

When the SASS is compiled the stylesheet is updated with additional classes, which are based on the values we passed into the mixin:

```
/* Default style example */
.x-btn-default-small {
  border-color: #d1d1d1;
}

/* Accept style example */
.x-btn-accept-small {
  border-color: #90ee90;
}
```

```
/* Reject style example */
.x-btn-reject-small {
  border-color: #f08080;
}
```

See also

▶ For more information about creating buttons, check out *Chapter 9, Constructing Toolbars with Buttons and Menus.*

▶ The earlier recipes in this chapter give insight into the basics of SASS and Compass, which you will require for this recipe.

Creating your own theme mixins

Mixins are a feature of SASS that allow you to easily re-use CSS styles, properties, and selectors without the need for unnecessary duplication.

This recipe will demonstrate how to make use of mixins in your SASS and how to make use of the compiled CSS in your application.

Getting ready

This recipe will require SASS and Compass to be set up so we can compile our SASS stylesheets. If you haven't already done so, please revisit the first recipe in this chapter and follow the instructions to get you started. You'll need to prepare a `config.rb` file for compiling your SASS like so:

```
sass_path = File.dirname(__FILE__)

css_path = sass_path

output_style = :expanded
```

How to do it...

1. Start by creating a SASS file called `CustomTheme.scss`.

2. In your SASS file style the body by adding a background color to the body selector:

```
body {
  background-color: #CCC
}
```

3. Compile your SASS with the command `compass compile`.

4. Create an HTML file and reference the newly generated stylesheet. Your browser will display a blank page with a gray background:

```html
<html>
<head>
    <title>5. Creating your own Theme Mixins</title>
    <link rel="stylesheet" type="text/css" href="CustomTheme.css">
</head>
<body>
</body>
</html>
```

5. We are now going to create a mixin for our emphasized text. In your SASS file add a mixin with the @mixin directive called emphasis-text. The font color can be defined as a global variable and referenced inside the mixin:

```scss
...
$font-color: #3868AA;

@mixin emphasis-text {
  font: {
    family: arial;
    weight: bold;
  }
  color: $font-color;
}
```

6. Include the mixin, using the @include directive, in a rule for heading tags and a title class:

```scss
h1, h2, h3, span.title {
  @include emphasis-text;
}
```

7. Re-compile the SASS with the command compass compile.

8. Add some content to your HTML to see the new styles applied:

```html
<body>
<h1>ExtJS 4 Cookbook</h1>
    <h2>Chapter 11 - Theming Your Application</h2>
    <h3>Creating your own Theme Mixins</h3>
    <span class="title">emphasis-text mixin</span>
    <p>Paragraph text</p>
</body>
```

ExtJS 4 Cookbook

9. It is also possible to pass arguments into a mixin that will be available within the mixin as variables. Create a second mixin for a text shadow with default values for each argument:

```
@mixin text-shadow($color: white, $h: 1px, $v: 1px, $blur: 0px ) {
    text-shadow: $h $v $blur $color;
}
```

10. Call the mixin from a rule for h1 and h3 selectors. We can even add further styling to each:

```
h1 {
    @include text-shadow(#333, 3px, 3px, 2px);
    font-size: 3.5em;
    margin: 0px;
}

h3 {
    text-transform: uppercase;
    @include text-shadow;
}
```

11. Re-compile the SASS with the command `compass compile`. The output should be:

How it works...

A mixin is defined using the `@mixin` directive and called using the `@include` directive. The first mixin, `emphasis-text`, demonstrates how we make use of a mixin to re-use the same styles again and again without the need to repeat them. Although the example is very simple you can imagine how this might help when working with many more styles. As soon as you need your class to emphasize the text, it's a simple case of including the mixin.

A mixin's arguments are very similar to arguments in JavaScript. We separate each variable name with a comma but we can also define default values for each argument. The variable is now available for use within the mixin:

```
@mixin text-shadow($color: white) {}
```

This mixin takes a `color` argument, but will default it to `white` if no value is passed in. This is demonstrated in the example on the h3 selector, which has `@include text-shadow;` without any arguments passed to the mixin.

▶ The first two recipes of this chapter go into detail about setting up Compass and getting start with SASS. This will be useful to learn about some of the terms used in this recipe.

▶ The Compass API documentation that details the huge range of mixins built into the framework.

Restyling a panel

Restyling a panel with SASS and Ext JS 4 is surprisingly straightforward. By following the examples shown throughout this chapter, in particular the recipe demonstrating SASS variables, you are likely to find that panels and other components in your app will already be restyled.

This recipe will demonstrate the specific steps you need to take in order to restyle a panel and how to make use of more than one style set with panels.

 We will not go as far as demonstrating support for legacy browsers (for example, Internet Explorer 6) in this recipe as this is covered in a later recipe.

Getting ready

As with previous recipes we will be using SASS with Compass so please ensure that you have everything setup on your development computer.

You'll need to prepare a `config.rb` file for compiling your SASS like so:

```
$ext_path = "../extjs"

sass_path = File.dirname(__FILE__)

css_path = sass_path

output_style = :expanded

load File.join(File.dirname(__FILE__), $ext_path, 'resources',
'themes')
```

How to do it...

1. Start by creating a panel and rendering it to the document's body. This will show a panel:

```
Ext.onReady(function(){
    Ext.create('Ext.panel.Panel', {
        width: 200,
        height: 100,
        title: 'Panel Example',
        renderTo: Ext.getBody(),
        style: 'margin: 50px'
    });
});
```

2. Now create an SCSS file called `CustomTheme.scss` and add SCSS configuration to it. We're only going to include the styles required for panels here:

```
$include-default: false;
$include-missing-images: true;
$theme-name: 'LegacyBrowsers';
$base-color: lighten(#BADA55, 15);

@import 'ext4/default/all';

@include extjs-panel;
```

 We have named this theme `LegacyBrowsers` to make this example compatible with the next recipe in this chapter.

3. Compile your SASS by running the command `compass compile`. This will generate a file called `CustomTheme.css`.

4. Swap the CSS file for the newly generated one:

```
<link rel="stylesheet" type="text/css" href="CustomTheme.css">
```

5. Refreshing your browser should now show you a panel with pink styling:

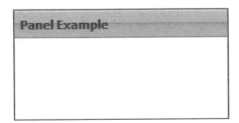

6. Now add an `extjs-panel-ui` mixin to the SASS with the following configuration and re-compile using the command `compass compile`:

```
@include extjs-panel-ui(
    'warning',

    $ui-base-color: $base-color,

    $ui-border-color: #EB5982,
    $ui-border-radius: 6px,
    $ui-border-width: 1px,

    $ui-header-color: #6E0C24,
    $ui-header-font-family: 'georgia, serif',
    $ui-header-font-size: 12px,
    $ui-header-font-weight: bold,
    $ui-header-border-color: #EB5982,
    $ui-header-background-color: #EB5982,
    $ui-header-background-gradient: matte,
    $ui-header-inner-border-color: null,

    $ui-body-color: null,
    $ui-body-border-color: #EB5982,
    $ui-body-border-width: 1px,
    $ui-body-border-style: solid,
    $ui-body-background-color: #F7CBD6,
    $ui-body-font-size: null,
    $ui-body-font-weight: bold
);
```

7. Set the `ui` config option to warning and add some text to the panel's body:

```
Ext.create('Ext.panel.Panel', {
    width: 200,
    height: 100,
    title: 'System Status',
    ui: 'warning',
    bodyPadding: 5,
    html: 'We are currently investigating a service outage.',
    renderTo: Ext.getBody(),
    style: 'margin: 50px'
});
```

8. Refresh your browser to see the updated panel:

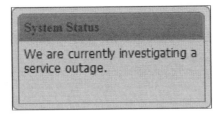

How it works...

When we compile the SASS with Compass a CSS file is produced that contains all the styles we need from the default Ext JS 4 theme but with our customizations (for example, the theme's `base-color`). This means we can completely remove the default CSS stylesheet and replace it with our newly generated one.

We can see how SASS alters the CSS by looking at the differences between the two stylesheets. An example class can be seen below, the first snippet from the CustomTheme.css file and the second from the stylesheet shipped with the framework (the comments regarding the color have been added by us).

```
/* CustomTheme.css */
.x-panel-body-default {
    background: white;
    border-color: #f47095; /* Pink */
    color: black;
    border-width: 1px;
    border-style: solid;
}
/* ext-all.css */
.x-panel-body-default {
    background: white;
    border-color: #99bce8; /* Blue */
    color: black;
    border-width: 1px;
    border-style: solid
}
```

With the new stylesheet applied, our browser will render the panel in our custom color.

See also

▶ The *Compiling SASS with Compass* and *Introduction to SASS* recipes will help remind you of the steps needed to set up the Compass and the SASS syntax used to create these styles.

Creating images for legacy browsers

As we all know, web developers are constantly battling with legacy browsers to make their designs consistent across all platforms. The abilities of CSS3 are well known and we want to use it as often as possible to easily create beautiful interfaces with rounded corners, gradients, and shadows, but Internet Explorer quickly stops us in our tracks.

Sencha also feels this pain and have created an ingenious slicer tool that allows us to think purely in terms of CSS3 and lets it take care of generating and slicing the images required to have those gradients and other CSS3 styles displayed exactly as we want in the older browsers.

The framework's new Split DOM feature, which causes each component's markup to be rendered differently based on the current browser's capabilities, means the images are used only as a fallback when necessary and the competencies of each individual browser are utilized to their fullest. This recipe will step through the process of using this SDK tool to generate the required images for our previously created custom theme making it fully compatible with IE6 and other legacy browsers.

Getting ready

Before we can use the slicing tool we must have a compiled Ext JS theme stylesheet, which the tool will use to create the images from. We are going to use the custom theme created in the previous recipe but you can apply the same steps to your own custom theme, being careful to alter the paths accordingly.

How to do it...

1. First we must download and install the Sencha SDK tools. This can be found on the Sencha website (`http://www.sencha.com/products/sdk-tools/`).

2. Once installed, open a new command prompt/Terminal window and navigate to this chapter's source folder.

 You can execute the slicer tool from any location—it doesn't have to be the location of your CSS file. Choose a location that makes it easy to configure the relative paths correctly.

3. Next we execute the following command that tells the slicer where to find the Ext JS directory, our custom CSS file, and where we want our images to be created:

```
sencha slice theme -d extjs -c LegacyBrowsers/LegacyBrowsers.css
-o extjs/resources/themes/images/LegacyBrowsers -v
```

4. While the tool does its work we will see each of the theme's images appearing in the output folder. Once it is complete we are able to navigate to our application in IE6 and see the theme appear exactly as it does in a modern browser.

How it works...

The slicer SDK Tool works by rendering each of Ext JS components in memory with the custom theme applied. It then starts slicing the rendered output into individual images. These images are then combined into sprites as needed and saved to your output folder.

The 'slice theme' command accepts various arguments to configure the tool's process:

- ▶ -c: This configures the path to your theme's custom CSS file (including the file name itself).

- ▶ -d: The path to the Ext JS framework directory.

- ▶ -m: This allows you to specify the path to a custom manifest file. This is used when we have defined custom UIs and allows us to define which components should be sliced using these new UIs. For example, indicating that the tool should slice a button with a new UI of 'fancy-button'. This is optional and if omitted will use the default manifest file.

- ▶ -o: The path to the folder the generated images will be saved to.

- ▶ -v: If included, a message will be displayed in the console as each image is created.

12
Advanced Ext JS for the Perfect App

In this chapter, we will cover:

- ▶ Advanced functionality with plugins
- ▶ Architecting your applications with the MVC pattern
- ▶ Attaching user interactions to controller actions
- ▶ Creating a real-life application with the MVC pattern
- ▶ Optimizing and building your application for a production environment with Sencha's SDK tools
- ▶ Getting started with Ext Direct
- ▶ Loading and submitting forms with Ext Direct
- ▶ Handling errors throughout your application

Introduction

This chapter will cover advanced topics in Ext JS that will help make your application stand out from the crowd. We will start by explaining how to extend and customize the framework through plugins, where we will write a plugin to toggle text fields between an editable and display state.

The next recipes will focus on the MVC pattern that has become the recommended way of structuring your applications. These recipes will start by explaining the file and class structure we need, leading into how to connect your application's parts together. Finally we will take one of our earlier examples and demonstrate how to create it following the MVC pattern.

We will also focus on `Ext.Direct` and how it can be used to handle server communications in conjunction with forms and stores.

Other advanced topics such as state, advanced exception handling, history management, and task management will also be described.

Advanced functionality with plugins

Ext JS' functionality can be easily extended and modified by attaching plugins to components. Plugins allow us to create reusable code that will modify or add to a component's look and behavior during or after its instantiation.

The Ext JS community is prolific in their creation of plugins to extend the framework and there are some excellent contributions with both open source and commercial licenses. You can browse through the available plugins (and submit your own!) on the Sencha forums or on the Sencha marketplace (`http://market.sencha.com/`).

In this recipe, we are going to create a plugin called `Ext.ux.ReadOnlyField` that can be attached to text fields. This will allow them to be switched between a read-only mode, which hides the input field, and an edit mode. The plugin will create a new `DIV` element as part of the field and show and hide it when the mode is changed.

The following screenshot shows the plugin in action with the left image showing the text field in edit mode and the right in read-only mode:

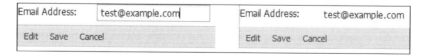

Getting ready

We will first need a simple form to demonstrate our plugin in action so we will start by creating one with a simple text field and three buttons, which we will attach functionality to later.

```
var form = Ext.create('Ext.form.Panel', {
    renderTo: Ext.getBody(),
    bbar: [{
        xtype: 'button',
        text: 'Edit'
    }, {
        xtype: 'button',
        text: 'Save'
    }, {
        xtype: 'button',
        text: 'Cancel'
    }],
    items: [{
        xtype: 'textfield',
        fieldLabel: 'Email Address'
    }]
});
```

How to do it...

1. Plugins are simply classes, in the same way that all components are, so we start by defining our `Ext.ux.ReadOnlyField` class that will, by default, extend the `Ext.Base` class:

    ```
    Ext.define('Ext.ux.ReadOnlyField', {
    });
    ```

     It is generally a good practice to create plugins in the `Ext.ux` namespace so they can be included in future projects easily and to ensure that they won't conflict with built-in framework classes.

2. The next step is to define our plugin's `init` method, which is the starting point of every plugin. To start with, we simply cache a reference to the plugin's parent component (that is, the text field) so we can easily access it later:

    ```
    Ext.define('Ext.ux.ReadOnlyField', {
        init: function(parent){
            this.parent = parent;
        }
    });
    ```

3. We will use the parent component's `render` event to create our plugin's extra markup. We attach a handler method that creates a new `DIV` element inside the field's body element:

```
Ext.define('Ext.ux.ReadOnlyField', {
    init: function(parent){
        this.parent = parent;
        this.initEventHandlers();
    },

    initEventHandlers: function(){
        this.parent.on({
            render: this.onParentRender,
            scope: this
        });
    },

    onParentRender: function(field){
        field.displayEl = Ext.DomHelper.append(field.bodyEl, {
            tag: 'div',
            style: {
                height: '22px',
                "line-height": '18px',
                margin: '2px 0 0 5px'
            }
        }, true).setVisibilityMode(Ext.Element.DISPLAY);

        field.inputEl.setVisibilityMode(Ext.Element.DISPLAY);
    }
});
```

4. We now add three methods, which will switch between read-only and edit modes. These methods show and hide the appropriate elements and set the values of them as needed:

```
...
edit: function(){
    if(this.rendered){
        this.displayEl.hide();
        this.inputEl.show();

        this.cachedValue = this.getValue();
    }
},
```

```
save: function() {
    if(this.rendered) {
        this.displayEl.update(this.getValue());

        this.displayEl.show();
        this.inputEl.hide();
    }
},
cancel: function() {
    if(this.rendered) {

        this.setValue(this.cachedValue);

        this.displayEl.show();
        this.inputEl.hide();
    }
}
...
```

5. In order for these methods to be called from the field directly we create a reference to them in the field's class inside the `init` method:

```
init: function(parent) {
    this.parent = parent;
    this.initEventHandlers();
    this.parent.edit = this.edit;
    this.parent.save = this.save;
    this.parent.cancel = this.cancel; }
```

6. We can now add handlers to our three toolbar buttons to call the relevant method:

```
...
bbar: [{
    xtype: 'button',
    text: 'Edit',
    handler: function() {
        form.items.get(0).edit();
    }
}, {
    xtype: 'button',
    text: 'Save',
    handler: function() {
        form.items.get(0).save();
    }
}, {
```

```
        type: 'button',
        text: 'Cancel',
        handle: function(){
            form.items.get(0).cancel();
        }
    }]
    ...
```

7. Finally, we attach the plugin to our text field by creating a new plugin instance and including it in the field's `plugins` array:

```
{
    xtype: 'textfield',
    fieldLabel: 'Email Address',
    plugins: [Ext.create('Ext.ux.ReadOnlyField')]
}
```

How it works...

Plugins must be a class and, as a minimum, have an `init` method. This method is called within the component's `constructor`, just before its `initComponent` method, and provides the opportunity to perform the setup required to make the plugin function correctly. The `init` method is passed one parameter, which is a reference to the component that it is attached to, in our case the text field.

In our plugin's `init` method we cache a reference to the parent text field and attach a listener function to the field's `render` event. Our handler function performs the modifications to the field's markup required for our plugin to work.

We use the `append` method of `Ext.DomHelper` to add a new HTML element to the field's body element. The new element is configured by the second parameter that contains the desired tag and some styling. The following screenshot shows the result of this code, with the new, hidden `div` at the bottom:

```
<div id="textfield-1015-bodyEl" class="x-form-item-body
" role="presentation" style="width: 150px;">
    <input id="ext-gen1010" class="x-form-field
    x-form-text" type="text" autocomplete="off" size="20" name="ext-
    gen1010" aria-invalid="false" role="textbox" aria-describedby="textfield-
    1015-errorEl" aria-required="false" style="-moz-user-select: text; width:
    150px;" data-errorqtip="">
    <div id="ext-gen1021" style="height: 22px; line-height: 18px; margin: 2px 0pt 0pt
    5px; display: none;"></div>
</div>
```

We then call the `setVisibilityMode` on the new `displayEl` and the `inputEl`'s `Ext.Element` so they do not take up space when they are hidden.

 The display mode of an element can be set to either `Ext.Element.VISIBILITY`, `Ext.Element.DISPLAY`, `Ext.Element.OFFSETS`, or `Ext.Element.ASCLASS`. The first uses the `visibility: hidden` CSS property, which means the element still takes up space. The second uses the `display: none` property, which means the element does not take up any space. The third option uses offset positions to hide the element by moving it off-screen. The final choice means that a CSS class will be applied to the element in order to hide it.

Finally we call the field's `edit` method to force it into edit mode from the start. The behavior of the plugin is controlled by the `edit`, `save`, and `cancel` methods. We will take these in turn and explain how they work:

- The `edit` method starts by checking if the component is rendered or not. If it isn't then our `displayEl` won't be created, so we don't have to do anything. If it is rendered, then we hide the `displayEl` (our custom `div`) and show the `inputEl`. We also store a copy of the field's current value in case we want to cancel the change and revert back to its previous value.

- The `save` method starts with the same check and if it is rendered then the `save` method updates the contents of the `displayEl` with the field's value. It then hides the `inputEl` and shows the `displayEl`.

- The `cancel` method reverts the field's changes back to what it was before the edit and shows the `displayEl` again. It does this by passing the cached value (set in the `edit` method) to the field's `setValue` method. It then shows the `displayEl` and hides the `inputEl`.

In order for these three methods to be called from the field itself, we create references to them on the field's class so they can be called directly without having to go through the plugin's instance. By doing this, the scope that the functions will be executed in is the field instance itself, not the plugin (that is, "this" will refer to the field).

See also

- For more information about extending Ext JS classes using inheritance see the *Utilizing inheritance in your classes* recipe in *Chapter 1, Classes, Object-Oriented Principles, and Structuring your Application*.

- If you need to change some of the internal workings of the framework in your plugin, check out the recipe titled *Overriding Ext JS' functionality*, also in *Chapter 1*.

▶ Plugins often require the need to create custom HTML so the recipes at the start of *Chapter 2, Manipulating the Dom, Handling Events, and Making AJAX Requests* will help you get started.

Architecting your applications with the MVC pattern

Ext JS 4 introduces the MVC application architecture, which Sencha define as:

▶ **Model**: A model contains the definition of your data, which is, in effect a definition of a data entity. In Ext JS 4 models can link to each other through associations and will remain persistent. Most commonly a model will be bound to a store, which can be used in components such as grids.

▶ **View**: Views are your UI components/widgets, for example, panels, forms, grids, and windows.

▶ **Controller**: A controller pulls everything together. They contain your application's logic and will perform tasks, such as referencing your stores and models from views. They will also be in charge of listening for events from views (for example, button clicks, grid selections, and so on) and hooking actions up to them.

In this recipe we are going to demonstrate how to architect a simple `Enhancement Log` application consisting of a grid displaying a list of enhancements.

Getting ready

Create the MVC file and folder structure described in the recipe *Creating Your Application's Folder Structure* in *Chapter 1*.

How to do it...

1. Start by editing `index.html` and add the files we require for our app:

```
<html>
    <head>
        <title>Enhancement Log</title>

        <!-- Library Files -->
        <link rel="stylesheet" type="text/css" href="extjs/
resources/css/ext-all.css">
            <script type="text/javascript" src="extjs/ext-all-debug.
js"></script>

        <script type="text/javascript">
            Ext.Loader.setConfig({
```

```
            enabled: true
        });

    </script>

    <!-- Application Logic -->
    <script type="text/javascript" src="app.js"></script>
</head>
<body>
</body>
</html>
```

2. We start the application with an instance of the `Ext.app.Application` class. This contains our application name, a reference to the controller(s), and the launch method that runs once everything has loaded. In `app.js` add:

```
Ext.application({
    name: 'EnhancementLog',

    controllers: ['Enhancement'],

    launch: function(){
        Ext.create('Ext.container.Viewport', {
            layout: 'fit',
            items: [{
                xtype: 'EnhancementGrid'
            }]
        });
    }
});
```

3. Now that we have our application defined and ready to launch, let's deal with the controller. Add the following code to `Enhancement.js` in the controller directory:

```
Ext.define('EnhancementLog.controller.Enhancement', {
    extend: 'Ext.app.Controller',

    stores: ['Enhancement'],

    models: ['Enhancement'],

    views: ['enhancement.EnhancementGrid'],

    init: function() {
        //initialization code
    }

});
```

4. Then define the view (in our case an enhancement grid) in `EnhancementGrid.js`:

```
Ext.define('EnhancementLog.view.enhancement.EnhancementGrid', {
    extend: 'Ext.grid.Panel',
    alias: 'widget.EnhancementGrid',

    title: 'System Enhancements',
    store: 'Enhancement',

    columns: [{
        header: 'Title',
        dataIndex: 'title',
        flex: 1
    }, {
        header: 'Enhancement Description',
        dataIndex: 'description',
        flex: 3
    }]
});
```

5. We now need to create a model and bind it to a store. The model is defined as follows:

```
Ext.define('EnhancementLog.model.Enhancement', {
    extend: 'Ext.data.Model',
    fields: ['id', 'title', 'description']
});
```

6. Finally we define a store (with some pre-defined data) like so:

```
Ext.define('EnhancementLog.store.Enhancement', {
    extend: 'Ext.data.Store',

    model: 'EnhancementLog.model.Enhancement',

    data: [{
        id: 1,
        title: 'Search Field Autocomplete',
        description: 'Could the main search field have an
autocomplete facility to increase my productivity.'
    }]
});
```

With all the pieces put together, when we run the application, you will see a grid with a list of enhancement requests:

System Enhancements	
Title	**Enhancement Description**
Search Field Autocomplete	Could the main search field have an autocomplete facility to increase my productivity.

How it works...

There are four key aspects to this MVC application.

Firstly, the application definition in `app.js` starts with the `Application` class. This class is where we put the main application logic and define key components:

- ▶ The application has a name `EnhancementLog`; this is the global namespace for the application.
- ▶ We then tell our application about its controllers. We only have one controller—`Enhancement` (if we had more than one, we'd simply add them to the array). If we have the `Ext.Loader` enabled, the classes in this array will be automatically loaded.
- ▶ Finally, in the `launch` property we add a function that creates the viewport for the application with our grid `xtype`. The `launch` property is automatically called as soon as the application is ready (that is, has loaded).

 The `xtype` is the `alias` (without the `widget.` prefix) that we defined in the `EnhancementGrid` class.

Now that the application knows about our the `Enhancement` controller, we add the second piece of the puzzle. The controller should contain a reference to its views and its models:

- ▶ Firstly, in the controller, we indicate the store(s) and model(s) it requires (these will be picked up by `Ext.Loader` if you wish—see the recipe on *Dynamically Loading Ext JS Classes*).
- ▶ We finish off by telling it about the view(s) it requires.
- ▶ The `init` method can be used to perform any pre-launch initialization and is run before your application launches.

With the controller ready, we create the view to display the enhancement requests. In this case, we've created a simple grid to list our enhancement requests. To create the grid we first extend `Ext.grid.Panel` and define the configuration it requires:

- ▶ We alias our grid with `widget.EnhancementGrid` so we can call the `alias` `EnhancementGrid` anywhere in our app
- ▶ Our grid has a title and columns (this configuration is explained in *Chapter 8*)
- ▶ Finally, we bind the grid to our store so it knows where to get its data from

The last part is adding the model that we referenced in our controller and a store to bind to the grid. The model is where we add the data definition. We start by extending the `Ext.data.Model` class. It's then simply a case of listing the fields our data contains.

With the model in place we add a store by extending `Ext.data.Store`. First we tell the store where to get the data definition from; in this case it's `EnhancementLog.model.Enhancement`. Next we add the method for retrieving the data. For the purposes of this demonstration we have defined some inline data. *Chapter 7, Working with the Ext JS Data Package* explains data and stores in more detail.

The controller is capable of dynamically loading stores, models, and views by adding an array for each. It's able to do this so long as your folder structure and class names adhere to Sencha's conventions. For example, the controller contains the following code:

```
stores: ['Enhancements'],
```

The framework will load and instantiate our enhancements store, which is named as `EnhancementLog.store.Enhancement` and located in the `enhancementLog/app/store/Enhancement.js` file.

See Also

- For more information on using MVC and Ext JS it's worth looking at Sencha's MVC guide that is supplied with the documentation.

- For more information about stores and models look back to *Chapter 7, Working with the Ext JS Data Package*.

Attaching user interactions to controller actions

The MVC architecture provides us with a standard way of organizing our applications and means that the code can be easily read and understood by other developers because things are always in the same place.

After creating our application's views we must start handling events raised after a user interacts with them, and use our controller actions to provide a path through our application.

Before the MVC architecture existed, this interaction was usually dealt with inside the view itself, that is, a tight coupling between application logic and presentation definitions. MVC allows us to remove this coupling and let views solely focus on displaying data and have the controllers tie everything together.

In this recipe, we will demonstrate how to listen for user interactions on our views and have the controller deal with the logic needed to move the user through our application.

Getting ready

We will start by creating a very simple MVC application structure to which we will add code to during this recipe. Our application will have one controller and one view that will display a login form to the user. Our folder structure can be seen as follows with the various files we will need:

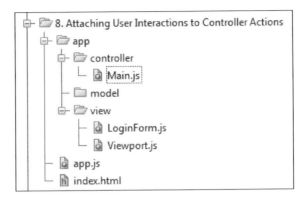

Our `app.js` file contains our `Ext.Loader` configuration and the application's definition using the following code:

```
Ext.Loader.setConfig({
    enabled: true
});

Ext.application({

    name: 'Cookbook',

    autoCreateViewport: true,

    launch: function(){
        console.log('App Launch');
    }
});
```

We have named the application as `Cookbook` and so will use this as its root namespace with all views, models, and controllers coming underneath this. We also set the `autoCreateViewport` config to true so the framework will look for a view called `Cookbook.view.Viewport` and automatically create it. We have created two views—`Viewport` and `LoginForm`. The `Viewport` view is automatically created and contains an instance of the `LoginForm` view.

```
Ext.define('Cookbook.view.Viewport', {
    extend: 'Ext.container.Viewport',

    initComponent: function(){

        Ext.apply(this, {
            layout: 'fit',
            items: [Ext.create('Cookbook.view.LoginForm')]
        });

        this.callParent(arguments);
    }
});
```

The `LoginForm` view extends the `Ext.form.Panel` class and contains a `Username` and `Password` field and a `Login` button:

```
Ext.define('Cookbook.view.LoginForm', {
    extend: 'Ext.form.Panel',

    initComponent: function(){

        Ext.apply(this, {
            items: [{
                xtype: 'textfield',
                name: 'Username',
                fieldLabel: 'Username'
            }, {
                xtype: 'textfield',
                inputType: 'password',
                name: 'Password',
                fieldLabel: 'Password'
            }, {
                xtype: 'button',
                text: 'Login',
                action: 'login'
            }]
        });

        this.callParent(arguments);
    }
});
```

If we now add references to the framework's JS file and `app.js` within our `index.html` and open it, we will see our application's login form:

Username:	
Password:	
Login	

Now that we have this structure in place, we can look into hooking up a click of our `Login` button to a controller action.

How to do it...

1. We start by creating a controller that will contain our login logic. We do this by creating a file in our `controller` folder called `Main.js` and define a class called `Cookbook.controller.Main` extending from the `Ext.app.Controller` class:

```
Ext.define('Cookbook.controller.Main', {
    extend: 'Ext.app.Controller',
});
```

2. Next we add the `init` method to our controller, which will be executed when the controller is loaded:

```
Ext.define('Cookbook.controller.Main', {
    extend: 'Ext.app.Controller',

    init: function(){
        console.log('Main Controller Init');
    }
});
```

3. Add a configuration option called `controllers` to our application definition, located in our `app.js` file. This will tell our application that we have a controller called `Main` to load and initialize:

```
Ext.application({

    name: 'Cookbook',

    autoCreateViewport: true,
    controllers: ['Main'],

    launch: function(){
        console.log('App Launch');
    }
});
```

4. Now that our controller is being initialized, we can hook up the `Login` button's click event to an action. We start by creating an action method called `onLoginButtonClick` in our `Main` controller and simply output a console message:

```
. . .
onLoginButtonClick: function(){
    console.log('Log me in!');
}
. . .
```

5. Now, in our `Main` controller's `init` method we use the `control` method to attach this `action` method to the `Login` button's click event:

```
. . .
init: function(){
    console.log('Main Controller Init');

    this.control({
        'button[action=login]': {
            click: this.onLoginButtonClick,
            scope: this
        }
    });
}
. . .
```

How it works...

Once we have defined our controller we use the `controllers` configuration to have it dynamically loaded and initialized by our application. This process will automatically call the controller's `init` method, allowing us to add our event handlers.

You can add as many controllers to this array and each will be loaded and initialized in turn.

The `control` method forms part of the `Ext.app.Controller` class and allows us to target specific components, using the `Ext.ComponentQuery` syntax, and attach handlers to their various events.

We do this by passing an object literal containing a component query as the key and another object literal as the value. This object is identical to the one you might give to a component's `listeners` configuration or the `on` method.

In our example we target the `Login` button by looking for all components with an `xtype` of button and with an `action` property set to login. If this query returned multiple components, they will all have their events bound.

Although executed when the controller is created, the targeted components don't have to exist at this point for the `control` method call to bind the event handlers. It works in a similar way to event delegation and so will still execute the handlers if the components are instantiated after this is called.

The object literal tells the control method that the `onLoginButtonClick` method will be bound to any click events raised on the queried component(s) and executed in the scope of the controller.

Any number of component queries can be included in this object literal with each of them binding to any number of events.

It is important to note that by using these component queries we are coupling our controllers to the views by varying degrees. In order to reduce this coupling and minimize the knowledge of the view's structure given to the controller, we should use as simple queries as possible to target the correct component. For example, it would be perfectly valid, but unwise, to target the button with a query such as:

```
. . .
'viewport > form > button[action=login]': {
    click: this.onLoginButtonClick,
    scope: this
}
. . .
```

By using a query such as this, we are forcing the view structure to remain as it is, meaning that this code must be changed if we wanted to, for example, introduce another level of nesting.

There's more...

At the moment all our `Login` button does is log a message to say it has been clicked. Obviously to make this functional we will need to collect the values entered in the `Username` and `Password` fields. We will now introduce the `refs` configuration option and show how this can be used to get references to components.

The `refs` config allows us to specify a component query string, which is used to automatically get a reference to a component. It accepts an array of object literals that must each have a `ref` and `selector` property. The `ref` property defines what name will be used to access this reference and the `selector` indicates the component query used to find it.

The following code shows this in action within our `Main` controller to create `refs` to our `Username` and `Password` fields:

```
...
refs: [{
    ref: 'usernameField',
    selector: 'textfield[name=Username]'
}, {
    ref: 'passwordField',
    selector: 'textfield[name=Password]'
}]
...
```

When our controller is constructed these `refs` are processed and a `get` method (getUsernameField and getPasswordField) is created for each of them that returns the reference found.

It is important to note that, in a similar way as the `control` method works, the targeted component does not have to exist at the time the controller is instantiated as the `get` methods will execute the query when called and cache its result. If the component has been destroyed since the last execution, it will be run again to get the new component.

We can now use these getter methods in our `onLoginButtonClick` method to get the value entered into each field:

```
onLoginButtonClick: function(){
    console.log('Log me in!');

    console.log(this.getUsernameField().getValue());
    console.log(this.getPasswordField().getValue());
}
```

See also

- ▶ Be sure to read about creating the standard application folder structure in the *Creating your Application's folder structure* recipe found in *Appendix, Ext JS 4 Cookbook-Exploring Further*.

- ▶ See the *Architecting your applications with the MVC pattern* recipe.

Creating a real-life application with the MVC pattern

Having talked through how to structure a MVC application and how we hook up our controller's actions to the application views' events, we are now going to look at creating a more real-life example.

In *Chapter 4, UI Building Blocks—Trees, Panels, and Data Views* we created a data view to display bugs, which links into a form for editing each bug. We are now going to port that application into the MVC architecture and show how we go about using the MVC pattern with an application with multiple views and user interactions.

If you aren't already familiar with the recipe from *Chapter 4* we recommend you revisit it and familiarize yourself with it before starting.

Getting ready

We will start by creating our standard application folder structure with folders for our controllers, models, stores, and views. We will also require an HTML file that references the Ext JS framework's JS and CSS files, and which also enables the `Ext.Loader` class so our files will be automatically loaded when required. To do this we add the following code snippet to the HEAD of the document:

```
<script type="text/javascript">
    Ext.Loader.setConfig({
        enabled: true,
        paths: {
            Ext: '../../../src'
        }
    });
</script>
```

In the original recipe in *Chapter 4, UI Building Blocks—Trees, Panels, and Data Views,* we also added some CSS styling to make our DataView look a little nicer. We will also require you to add these styles to a CSS file and link to it in the `index.html` file.

How to do it...

1. Our first step is to create our `app.js` file, which will provide our application's launch point. We create this file in the root of our application alongside our `index.html`. At this stage we will give our application the name `BugTracker` and an empty `launch` function:

```
Ext.application({
    name: 'BugTracker',
    launch: function(){
        console.log('App Launch');
    }
});
```

2. Next we will define our bug model and store. These will be placed in two files named `Bug.js` in the `model` folder and `BugStore.js` in the `store` folder respectively. The contents of each can be seen as follows:

```
// model/Bug.js
Ext.define('BugTracker.model.Bug', {
    extend: 'Ext.data.Model',
    fields: [
        'title',
        'status',
        'description',
        'severity'
    ]
});


// store/BugStore.js
Ext.define('BugTracker.store.BugStore', {
    extend: 'Ext.data.Store',
    model: 'BugTracker.model.Bug',
    data: [ ... ]
});
```

3. We have created our main model and store, now we want to make the application aware of them so the framework loads them when required. We do this by adding `stores` and `models` configs to the `Ext.application` call of `app.js`. These configs accept an array of strings that are then fully qualified with the relevant namespace (for example, `MyModel` becomes `BugTracker.model.MyModel`).

```
Ext.application({
    name: 'BugTracker',
    models: [
        'Bug'
    ],
    stores: [
        'BugStore'
    ],
    launch: function(){
        console.log('App Launch');
    }
});
```

> If your models or stores are contained in further namespaces (for example, `BugTracker.model.AdminApp.Bug`) then you must include all namespaces after the default `BugTracker.model` for the `Ext.Loader` to load them correctly.

4. Our next step is to create our views. In our application we have a DataView that displays our set of bugs, a panel to wrap the DataView, a Form panel to allow us to edit a bug, a window to house the Form panel when it is displayed, and a Viewport container. We are going to create each of these views as their own class, extending the relevant framework class, starting with our `BugDataView`:

```
// view/BugDataView.js
Ext.define('BugTracker.view.BugDataView', {

    extend: 'Ext.view.View',

    alias: 'widget.BugDataView',

    config: {
```

```
        store: Ext.create('BugTracker.store.BugStore'),
        tpl: '<tpl for=".">' +
          '<div class="bug-wrapper">' +
          '<span class="title">{title}</span>' +
          '<span class="severity severity-{severity}">{severity}</
span>' +
          '<span class="description">{description}</span>' +
          '<span class="status {[values.status.toLowerCase().
replace(" ", "-")]}">{status}</span>' +
          '</div>' +
          '</tpl>',
        itemSelector: 'div.bug-wrapper',
        emptyText: 'Woo hoo! No Bugs Found!',
        deferEmptyText: false
    }
});
```

5. Next we create the `BugPanel` that will have an instance of the `BugDataView` within it. Notice the new `action` config we have given to each of the toolbar buttons; we will use these later on to hook up their click events:

```
// view/BugPanel.js
Ext.define('BugTracker.view.BugPanel', {
    extend: 'Ext.panel.Panel',
    alias: 'widget.BugPanel',
    config: {
        title: 'Current Bugs,
        height: 500,
        width: 580,
        layout: 'fit',
        style: 'margin: 50;',
        tbar: [{
            xtype: 'combo',
            name: 'status',
            width: 200,
            labelWidth: 100,
            fieldLabel: 'Severity Filter',
            store: ['1', '2', '3', '4', '5'],
            queryMode: 'local'
        }, '-', {
            text: 'Sort by Severity',
            action: 'sortBySeverity'
        }, {
            text: 'Open all Bugs',
            action: 'openAllBugs'
```

```
        }, '->', {
            text: 'Clear Filter',
            action: 'clearFilter'
        }],
        items: [{
            xtype: 'BugDataView'
        }]
    }
});
```

6. The Bug form panel is next and we follow the same pattern as the other views and create it in its own file whose name matches the class name that it contains:

```
// view/BugForm.js
Ext.define('BugTracker.view.BugForm', {

    extend: 'Ext.form.Panel',

    alias: 'widget.BugForm',

    config: {
        border: 0,
        items: [{
            xtype: 'textfield',
            name: 'title',
            width: 300,
            fieldLabel: 'Title'
        }, {
            xtype: 'textarea',
            name: 'description',
            width: 300,
            height: 100,
            fieldLabel: 'Description'
        }, {
            xtype: 'numberfield',
            name: 'severity',
            width: 300,
            fieldLabel: 'Severity',
            value: 1,
            maxValue: 5,
            minValue: 1
        }, {
            xtype: 'combo',
            name: 'status',
            width: 300,
```

```
            fieldLabel: 'Status',
            store: ['Open', 'In Progress', 'Complete'],
            queryMode: 'local'
        }]
    }
});
```

7. Now we create a window that contains an instance of the `BugForm` as well as a single `Save` button:

```
Ext.define('BugTracker.view.BugFormWindow', {
    extend: 'Ext.window.Window',
    alias: 'widget.BugFormWindow',
    config: {
        height: 250,
        width: 500,
        title: 'Edit Bug',
        modal: true,
        items: [{
            xtype: 'BugForm'
        }],
        closeAction: 'hide',
        buttons: [{
            text: 'Save',
            action: 'saveBug'
        }]
    }
});
```

8. Our Viewport container is our final view and is a simple component that extends the `Ext.container.Viewport` class and creates an instance of the `BugPanel` class within its `items` collection. To have this class instantiated automatically we also add the `autoCreateViewport: true` configuration to our application definition in `app.js`:

```
// view/Viewport.js
Ext.define('BugTracker.view.Viewport', {
    extend: 'Ext.container.Viewport',

    initComponent: function(){
        Ext.apply(this, {
            layout: 'fit',
```

```
            items: [{
                xtype: 'BugPanel'
            }]
        });

        this.callParent(arguments);
    }
});
```

9. At this point if we open our `index.html` page we will see the application displaying our bugs, but clicking on the buttons or bugs doesn't do anything! To bring it all to life we need to create a controller, which will tie everything together. Start by creating a new file called `Bugs.js` in the controller folder and give it the following skeleton code. At this point we must also add a `controllers` config to the application definition of `app.js` with a value of `['Bugs']` so the controller is automatically loaded and initialized:

```
// controller/Bugs.js
Ext.define('BugTracker.controller.Bugs', {
    extend: 'Ext.app.Controller',
    views: [
        'BugDataView',
        'BugPanel',
        'BugForm',
        'BugFormWindow'
    ],
    init: function(){
        console.log('Bugs Controller Init');
    }
});
```

10. Next we use the `refs` config option to adds some accessor methods for each of the main components so we can access references to them in our action methods:

```
refs: [{
    ref: 'bugDataView',
    selector: 'BugPanel BugDataView'
}, {
    ref: 'bugFormPanel',
    selector: 'BugFormWindow BugForm'
}, {
    ref: 'bugFormWindow',
    selector: 'BugFormWindow'
}]
```

11. We now use the `control` method (which we introduced in the previous recipe) to wire up our button clicks to a controller action. We use a simple component query to target the correct button using the `action` property that we gave each button and then hook its click event to a method within the controller:

```
init: function(){
    console.log('Bugs Controller Init');
    this.control({
        'BugPanel button[action="sortBySeverity"]': {
            click: this.onSortBySeverityButtonClick,
            scope: this
        }
    });
},

onSortBySeverityButtonClick: function(btn){
    this.getBugDataView().getStore().sort('severity', 'DESC');
}

onSortBySeverityButtonClick: function(btn){
        this.getBugDataView().getStore().sort('severity', 'DESC');
}
```

12. We do this for the remaining buttons, the DataView's `itemclick` event and the comboboxes' change event:

```
init: function(){
    console.log('Bugs Controller Init');

    this.control({
        'BugPanel BugDataView': {
            itemclick: this.onBugDataViewItemClick,
            scope: this
        },
        'BugPanel button[action="sortBySeverity"]': {
            click: this.onSortBySeverityButtonClick,
            scope: this
        },
        'BugPanel button[action="openAllBugs"]': {
            click: this.onOpenAllBugsButtonClick,
            scope: this
        },
        'BugPanel button[action="clearFilter"]': {
            click: this.onClearFilterButtonClick,
            scope: this
        },
        'BugPanel combo[name="status"]': {
            change: this.onBugStatusComboboxChange,
```

```
                        scope: this
                },
                'BugFormWindow button[action="saveBug"]': {
                        click: this.onSaveBugButtonClick,
                        scope: this
                }
        });
},

onSaveBugButtonClick: function(btn){
        var form = this.getBugFormPanel();

        // get the record loaded into the form
        var selectedRecord = form.getRecord();

        selectedRecord.set(form.getValues());

        // refilter
        this.getBugDataView().getStore().filter();

        this.getBugFormWindow().close();
},

onBugDataViewItemClick: function(view, record, item, index,e){
        var win = this.getBugFormWindow();

        if(!win){
                win = Ext.create('BugTracker.view.BugFormWindow');
        }

        win.show();

        // populate the form with the clicked record
        this.getBugFormPanel().loadRecord(record);
},

onSortBySeverityButtonClick: function(btn){
        this.getBugDataView().getStore().sort('severity', 'DESC');
},

onOpenAllBugsButtonClick: function(btn){
        this.getBugDataView().getStore().each(function(model){
                model.set('status', 'Open');
                model.commit();
```

```
        }, this);
    },

    onClearFilterButtonClick: function(btn){
        this.getBugDataView().getStore().clearFilter();
    },

    onBugStatusComboboxChange: function(combo, value, options){
        this.getBugDataView().getStore().clearFilter();

        this.getBugDataView().getStore().filter('severity', combo.
getValue());
    }
}
```

How it works...

As we have done in the previous MVC recipes each type of class (models, stores, views, and controllers) is defined in its own separate file that mirrors the class's namespace structure. This keeps our code separated and easy to follow without cluttering any one file with too much code.

We have taken the views that we created in the *Chapter 4* recipe and split them into their own files and turned them into classes, extending their relevant base class. Each of them is also given an alias, which we make use of when instantiating them in other views.

In the views that have buttons we have also added an `action` property to each button that is used to identify that button when we go to target it, using the `ComponentQuery` syntax. Using `action` is simply a handy property that isn't used by the framework but could equally be replaced with something of your own choosing.

We have also removed all event-handling code from these views to maintain the separation of concerns demanded by the MVC pattern. The views should only be in charge of presentation and so this logic does not belong here.

The logic we removed from these event handlers is moved into the Bugs controller and is hooked up using the `control` method, which uses component queries to target the specific component and attach handling functions to its events.

We have also made use of the `refs` configuration, which allows us to have accessor methods automatically created for components that match the given `ComponentQuery` selector. We have created refs for the `BugDataView`, `BugForm`, and `BugFormWindow` views so they can be easily accessed from our controller's `action` methods.

You can see these in use in the `onBugDataViewItemClick` method, which accesses the `BugFormWindow` component through the `getBugFormWindow` method that is automatically created for us. If no component matching the query is found then `null` is returned. We use this fact to determine if we have to create an instance of the `BugFormWindow` after a `Bug` is clicked. If a component is returned then we can simply repopulate it and show it again rather than creating a new one.

See also

▶ The *Displaying a detailed Window after clicking a Data View node* in *Chapter 4*, which forms the basis of this recipe.

▶ The previous two recipes about the MVC pattern, which explain how to structure your application, have more detailed information about the `control` method and the `refs` configuration option.

Building your application with Sencha's SDK tools

Sencha's SDK tools, which we introduced with our recipe on theming for legacy browsers, provide two commands for preparing your application for use in a production environment—`create jsb` and `build`.

These commands allow us to create a custom build of the Ext JS framework, so we only include the components and classes that we have used, and minify the code to reduce its file size.

In this recipe we will take a very small 'Hello World!' example application and demonstrate the steps needed to build and minify it for use in production.

Getting ready

This recipe requires you to have the Sencha SDK Tools installed on your development machine. They can be found on the Sencha website (`http://www.sencha.com/products/sdk-tools/`).

Our sample application will be very simple and follow the standard MVC folder structure, as the following screenshot shows:

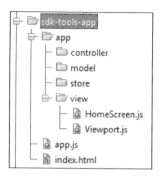

We have two views (`Viewport.js` and `HomeScreen.js`) with the following definitions:

```
Ext.define('Cookbook.view.Viewport', {
    extend: 'Ext.Viewport',
    requires: ['Cookbook.view.HomeScreen'],
    layout: 'fit',
    items: [{
        xtype: 'HomeScreen'
    }]
});

Ext.define('Cookbook.view.HomeScreen', {
    extend: 'Ext.Panel',
    alias: 'widget.HomeScreen',
    html: 'Hello World!'
});
```

Our `app.js` configures the `Ext.Loader` class and defines our application, which simply creates and shows our `Cookbook.view.Viewport` component:

```
// Enable & configure the Loader
Ext.Loader.setConfig({ enabled: true });

// Create our Application
Ext.application({
    name: 'Cookbook',

    launch: function() {
        // create and show our Viewport
        Ext.create('Cookbook.view.Viewport').show();
    }
});
```

Finally, our `index.html` references the framework's `ext.js` and our `app.js` files, along with the `ext-css.css` stylesheet:

```
<html>
<head>
    <title>SDK Tools</title>

    <link rel="stylesheet" type="text/css" href="../extjs/resources/
css/ext-all.css">
    <script type="text/javascript" src="../extjs/ext.js"></script>
    <script type="text/javascript" src="app.js"></script>
</head>
<body>
</body>
</html>
```

There are a few important things to note about this basic application, namely:

▶ We are using the `Ext.Loader` class to dynamically load the framework's and our own classes

▶ We are including the `ext.js` library file, which contains only the very basic framework code, as opposed to the `ext-all(-debug).js` file, which has the complete library

▶ We have followed the standard of adding the `required` configuration containing any classes that the component uses so these can be dynamically loaded

▶ We instantiate classes using the `Ext.create` syntax

These points are very important as the SDK tools rely on these to parse your application and find all of its dependencies.

How to do it...

Now that we have our simple application up and running we can start using the SDK tools to create our application's 'dependency list' in the form of a JSB3 file, which can then be used to build it into a single, minified file:

1. First we must open a command-line window and navigate to our application's source folder.

2. Once there we run the following command:

```
sencha create jsb -a http://localhost/sdk-tools-app/index.html -p
app.jsb3 -v
```

Notice that we used a URL instead of simply `index.html`. By doing this we ensure that the paths to the source files are correct.

3. Once this process has completed you will notice a new file called `app.jsb3` in your application's folder. If you open this you will see a list of all the Ext JS framework files that our application requires to run. A small sample of it can be seen as follows:

```
{
    "projectName": "Project Name",
    "licenseText": "Copyright(c) 2011 Company Name",
    "builds": [
        {
            "name": "All Classes",
            "target": "all-classes.js",
            "options": {
                "debug": true
            },
            "files": [
                {
                    "path": "../extjs/src/util/",
                    "name": "Observable.js"
                }
                . . .
            ]
        }
        . . .
    ]
}
```

4. Our next step is to use this definition file to build our application into a single, minified file. We do this by running the following command:

```
sencha build -p app.jsb3 -d .
```

How it works...

The first command we used, `create jsb`, generates a JSON definition file that can be parsed by JSBuilder and is used to decide what the build output will be like, what files will be included, and how it will be processed. The command accepts four arguments:

▶ `-app-entry (-a)`: defines the HTML page of the application
▶ `-project (-p)`: defines the location and name of the outputted JSB3 file
▶ `-target (-t)`: defines the JSB build target
▶ `-verbose (-v)`: output is printed to the command line

The SDK tool creates this file by parsing the application's `index.html` file and following all of the required classes (this is possible because we used the `requires` option and the `Ext.create` syntax in our definitions) and builds a list of them, in a similar way as the framework does at runtime when the classes are loaded.

The JSB3 file that is created contains a property called `builds`. This property contains an array of objects that define a single file that will be output by the build process. In our file there are two items in this array—All Classes and Application.

The `All Classes` definition tells the builder to create a file called `all-classes.js` (our `target`), to build in debug mode and to include all the files in the files property. This file contains all of the Ext JS classes that are required and all of our custom application classes.

The second tells the builder that a compressed file (`app-all.js`) will be built containing the `all-classes.js` file outputted from the first build item and the `app.js` file.

Step 4 shows the command to process this JSB3 definition file and have JSBuilder combine and minify the files based on its contents.

The command to perform this action is `sencha build` and accepts two required arguments:

- ▶ `-deployDir` (`-d`): defines where the combined and minified output files will be saved
- ▶ `-projectFile` (`-p`): defines the path and name of the JSB3 file

Getting started with Ext Direct

Ext Direct allows you to seamlessly integrate your Ext JS frontend with the server-side technologies running the backend.

As you already know, it's not possible to have our JavaScript make calls to methods in our server code directly. At present the requests we make call the necessary method and return the results back to the browser.

Ext Direct helps by exposing server-side classes and methods and allowing you to call them directly from your JavaScript, for example, `ClassName.MethodName()`. You'll have neat code, consistent naming between the client and server-side, and having invested a small amount of time in setup/configuration, you will undoubtedly save time in the long run.

 It's straightforward working with Ext Direct no matter what your server-side environment is. Integration is already provided for PHP, .NET, Ruby, ColdFusion, Java, and others.

We're going to use this recipe to demonstrate how to use Ext Direct in your application. For the purposes of this recipe we will use a server-side stack for PHP. However, you can download a stack for your environment from Sencha's website: `www.sencha.com/forum/showthread.php?67992-Ext.Direct-Server-side-Stacks`.

Getting ready

For this recipe you will require a working web server capable of parsing PHP and the server-side stack entitled "Extremely Easy Ext.Direct integration with PHP." The stack is provided by community member *j.bruni* and can be downloaded from here: `http://www.sencha.com/forum/showthread.php?102357-Extremely-Easy-Ext.Direct-integration-with-PHP`.

How to do it...

1. Start by extracting the downloaded server stack to the directory `Server`.

2. Create a PHP file called `GettingStarted.php` and add the following code. The class `GettingStarted` will be exposed to the client side with Ext Direct:

```php
<?php

require 'Server/ExtDirect.php';

class GettingStarted {

  public function simple() {
    return "Returned a String";
  }

  public function parameterExample($name) {
    return "Your Name is " . $name;
  }

}

ExtDirect::provide('GettingStarted');
?>
```

3. In your HTML file include the `GettingStarted.php` file inside a `<script>` tag. Pass the parameter `javascript` to ensure that the PHP file returns JavaScript (this is handled by the server-side stack we downloaded):

```
<link rel="stylesheet" type="text/css" href="../../../resources/
css/ext-all.css">
<script type="text/javascript" src="../../../ext-all-debug.js"></
script>

<script type="text/javascript" src="GettingStarted.
php?javascript"></script>
```

4. Now that Ext Direct is ready to use, we'll call the `simple` method from our `GettingStarted` class. The default namespace (`Ext.php`) is required, however, this is configurable from the server-side stack. The parameter is used for a callback function to display the output of the request:

```
Ext.php.GettingStarted.simple(function(result) {
    console.log(result);
});
```

5. To demonstrate passing a parameter via Ext Direct call the `parameterExample` method. The first argument is parameter one and the second argument is our callback function. In this case we'll pass the string `Joe` to the server-side. The server-side is ready to parse the parameter and return a result accordingly:

```
Ext.php.GettingStarted.parameterExample("Joe", function(result,
response) {
    console.log(result);
});
```

6. Run the code on your web server and your console should display **Returned a String** and **Your Name is Joe**.

How it works...

Having run the previous code you now have an, albeit basic, app running with Ext Direct. We've successfully managed to call a class and its methods directly from the client side.

There are three core components that we must be aware of before we can use Ext Direct with our server-side code:

1. Configuring our server side correctly so it exposes the correct components to the client side. We've done this by including the `ExtDirect.php` stack and exposing the `GettingStarted` class with `ExtDirect::provide('GettingStarted');`

2. The API that we use to generate a client-side descriptor of the server side based on the configuration. The API, in our example, is generated dynamically by including the file `GettingStarted.php?javascript` as in step 3 above.

3. The router for directing requests to the appropriate class and method. In this case we don't need to worry too much about the router because the server-side stack (ExtDirect.php) is taking care of that for us. The API that's generated by the server-side stack outputs the following:

```
if ( Ext.syncRequire )
   Ext.syncRequire( 'Ext.direct.Manager' );

Ext.namespace( 'Ext.php' );
Ext.php.REMOTING_API = {
   "url":"\/ExtDirect\/GettingStarted.php",
   "type":"remoting",
   "namespace":"Ext.php",
   "descriptor":"Ext.php.REMOTING_API",
   "actions":{
       {"name":"simple","len":0},
       {"name":"parameterExample","len":1}
     ]
   }
};
Ext.Direct.addProvider( Ext.php.REMOTING_API );
```

There are four items to note here:

▶   Ensure Ext Direct is ready to run on the client side as the class `Ext.direct.Manager` is required.

▶   Define a namespace for the components we may wish to call. In our example we have used the default namespace, `Ext.php`, from the stack. If you wish to change this add the line `ExtDirect::$namespace = 'MyNamespace.Name';` to your configuration.

▶   The `REMOTING_API` is simply an output of the stubs that the client side needs to create everything we need. As you can see here, we have a reference to the URL that the framework must route all requests to and the various actions available. The number of parameters for a method is also described here.

▶   We must add the `RemotingProvider` to ensure Ext JS creates the necessary proxy and stub methods that will call the server-side methods. This is done using the `addProvider` method in `Ext.direct.Manager`.

Now that the framework knows what classes and methods are available it's an easy task for us to make requests to the server.

Ext Direct does other clever things for us, such as method batching. This reduces the number of requests to a server by batching all requests within a certain time period together. This defaults to 10-millisecond batches, however, this is easily configurable with the `enableBuffer` configuration.

See also

▶ The next recipe in this chapter that focuses on loading and submitting forms with Ext.Direct.

Loading and submitting forms with Ext Direct

Loading and submitting forms with Ext Direct is relatively simple and this recipe will show you how and what you need to look out for. We'll make a simple contact form that is capable of loading and submitting data to and from our server with Ext Direct. The requests will also include a `UserID` parameter as we may wish to use this for loading/submitting data against a specific account.

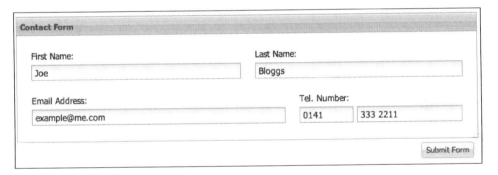

Getting ready

We're going to need our working web server again that's capable of parsing PHP and the server-side stack entitled "Extremely Easy Ext.Direct integration with PHP." The stack is provided by community member *j.bruni* and can be downloaded here: `http://www.sencha.com/forum/showthread.php?102357-Extremely-Easy-Ext.Direct-integration-with-PHP`.

If you followed the steps successfully in the previous recipe, you should have this already.

How to do it...

1. We're going to need server-side code for this to run. Create a `FormClass` class and configure it for Ext Direct:

```php
<?php

require 'Server/ExtDirect.php';

class FormClass {

  public function load($UserID) {

    $data = array(
      'FirstName' => 'Joe',
      'LastName' => 'Bloggs',
      'EmailAddress' => 'example@me.com',
      'TelNumberCode' => '0141',
      'TelNumber' => '333 2211');

    $arr = array('success' => true, 'data' => $data);
    return $arr;

  }

  public function submit($UserID, $FirstName, $LastName,
$EmailAddress, $TelNumberCode, $TelNumber) {
    return array('success' => true);
  }

}


ExtDirect::$form_handlers = array('FormClass::submit');
ExtDirect::provide('FormClass');

?>
```

2. Add the API configuration to your HTML file, placed inside a `<script>` tag:

```html
<script type="text/javascript" src="FormRouter.php?javascript"></
script>
```

3. Create a Form panel with some fields. Render the panel to the document's body:

```
var formPanel = Ext.create('Ext.form.Panel', {
    title: 'Contact Form',
    width: 650,
    height: 200,
    bodyPadding: 10,
    items: [{
        xtype: 'container',
        layout: 'hbox',
        items: [{
            xtype: 'textfield',
            fieldLabel: 'First Name',
            name: 'FirstName',
            labelAlign: 'top',
            cls: 'field-margin',
            flex: 1
        }, {
            xtype: 'textfield',
            fieldLabel: 'Last Name',
            name: 'LastName',
            labelAlign: 'top',
            cls: 'field-margin',
            flex: 1
        }]
    }, {
        xtype: 'container',
        layout: 'column',
        items: [{
            xtype: 'textfield',
            fieldLabel: 'Email Address',
            name: 'EmailAddress',
            labelAlign: 'top',
            cls: 'field-margin',
            columnWidth: 0.6,
            msgTarget: 'side'
        }, {
            xtype: 'fieldcontainer',
            layout: 'hbox',
            fieldLabel: 'Tel. Number',
            labelAlign: 'top',
            cls: 'field-margin',
```

```
            columnWidth: 0.4,
            items: [{
                xtype: 'textfield',
                name: 'TelNumberCode',
                style: 'margin-right: 5px;',
                flex: 2
            }, {
                xtype: 'textfield',
                name: 'TelNumber',
                flex: 4
            }]
        }]
    }],
    renderTo: Ext.getBody(),
    style: 'margin: 50px'
});
```

4. Add an `api` configuration to your `BasicForm` with references to the `load` and `submit` stubs:

```
var formPanel = Ext.create('Ext.form.Panel', {
  ...
  api : {
    load : Ext.php.FormClass.load,
    submit : Ext.php.FormClass.submit
  },
  ...
});
```

5. Add the `paramOrder` configuration to ensure that we are able to submit a `UserID` with every request:

```
var formPanel = Ext.create('Ext.form.Panel', {
  ...
  paramOrder : ['UserID'],
  ...
});
```

6. Use the `load` method to load the form:

```
formPanel.getForm().load({
  params : {
    UserID : 1
  }
});
```

7. Add a button for submitting the form:

```
var formPanel = Ext.create('Ext.form.Panel', {
  ...
  buttons : [{
    text : 'Submit Form',
    handler : function() {
      formPanel.getForm().submit({
        params : {
          UserID : 1
        }
      });
    }
  }],
  ...
});
```

How it works...

We've started by providing the framework with our RemotingProvider
(Ext.php.REMOTING_API). This describes the server-side classes
and methods we are exposing to the client side.

The output from the server-side stack is:

```
{
    "url": "/ExtDirect/FormRouter.php",
    "type": "remoting",
    "namespace": "Ext.php",
    "descriptor": "Ext.php.REMOTING_API",
    "actions": {
        "FormClass": [
            {
                "name": "load",
                "len": 1
            },
            {
                "name": "submit",
                "len": 6,
                "formHandler": true
            }
        ]
    }
}
```

We have two actions in the FormClass action.

1. The `load` method accepts one parameter, which is represented by the key/value pair `"len": 1`. The method is looking for the value `$UserID`. When we populate the form using the `load` method the output from `FormRouter.php` is:

```
{
    "type": "rpc",
    "tid": 1,
    "action": "FormClass",
    "method": "load",
    "result": {
        "success": true,
        "data": {
            "FirstName": "Joe",
            "LastName": "Bloggs",
            "EmailAddress": "example@me.com",
            "TelNumberCode": "0141",
            "TelNumber": "333 2211"
        }
    }
}
```

The data that our form works with is found inside the `result` object. As you might expect it requires a `success` flag and a `data` object before the form is populated with data.

2. The `submit` method accepts six parameters (five form fields and one additional parameter for UserID). Note the `"formHandler": true`. Our server-side stack has added that for us because we have configured it to know that the `submit` method is for submitting form data. We added `ExtDirect::$form_handlers = array('FormClass::submit');` to our PHP for this reason. When we press the **submit** button our form `submit` method is called and the following data is posted to the router for parsing:

```
Referer: http://localhost:8888/ExtDirect/Loading%20and%20Submitting%20form
User-Agent: Mozilla/5.0 (Macintosh; Intel Mac OS X 10_7_2) AppleWebKit/535
X-Requested-With: XMLHttpRequest
▼ Form Data        view URL encoded
    extTID: 2
    extAction: FormClass
    extMethod: submit
    extType: rpc
    extUpload: false
    UserID: 1
    FirstName: Joe
    LastName: Bloggs
    EmailAddress: example@me.com
    TelNumberCode: 0141
    TelNumber: 333 2211
▼ Response Headers        view source
    Connection: Keep-Alive
```

- ▶ For an introduction to Ext.Direct take a look at the previous recipe.

- ▶ To learn about how to use Ext.Direct in conjunction with stores and grids, read through the next recipe.

- ▶ For details about exception handling with Ext.Direct see the recipe titled *Handling Exceptions with Ext Direct* later in this chapter.

Handling errors throughout your application

Reporting feedback to the user is, as I am sure you already know, vital in **Rich Internet Applications** (**RIA**). We must always prepare for the worst when the application doesn't function as expected and in these situations feedback is important to stop the user getting frustrated when they later learn that their work or data couldn't be saved, for example.

If you are already building an application with Ext JS, You've probably already given this some thought and have already implemented a method for reporting feedback to users when there are errors between the client side and server side.

In a large application it can be cumbersome, however, to write and maintain individual error response handlers for all your AJAX requests as it's likely you'll have hundreds.

In this recipe we will show a few techniques you can use to implement application-wide error handling and provide consistency and clarity to your users.

How to do it...

1. Register the 'Cookbook' namespace:

   ```
   Ext.ns('Cookbook');
   ```

2. Define a default error message for unknown situations:

   ```
   Cookbook.SYSTEM_GENERIC_ERROR = 'Unknown Error, contact support.';
   ```

3. Write a function that we can use for displaying an error message to the user. We need to keep this fairly generic so it can be used for all error messages. If something goes wrong, we'll display the generic system error here:

   ```
   Cookbook.GenericErrorMessage = function(message) {

     if(Ext.isEmpty(message)) {
       message = Cookbook.SYSTEM_GENERIC_ERROR;
     }

     Ext.Msg.show({
   ```

```
          title : 'An Error has occurred',
          msg : message,
          modal : true,
          icon : Ext.Msg.ERROR,
          buttons : Ext.Msg.OK
      });

  };
```

4. We now require a function that will process failures with our AJAX requests. This function can be split in two:

   ❑ If the connection is successful but the server returns an error message.

   ❑ If the connection is unsuccessful.

   Either way the outcome is that we require an error message to display to the user.

```
Cookbook.DataConnectionFailureHandler = function(response,
options) {
    if(Ext.isEmpty(response.status)) {
       response = options.response;
    }
    if((message === undefined || message === '') && response.status
=== 200) {
        if(!Ext.isEmpty(response.responseText)) {
           jsonResponse = Ext.util.JSON.decode(response.responseText);
        }
        displayMessage = jsonResponse.msg;
    } else if(response.status !== 200 && response.status !==
undefined && response.status !== null) {
        displayMessage = response.statusText;
    }

    //Display a message to the user
    Cookbook.GenericErrorMessage(displayMessage);
};
```

5. When a store request fails this function will be called. Just as the previous function this is also capable of handling errors when the HTTP response code is 200:

```
Cookbook.StoreExceptionHandler = function(proxy, response,
operation, eOpts) {

    if(response.status !== 200) {
        // call the AJAX Error Handler
        Cookbook.DataConnectionFailureHandler(response, null);
    } else {
        //Read the contents of the "msg" returned from the server
        var displayMessage = response.raw.msg;
```

```
       Cookbook.GenericErrorMessage(displayMessage);
    }

};
```

6. Now we'll prepare a basic handler for Ext Direct exceptions:

```
Cookbook.DirectExceptionHandler = function(eventException) {
    // call the Generic Response Handler
    Cookbook.GenericErrorMessage(eventException.message);

};
```

7. Finally, we're going to listen out for the firing of an `exception` event from the `ServerProxy`. When the event is fired we'll call the `StoreExceptionHandler` function above. We can do the same for Ext Direct:

```
Ext.util.Observable.observe(Ext.data.proxy.Server);
Ext.data.proxy.Server.on('exception', Cookbook.
StoreExceptionHandler);

Ext.Direct.on('exception', Cookbook.DirectExceptionHandler);
```

How it works...

Although the previous example is relatively basic, it demonstrates how straightforward it is to add generic exception handling for the data requests in your app.

The line `Ext.util.Observable.observe(Ext.data.proxy.Server);` is extremely useful as it allows us to centrally manage the firing of the `exception` event from all instances of the `Ext.data.proxy.Server` class.

When the application encounters a problem the `StoreExceptionHandler` is fired, which determines if the error is because our server side is reporting a handled error (in the form of a `msg`) or if it's an error where the HTTP status code is not 200 (that is, OK). No matter what the outcome we are able to extract some form of error message from one of the following sources:

▶ `response.responseText.msg`: a message returned in the JSON

▶ `response.statusText`: the associated text that accompanies the HTTP status code, for example, 404 "Not Found"

▶ If something goes wrong and we are unable to figure out what error message we should be displaying to the user then we'll fallback to a generic system message that is found in the global variable `Cookbook.SYSTEM_GENERIC_ERROR`

See also

▸ For a more detailed example of handing exceptions in forms, see the last recipe in Chapter 5, *Loading, Submitting, and Validating Forms*.

▸ The recipe *Handling store load exceptions* in *Chapter 7, Working with the Ext JS Data Package*, explores how exception handling can be added to store loads.

Index

Thank you for buying
Ext JS 4 Web Application
Development Cookbook

About Packt Publishing

Packt, pronounced 'packed', published its first book "*Mastering phpMyAdmin for Effective MySQL Management*" in April 2004 and subsequently continued to specialize in publishing highly focused books on specific technologies and solutions.

Our books and publications share the experiences of your fellow IT professionals in adapting and customizing today's systems, applications, and frameworks. Our solution based books give you the knowledge and power to customize the software and technologies you're using to get the job done. Packt books are more specific and less general than the IT books you have seen in the past. Our unique business model allows us to bring you more focused information, giving you more of what you need to know, and less of what you don't.

Packt is a modern, yet unique publishing company, which focuses on producing quality, cutting-edge books for communities of developers, administrators, and newbies alike. For more information, please visit our website: www.packtpub.com.

About Packt Open Source

In 2010, Packt launched two new brands, Packt Open Source and Packt Enterprise, in order to continue its focus on specialization. This book is part of the Packt Open Source brand, home to books published on software built around Open Source licences, and offering information to anybody from advanced developers to budding web designers. The Open Source brand also runs Packt's Open Source Royalty Scheme, by which Packt gives a royalty to each Open Source project about whose software a book is sold.

Writing for Packt

We welcome all inquiries from people who are interested in authoring. Book proposals should be sent to author@packtpub.com. If your book idea is still at an early stage and you would like to discuss it first before writing a formal book proposal, contact us; one of our commissioning editors will get in touch with you.

We're not just looking for published authors; if you have strong technical skills but no writing experience, our experienced editors can help you develop a writing career, or simply get some additional reward for your expertise.

Ext JS 4 First Look

ISBN: 978-1-84951-666-2   Paperback: 340 pages

A practical guide including examples of the new features in Ext JS 4 and tips to migrate from Ext JS 3

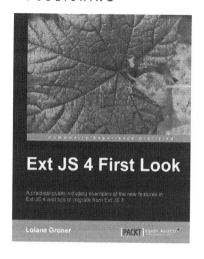

1. Migrate your Ext JS 3 applications easily to Ext JS 4 based on the examples presented in this guide

2. Full of diagrams, illustrations, and step-by-step instructions to develop real word applications

3. Driven by examples and explanations of how things work

Sencha Touch Mobile JavaScript Framework

ISBN: 978-1-84951-510-8   Paperback: 316 pages

Build web applications for Apple iOS and Google Android touchscreen devices with this first HTML5 mobile framework

1. Learn to develop web applications that look and feel native on Apple iOS and Google Android touchscreen devices using Sencha Touch through examples

2. Design resolution-independent and graphical representations like buttons, icons, and tabs of unparalleled flexibility

3. Add custom events like tap, double tap, swipe, tap and hold, pinch, and rotate

Please check **www.PacktPub.com** for information on our titles

Learning Ext JS 3.2

ISBN: 978-1-849511-20-9   Paperback: 432 pages

Build dynamic, desktop-style user interfaces for you data-driven web applications using Ext JS

1. Learn to build consistent, attractive web interfaces with the framework components

2. Integrate your existing data and web services with Ext JS data support

3. Enhance your JavaScript skills by using Ext's DOM and AJAX helpers

4. Extend Ext JS through custom components

Ext JS 3.0 Cookbook

ISBN: 978-1-847198-70-9   Paperback: 376 pages

109 greate recipes for building impressive rich internet applications using the Ext JS JavaScript library

1. Master the Ext JS widgets and learn to create custom components to suit your needs

2. Build striking native and custom layouts, forms, grids, listviews, treeviews, charts, tab panels, menus, toolbars and much more for your real-world user interfaces

3. Packed with easy-to-follow examples to exercise all of the features of the Ext JS library

Please check **www.PacktPub.com** for information on our titles